Story of a
Santa Barbara Birder

Joan Easton Lentz

Story of a Santa Barbara Birder
by Joan Easton Lentz

ISBN: 978-0-929702-12-4

 Mission Creek Studios
Santa Barbara, CA
www.missioncreek.com

Design and Layout, Anna Lafferty, Lafferty Design Plus

Editor - Kathy Jean Schultz

Imagery Credits - Note: Images with no credit names
are from the author's collection

Front Cover Images:
BACKGROUND: Cottonwood Canyon, Sierra Madre Mtns.,
    S.B. County, courtesy of Stuart Wilson,
PORTRAIT: courtesy of Ellen Easton

Back Cover Images:
LEFT: Goleta Slough, Coal Oil Pt., Jan. 2019,
    courtesy B. Dewey
RIGHT: Author with her father, 1945.

This book is dedicated to
Alex and Annabel

Preface

My Santa Barbara

When the wind sweeps the winter sky blue and clear, and the mountains in back of Santa Barbara show their sandstone ridges, I'm back to my childhood.

I remember the view from my bedroom window: the Channel Islands lying on a silver sea, white sailboats in the harbor, the red tile roofs of town, the brown Granada building always the tallest.

And closer was the green patch of the high school football field at Peabody Stadium.

I lived on the Riviera. Not many houses on those hillsides then. Vacant lots stood on either side of the secret staircases we climbed on our way home from school in the afternoons. Public stairways passed between the white walls of the Andalusian style houses, lovely houses built in the 1920s and '30s – old-fashioned and marvelous.

I knew the short cuts. My sunburned legs were scratched and bruised from climbing up the hill through brushy lots, my dress torn and wrinkled.

Sagebrush and eucalyptus, those were the smells. Pungent, acrid sagebrush grew on the hillsides. Not the Great Basin kind, but the wispy, gray coastal sagebrush. The eucalyptus dropped round pods that crunched underfoot, and the tree's branches roared on a windy day.

I absorbed these things. It's as if I felt the glad moisture of the heavy rains, the anguish of the long droughts. I could feel the weather, just as my body would cozy up to a warm sweater or shiver in a wet bathing suit.

A January day is my day – after a gulley-washer rain, when the runnels of water make the paths muddy, and the sound of rushing creeks gladdens my heart.

Wrapped in this landscape, my soul grew up, developed a sense of place. I didn't realize that it had settled.

I never planned to burrow in. I thought I was free to wander the world, live in new places, experience other landscapes.

But I'm not. I'm tethered to my Santa Barbara. It's as if all the years past are still with me – the smells, the weather, the bones of the land. The laughter, the love, the family, the life.

The older I am, the more I am tied, bound up, secured.

This is my Santa Barbara.

Introduction

Why I Wrote This Book

I wrote this book to share with you how birds and nature have influenced my life.

When I observe birds in their natural habitats, I am inspired by wonder and excitement. A feeling of deep joy and appreciation adds to these moments, intensifying the effect of the natural world.

Birding is time spent outdoors or indoors, with or without companions, safe and welcoming — a soothing accompaniment in harsh times, a heightened sensibility in good times. It is my go-to place. Whether I am getting in the car and exploring a new location, or just walking out the door, I pick up my binoculars and off I go. On a country road, or in a city park, at a sewage treatment plant, or in my backyard: there they are — birds.

I could not have written this book as a young woman. But over the years, as I renewed my commitment to observing birds — taught more classes, interacted with colleagues, wrote books, lived through the ups and downs — I became aware of how I relied upon birding.

Just the other day my husband commented, "You were so unfocused until you got serious about birding." Indeed, it molded my life.

Hand-in-hand with birding goes my affection for Santa Barbara and its surroundings. To love this land is to thrive and blossom in a place I've known since childhood. I was given an extraordinary chance to pursue my passion for birds in the region where I had roots. Growing up in Santa Barbara and returning here to spend my life pervades my feelings for birds and nature.

These interwoven facets scoop up my family, the houses we lived in and the places I visited as a child, and combines them with birds and natural history. It's a mish-mash, an agglomeration.

My life is no different from yours. Experiences buffet the winds of that life; some unbearably painful, others deliriously happy.

At first I set out to record only the perfect parts. Then, a year ago, I became suddenly ill with a life-threatening lung disease. As I lay in the hospital for weeks, I resolved that if I was lucky enough to pull through, I would write this book.

Miraculously, I survived. Each day, I start out at the bottom of the trail, figuratively speaking. My breathing capacity is so reduced that I need supplemental oxygen whenever I engage in physical activity. Decline is certain. Each day is a struggle to stay in the game and to adapt.

For the moment, I have my life back. I can go outdoors. I can go birding.

In addition to the love of family, friends, and community, I credit my good fortune to the restorative power of birding and nature.

This is my story.

Santa Barbara Region

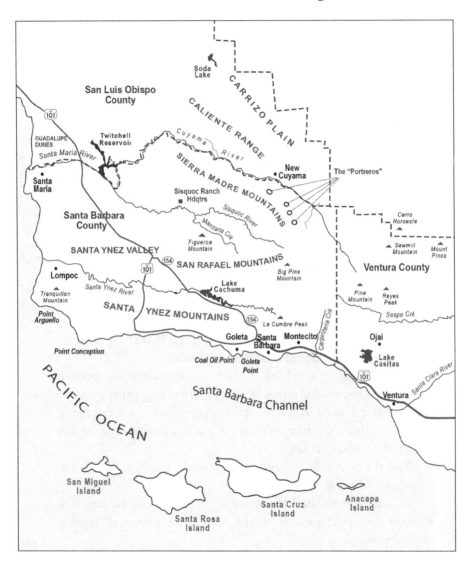

Table of Contents

Rancho Sisquoc headquarters

1.

Family Ties

The Eastons and Rancho Sisquoc

People ask me how I ended up living in Santa Barbara and why I like birds.

If I trace it all the way back, if I remember what influenced me as a child, and if I thought that *where* I grew up was a part of the answer to *why* I like birds, I'd have to say that it all started with the Sisquoc Ranch.

Not that I ever lived on the ranch or that I even visited the place more than once or twice as a child. I never rode horses there and by the time I was birding, the ranch wasn't accessible to me. But thinking back on it, if it hadn't been for the Sisquoc Ranch, how would Dad ever have known the hikes, the backpack destinations, all the places he later showed us when we were growing up so we could share his vision?

So why the Sisquoc?

The ranch was a working Spanish land grant rancho, located at the confluence of the Santa Maria and Sisquoc Rivers in what was a remote area of the central coast back in the 1890s. To get there you took the train to the tiny station in the town of Guadalupe. And it was often the middle of the night when the train pulled up.

That's where my grandfather, Robert E. Easton, found himself one chilly night in 1899. He was alone, newly graduated in civil engineering from Cal Berkeley, and needed a job. His brother-in-law, Tom Porter, from up in Santa Cruz County, knew this, and had suggested my grandfather come down and take a look at a piece of property he'd recently purchased as an investment. Not just any old investment property, mind you, but one that spanned 40,000 acres and was wild as a mountain lion and just as unruly.

It was true. The Sisquoc Ranch needed to be brought up-to-date with boundaries correctly surveyed, and rights-of-ways decided upon. The only map up to then was the old, hand-drawn "Desenio" from 1883. That was the original land grant, and it showed property corners illustrated by rock formations or a massive oak tree, just pen and ink sketches.

The ranch headquarters — located at the western edge of the property where the pasturelands were wide — held the barns, tackroom, and a bunkhouse. But up the Sisquoc River, back toward the eastern ridges, that's where the bulk of the ranch land lay in the shape of a large rectangle. And if you rode most of the day on horseback, you would at last come to the border with the national forest. Then you hit the public lands. But in this hardscrabble country with no regulation, it all might as well have been one big chunk, whether you were a homesteader further upriver, or a Chumash Native American who came and went along the secret pathways: boundaries were fluid.

We have a term for the watershed that's embraced like a big horseshoe by the San Rafael Mountains on the south and the Sierra Madre Mountains on the north: "the backcountry." Loosely defined, it's the area within what's now a portion of the Los Padres National Forest, called the San Rafael Wilderness.

My grandfather, my father, and I have in one way or another been involved in the Sisquoc Ranch or the wilderness area that surrounds it. From the hot canyons and cool rivers where my grandfather and father would ride chasing after errant cattle that had escaped from the ranch, to Dad's memories of those times recounted to me on our hikes, and, much later, through the work I did with bird surveys on Big Pine Mountain, a collective memory grew up around this area of our county.

My grandfather, later accompanied by his son, my dad, came to

know every corner of the ranch. He was eventually named superinten-
dent, and rode horseback to check on remote boundary fences. Father
and son grew to love the rough and inhospitable landscape; they fished
in the deep pools of the river, and marveled at the wildflowers after a
rainy winter.

In its heyday, the Sisquoc Ranch was a huge operation. It pastured
between two and three thousand head of cattle per year. Due to his
business acumen, my successful grandfather acquired a house in Santa
Maria, and then he proposed to my grandmother, Ethel Olney.

Ethel came from a prominent family in Oakland, and it took some
pursuing to entice her down to the hinterlands of Southern California.
Her father, Warren Olney I, was a well-known attorney. He adored the
wilderness, particularly Yosemite. He and John Muir were friends; it
was in Olney's office in San Francisco that Muir and others drew up the
bylaws of the Sierra Club.

Great grandfather Olney doted on his daughter Ethel. They had
traveled together throughout Europe and in the Sierra Nevada. Ethel
was a cultured, well-read woman who had a wide grasp of the world.
Would she agree to come to Santa Maria to marry a man who supervised a ranch out in the middle of nowhere?

She was almost forty years old, and did accept my grandfather's proposal. A year later, in 1915, my father, Robert Olney Easton, was born.

Dad treasured the times he spent riding with his dad, exploring
the Sisquoc Ranch and beyond. I attribute my attachment to the Santa
Barbara backcountry as a reason I later wished to survey it for birds and
other creatures.

One of the historic structures on the ranch was known as the
Tunnell House, which was located way up the Sisquoc River. A two-
story wooden cabin that was originally built by early homesteaders —
the Tunnell brothers — it was used by the ranch cowboys as a place to
bunk down after hard days in the saddle up the river.

Several years ago, my sister Ellen and I were invited by Elizabeth
Flood Stevenson, one of the current ranch owners, to set aside a day for
a jeep ride up along the river.

It was a chilly October afternoon with low shadows on the hills. I was surprised to see so much water flowing. We crossed and re-crossed the shallow riffles, avoiding the bigger rocks and climbing up the steep banks with the gears grinding. Overhead, the branches of low-hanging coast live oaks almost swept our hats off. The road was rough and the country looked dry. Gray pines dotted the hills as we got farther inland, and the grays and browns of chaparral blended into the arroyos as we bumped along.

We arrived at the Tunnell House at mid-day, and walked around. Ellen and I found Dad's name carved into one of the planks of the wood siding. Inside, we saw the old kitchen, complete with stove and iron pans hanging on the wall. We thought of the tired, dirty cowboys coming in, their horses tied in the corral, and the Chinese cook producing the meals. Climbing up a central staircase, we arrived at one big room on the second floor, where rows of iron bunk beds with thin mattresses were lined up.

We could feel the spirit of Grandfather and Dad, all the long horse rides out into the backcountry that might've started and ended here, all the brandings, all the cowboys sitting on the porch telling yarns.

Several miles up, the jeep road entered the national forest; we were near the far eastern border of the ranch.

I wandered over to the barbed wire fence and looked longingly into the distance. I wanted to explore the country on the other side of that fence; go birding, follow one of those faint game trails that led upstream through the oaks and sycamores.

That's when I realized that my history began with the Sisquoc Ranch and Grandfather getting off the train on that foggy night in 1899.

The Fausts And An Italian Villa

The details of my Easton ancestors on the Sisquoc Ranch are worlds away from my mother's upbringing in an Italian villa in Florence.

But there is one thread that holds it all together: writing.

My mother's father, Frederick Faust, was a prolific author of popular

4

Western novels and magazine stories throughout the 1920s and '30s. Eventually he produced more than 300 Western novels and stories, most of them under the pen name Max Brand. Later on, Faust created characters and screenplays for Hollywood. One of his books, "Destry Rides Again," became a movie and a Broadway play. Grandfather Faust also created the Dr. Kildare characters, which were serialized on television in the 1960s.

Grandfather Faust was a natural writer. From a young age, he wrote poetry and short stories, partly to escape the misery of his daily life, partly to emulate the books he read voraciously.

His background of poverty was unlike any of my Easton or Olney relatives. He was raised in the San Joaquin Valley, an orphan from the age of twelve. Shuttled from one family member to another in the Valley, he honed his strength in fights he had to endure every time he changed schools when he was growing up. Encouraged by a friendly high school principal, young Faust lost himself in books. He read constantly, especially admiring the classical Greek heroes that fired his imagination. The more he read, the more he wrote. His creative life was built upon the heroes he read about in Dickens, Thackeray, Goethe, and Hugo. He filled his notebooks with stories and poems, anything to take him away from the drudgery of Valley life. Eventually, my grandfather was admitted to U.C. Berkeley, where he excelled in everything to do with literature. Frederick Faust married his beautiful classmate at Berkeley, Dorothy Schillig ("Nin" to us grandchildren) and had three children. My mother, Jane, was the oldest.

Like many artists and writers of the 1920s and '30s, my grandfather discovered it was cheap to live abroad. He sought the peace and quiet of the Tuscan countryside to get away from the pressures of New York City and the stressful world of publishing.

In Italy, he realized his dream, remodeling a 15th century farmhouse into an enchanting villa where he could work and play together with his family. The villa stood on the edge of a valley in Fiesole, just outside Florence. A cypress-lined walk led down to the swimming pool and tennis court, which were surrounded by a large garden bursting with roses, jasmine, and fruit trees. Devoted servants cooked their meals, cleaned, gardened, and chauffeured. All of it was supported by Faust's writing. And his publishers were delighted, because he worked so fast, churning out novels in a matter of weeks.

The Fausts' Italian interlude came to an end with the rise of Mussolini and the threat of World War II. My grandparents decided to return to the U.S., where they settled in California. They lived in Brentwood, where Grandfather began writing for the Hollywood studios.

Many years later, on a visit to Florence as an adult, I toured the villa where my Faust grandparents had lived. The last time I was there, it had been donated permanently to New York University; filing cabinets and office desks filled the beautiful high-ceilinged rooms. I went upstairs to Grandfather's study. I could imagine him sitting in front of his old Royal typewriter, surrounded by these same bookshelves, although in his day they were filled with leather-bound editions of the classics.

I made my way outside across the broad terrace and down the steps into the garden, noticing where the pool and tennis court had been, now empty and neglected. But the smell of the Tuscan hills pulled me to Italy as much as it reminded me of Santa Barbara.

When I'm driving the streets of my beautiful Santa Barbara, I remember my mother's happiness in Italy. She longed for the Mediterranean light, the bright flowers, the sunny days, the beach. And she got all of that by living in Santa Barbara, where the beauty reminded her of Europe. And that has come down to me, too, in the way that I am happiest travelling in the countries around the Mediterranean Sea.

It was not long after the Fausts had relocated to Brentwood, just before World War II began, that my mother and father met on a blind date — arranged by my two grandmothers who had known each other at Cal.

Love at first sight.

Imagine any two families more different — the Fausts and the Eastons? This tall, larger-than-life author — Grandfather Faust — shaking hands with my short, business-oriented Grandfather Easton?

My handsome father, who had graduated from Santa Barbara High School, then gone to Andover and Harvard, was groomed in other words for a future in business or one of the professions. All he wanted was to be a writer.

My tall, elegant mother was knowledgeable in all sorts of subjects, having absorbed a great deal from living in Florence. But she never attended college, and all she ever wanted was to marry a writer.

It was indeed a match made in heaven, and I grew up with that powerful romantic love that enveloped my parents. Throughout their lives, they remained deeply in love. My teen-age friends used to comment on it; they noticed my parents were "still in love" into old age.

Mom and Dad

My father's writing career started off well, because his first book "The Happy Man," was a recognized success as a classic about the West. The book was a collection of stories about his experiences working as a cowboy on one of the large cattle ranches in the delta country between the Sacramento and San Joaquin Rivers in Northern California. He was dubbed the "Harvard Cowboy."

My parents spent the first year of their married life living in a modest house crammed between feedlots and pastures. Dad used the skills he'd acquired ranching on the Sisquoc to work physically hard all day, and then come home to write at night. To mother, it was all romantic and part of a new adventure.

All too soon, Pearl Harbor occurred, and Dad answered the call to fight for his country. He was a proud soldier, and spent four years in the U.S. Army, much of it overseas. This was the period when Mom and Dad wrote each other every day for the duration of the time they were apart. Later, Dad compiled all their letters to each other in a book, published in 1991 and entitled "Love and War."

Throughout their life together, mother was to be his muse, who inspired and encouraged his writing. He read aloud much of what he'd written to her, and she had the quick and true judgment of one who herself was a gifted writer, like her father.

Although Dad worked very hard, and published many books and articles, he never reached the financial success he wished to have with his writing. Fortunately, he liked teaching, and was an excellent addition to the English department at Santa Barbara City College.

However, most of Santa Barbara will remember my father as an early environmental activist, kick-started by his involvement with the 1969 Oil Spill here in the community he treasured. From there, Dad went on to have a hand in the establishment of the Community Environmental Council (CEC, our local recycling operation), the Environmental Defense Center, and the San Rafael Wilderness in our own backcountry.

These activities took a tremendous amount of time, phone calls, and attendance at community meetings. In many ways his participation in what was then thought of as radical causes was essential. The name Robert O. Easton on a committee meant stability and rationality, and if Bob was for it, other members of the community were more likely to get onboard. My father was good at that — bringing people together to protect the Santa Barbara that he cherished. Pearl Chase, the grande dame of Santa Barbara preservation, was a family friend of my Easton grandparents, and she got behind several of these causes while she was still alive.

For me, Mom was a strong influence, one quite different from Dad. Having been raised in Italy and traveled throughout Europe as a child, she had glamorous stories to tell. I heard about her youth in an Italian villa, listened to stories of her boarding school in Switzerland, and her travels in France and Germany. Also, Mom was good at languages and had an ear for them. She spoke Italian like a native, but also French and even some German, from the days she spent in Vienna just before World War II began in 1939.

Both my mother's siblings, John and Judy, ended up settling in Florence for the rest of their lives. Judy died of cancer at a relatively young age. Her daughter, Adriana, later became very close to all of us here in the U.S.; she was our only cousin and has kept our family's loving connection to Italy strong.

But back to my mother: she had an aura of European elegance about her in a subtle, feminine way. At six feet tall, her commanding figure and beautiful face stood out, but she was also charming. Speaking in her educated accent to whomever she encountered, that person would do anything for her. Whether with the guy stocking the shelves at Safeway or the countess who came to the villa when she was a child and subsequently bequeathed her a diamond ring (exquisite, I still have it), my mother was charismatic. And I saw all that, but I also saw how she'd turned her back on a certain kind of life she could have had in order to marry a writer and be a hands-on mother.

I worshipped the way she could be strong and get what she wanted in a quiet manner. She was not above using her feminine wiles, the way women of that era would do, but at the same time she wasn't one bit phony, nor did she ever put on airs. Also, Mom detested polite untruths, "safe talk" she would call them.

In addition, I wouldn't consider my parents intellectuals, in the true sense of the word. Although they were well-educated and read widely, both of them had a soft spot for the simple, less fortunate person of any race or creed. Overly generous, my parents were easily touched by people they'd decided were deserving of their help, at least in some small financial way. Both Mom and Dad had such faith in the average person, Dad even more so than Mom. They firmly believed that the high-minded aspects of life would triumph.

2.

A Santa Barbara Childhood

Mother said one of the first words I uttered as a toddler was "burr," while pointing to the birds on the lawn in Santa Barbara. I know this from a letter she wrote to my father, who was overseas during World War II.

"Yesterday two pretty little hummingbirds did the loveliest dance and flight over the lawn. Joan was enchanted and I explained to her, though she had no idea what I was chattering about — except that she loves to watch birds."

My first conscious memory was Dad coming home from the war. Mom's intense joy and anticipation at his return imprinted this moment on my brain. One day in November 1945, my father stood in uniform at the front door of our house. He opened his arms wide, and threw them around his wife and two children — me and Katherine. The excitement of Dad's return, rushing upstairs to show him my room, and the wave of happiness that came over our young family made this day unforgettable.

On the Riviera

Skipping many years ahead to the early 1950s, the Easton family had grown: I now had three younger sisters — Katherine plus Ellen and Jane. We had relocated to a George Washington Smith-designed house in the Riviera section of Santa Barbara. The house itself hadn't been touched since the 1920s, when it was built. My parents put in a dishwasher, but much of the house was in its original state. Beautiful imported tiles and authentic Spanish touches couldn't quite make up for the benign neglect.

French doors led to a flagstone terrace with steps on either side into a marvelous garden. Surrounded by over two acres of overgrown oak woodland, with unkempt pathways and natural landscaping, the garden was ideal. It afforded privacy and places for children to explore. This was my childhood home and I loved it: my own wild kingdom.

My parents didn't care about having a manicured garden or interior decorating. They had a dream of how they wanted to live and how they would raise their children. Mother was unconventional, Bohemian even. She had few clothes, although she loved luxuries, and everything in her life was focused around my father and his writing career. Their social life was quiet, so as not to interfere with writing. They seldom went out to dinner, and life was basically no frills. With four girls to raise, there was never enough money, but nobody mentioned that. My parents never discussed money issues; Mother said it was considered rude to ask about such things.

Books, books, and more books. Reading aloud, trips to the library, and above all, ideas and ideals filled our life. Conversation and letter writing, that's what I grew up with. Everything was focused on the beauty and wisdom of the printed word. As a child, I read everything, especially books that could be found in the masses of bookshelves in every room.

In winter when the north winds gusted over our hilltop, I heard the frightening sound of the eucalyptus trees thrashing against each other. In summer, I watched the fog roll in over the town of Santa Barbara below our house, covering everything with deep, white cotton. The massive oaks that bordered the house on either side had thick limbs for climbing. From my bedroom window, I had a view out to the Channel Islands — which reminded me of the ocean and the beaches that I loved.

Every day I walked down the hill to attend Jefferson Elementary School, and back up again. I never minded the walk. And soon I was on the last leg, up the hill through the vacant lot to our house. Once there, I ran up the back porch stairs into the kitchen and grabbed a snack. Then, I changed out of my dress — nobody wore pants to school in those days — and put on a pair of jeans. I headed outside.

Mom wasn't worried about us. She was casual.

We rode our bikes all over. I hopped on my green Schwinn bike and pedaled down Las Tunas Road. I felt the wind in my face, while I struggled with the brakes on the steepest part of the road. Where Las Tunas opens up after it turns a corner, I skidded to a stop. A patch of beavertail cactus grew on the upslope side of the road, and opposite it on the downslope side stood a gnarled California pepper tree.

Usually I was by myself, but sometimes Ellen joined me at our "fort" in the old pepper tree.

When I climbed up into the tree's branches, I could look way out across the open fields of the Riviera with few houses. Just the wild oats waving in the breeze, green after winter rains, gold all summer long.

This was my territory, and the pepper tree was my lookout.

My First Field Guide

Starting in 1952, Nin, my Faust grandmother, arranged for each of her grandchildren to come up to Berkeley for a short visit during the summer.

I arrived on the prop airplane from Santa Barbara wearing my navy blue plaid dress with the white collar, and little white gloves (considered proper for travel in those days). At the same time, I clutched a large jar filled with slimy water full of chorus frog tadpoles in various stages of development. These tadpoles (Pacific treefrogs) had been captured in Mission Creek. As adults, they would turn into tiny frogs no more than two inches long. Since I didn't want to miss out on their metamorphosis from tadpole to adult, I was still grasping this precious jar of frogs when I later returned from Berkeley.

Nin was now a widow, because Grandfather Faust had signed on as a war correspondent and was tragically killed in 1944. Nin lived in a shingled cottage with a splendid view of San Francisco Bay and a steep, flower-filled garden. I looked forward to my visits there.

One day, Nin drove me over to San Francisco to pay one of those duty visits — the kind children dread — to Miss Florence Greeley, a distant relative. We called her Tante (German for aunt, after the fashion of the day). She was proud that Horace Greeley was an ancestor.

I climbed the dark, narrow staircase of a respectable but dilapidated apartment house. Tante was in her seventies, a square-faced, heavy-set woman with a deep voice and a husky laugh. She wore loose-fitting print dresses and smoked. I still remember the click of her tortoise shell cigarette holder against her teeth as she paused between sentences. She told long, involved stories of her past, punctuated with sips from a glass of sherry.

We never stayed more than an hour, and Tante had a small present to give me before I left. She kept books and Victorian mementos crammed into her apartment, and from these she selected a treasure.

That summer my present was a much-used, faded copy of Chester Reed's "Field Guide to Birds East of the Rockies," published in 1906. Perhaps it was the small size of the book, hardly bigger than a pocket pamphlet and bound in imitation leather, or the way the description of each bird was placed neatly on the same page as the artist's illustration, but I was entranced. Up to that point, I had never known there was such a thing as a field guide.

Something about the idea of matching the birds I saw in the garden with those pictured in the field guide attracted me.

When I returned to Santa Barbara, I sought out the only binoculars in the house, a pair of German field glasses. They were small, but good.

I liked the fact that Dad had used them during the war.

Once I looked through the binoculars, I realized I could recognize details on birds. I took the binoculars out into our garden. If I sat quietly on a rock near a running sprinkler, birds would come in to drink. I tried my best to identify birds from the Reed field guide. I saw ruby-crowned kinglets, cedar waxwings, and Audubon's (now yellow-rumped) warblers.

And so my secret life began. In the soft, misty October evenings, and the clear, breezy winter afternoons I roamed the garden puzzling over what birds I saw. Usually I picked three or four favorite spots in our overgrown property. If I sat astride one of the limbs of the big oak trees, or hid behind a bush and stayed quiet, I realized the birds would come to me.

One difficulty was that my field guide showed only those land birds east of the Rockies. Surely, I surmised, there must be some overlap. However, it was all very confusing.

But it clicked — the beginning of a life-long passion for learning more about birds, their life histories, where they came from and where they were going. From then on, I was interested in anything to do with birds.

Pet Birds and Projects

For several years I owned caged birds. Some were canaries, which sang loudly. Another was a Cockatiel, very fancy and exotic, but not as appealing as the canaries.

Mother took me down to the pet store owned by kind Mr. Finley on Milpas Street. How thrilling to walk in and get a new cage or a new tidbit for my bird. The cage hung in my room on a stand, right in front of the window.

Why did I want a caged bird? Probably due to my reading of all the "Dr. Dolittle" stories by Hugh Lofting. These stories fascinated me, because I liked books where animals came alive and had personalities. One of the books, *Dr. Dolittle and the Green Canary*, described the adventures of a canary. Dr. John Dolittle was a man who could talk to animals in their own language; he was my hero.

When I was even younger, I enjoyed all of the Beatrix Potter books. And since, like Dr. Dolittle, they took place in England — the English being the best in the world at nature writing — it was the beginning of my adoration of all things English.

When it came to literature for young naturalists, I guess I was born on the wrong side of the U.S. Although I read with delight the Thornton Burgess stories about birds, they were all illustrated with *Eastern* bird species, as were most of the flash cards and other nature-oriented learning guides for children that I found in the library.

Books I borrowed from the library described how to make feeders or nest boxes for *Eastern* birds, but I hoped the design would work for Western birds as well. So I made a nest box and put it up on the big oak tree. Then I made a wooden feeder tray, and had Dad help me attach it to the ledge outside my bedroom window. I sprinkled bird seed on the tray, but was disappointed when only a few finches and jays came to feed.

* * *

In hindsight, it seems to me a child who is fortunate enough, as I was, to be isolated by circumstance, sometimes develops an interest in nature. My childhood homes weren't in city neighborhoods that fostered friends who drop in. "Having a play date" was a big deal, because my mother had to drive over and pick up the girl, bring her to our house, and then take her home.

Being the oldest, I was often alone.

I had time after school and on the weekends; Mom was busy with Dad and the younger children.

I had the freedom and space in which to explore. So the bird sounds, the smells of plants, the weather — I absorbed it all.

Thus I created my own private world; the world you dip into anytime you want. You are outdoors, but you are not alone. Being surrounded by birds, birds that you can put a name to, is like being among old friends.

So birds became a powerful symbol of an aspect of nature that belonged to me, all mine. For one thing, nobody else that I knew was interested in birds, nobody in my immediate family, and none of my friends.

Me and the birds. I couldn't help myself. Yes, I wanted to enjoy birds, to appreciate them as one sees beauty in nature, but it was more than that. To name it: what was this urge to identify, to learn, and to recognize which bird I was looking at? Why would that matter? The naming, the possessing, the reaching out and bringing into one's realm — was that what I was doing when I was ten years old with my funny binoculars and my Chester Reed field guide?

Growing Up in the Easton Household

Life in the Easton household was not luxurious. Possessions and modern conveniences were unimportant.

For example, we girls ate most meals in the kitchen, and our dinner was always earlier than our parents'. Since he was home, Dad did much of the grocery shopping. Often, Spam was on the menu. The Eastons lived in their Spanish-style mansion eating Spam. As a youngster, I didn't understand. And as I grew up, I had questions about our family's lifestyle and why we were different. Set against the 1950s, our family was an oddball: in ideas, in lifestyle, in the way we children were brought up.

By about 1960, Dad went back to UCSB and received his Master's degree, then began to teach English at Santa Barbara City College, but back in the 1950s he was writing full-time at home. And Mom was the gatekeeper. If Dad was in his study in the house, we girls had to be quiet. Instead of shouting and running up the tile staircase to our bedrooms, we were supposed to whisper. Occasionally, when my parents entertained, we girls would huddle on the balcony overlooking the front door and chuckle about the guests. Giggling fits would break out, however, and we'd rush back inside.

An e-mail I received recently from a friend describes how my family appeared to my peers in the 1950s: "A few times I was lucky enough to be invited over to play at Joan's and was very impressed with her beautiful big home. It seemed to me it was a Spanish style 'mansion' with beautiful grounds; large and with many rooms. Certainly not like my middle-class home.

"Once I was invited over for dinner and it turned out to be Joan's parents' anniversary. I was asked a question or two at dinner and I was so painfully shy and unsure of myself and in awe of the Eastons, that I could barely get anything out.

"Joan's Mother seemed to be very happy as a mom of 4 girls and never worked outside of the home. She had a 5-year-old daughter, Jane, who was about the same age as my younger sister. Ellen and Katherine shared a room and Joan had her own room with lots of filled bookcases and even a corner fireplace. I remember looking out the windows of her second floor bedroom and I could see the ocean.

"Joan's father didn't have a 'real' job like mine did. He was an author and spent time in his private office writing. My dad had a real job selling furniture and worked six days a week, so I again was in awe of someone who didn't seem to have to work to support a family. Joan's father was educated and my dad had graduated from Santa Barbara High School in 1929 and was put in business by his immigrant parents, so again the two families were quite different.

"I remember Joan's father had the children run around the outside of the house for exercise! That seemed odd to me. My Dad made popcorn at night and he and my Mom ate it in bed and we loved that special time. Can you imagine the Eastons doing THAT?"

* * *

One night a week, usually Sundays, the whole family was required (perhaps not Jane, she was too young) to sit by the fire in the living room and listen to a book Dad chose to read aloud to us. Enormous groaning and moaning greeted these family evenings. Part of the problem was that Dad had us listening to pretty grown-up material.

We'd be assigned parts in a Shakespeare play to read aloud. Sometimes, we were each required to memorize a poem and recite it, standing up in front of the fireplace. Dad was the driving force in our education.

He wanted me to write research papers. One project was on great religions of the world, taken from those terrific "Life" magazine series that were issued occasionally. I struggled trying to describe and summarize Mohammedanism (now Islam), Hinduism, Buddhism, and Christianity. None of the other sisters had to do these sorts of things.

Looking back, I realize how valuable this reading and writing was, and what a terrific opportunity it was for me, but at the time I thought, why couldn't I just relax and enjoy myself like other kids?

I worshipped my parents, and Dad's writing was the consuming purpose of their life. In many ways, there wasn't enough time or attention for us children. But I, being the oldest, was lavished with praise and love. In return, I did everything I could to please my parents.

However, the greatest gift from them was what I was born with — a happy outlook on life. I was certain my life was going to be a good one.

My Sisters

I was glad to have sisters — three of them — each of us very different.

Katherine was a year-and-a-half younger than I was, but two grades separated us at school. She was truly talented as an artist, and my parents encouraged her. When she was young, she went to the Santa Barbara Museum of Art for classes, and even took private lessons from Douglas Parshall for awhile.

Katherine had a lovely face, big dark eyes; she exuded femininity. But even as a child she was emotional, clung to Mom, and needed special handling. Today she might have been called bipolar.

Ellen has reminded me that she, being the next one down in the family, was tormented by Katherine. Katherine could be cruel. She pulled the hair off Ellen's dolls and did little things to Ellen that my parents were too busy to notice. Katherine could embellish the truth so skillfully that anyone would believe her.

As she got older, Katherine spent more and more time in her room. Some days she'd go to school, some days not. We all grew up knowing that Katherine had problems and that she was artistic. Suffice it to say that I had to be good. When there's a difficult child in the family, that child gets a lot of attention and the rest of us have to behave. So I was the responsible type, got good grades, did the sensible thing.

Ellen, the third in line, was the one with whom I formed a special bond early on. Despite the nearly five-year gap in our ages, we were on the same wavelength. Not that she liked birds, but she was passionate about horses, and she liked the outdoors and exploring around. The older we grew, the more I turned to Ellen. Also, she was the one to accompany Dad and me on hiking trips, which drew us closer.

And Jane, my youngest sis, well, we were robbed of our sisterhood, because there was nearly a 10-year gap between us in age. I was off to college just as she was coming into her own. Jane, my spiritually-minded sister, was always a mellow person. And being the youngest, she had a more relaxed upbringing than the rest of us.

Days at the Santa Barbara Museum of Natural History

On the weekends, I rode my bike down to the Museum of Natural History. I pressed the "rattlesnake button" in the display case as I entered the museum. The buzz it made was unforgettable. Until I heard one in the backcountry later, I couldn't believe the rattle would be so loud. And the rattlesnake button is still there today.

I wandered through the cool dark halls.

The Sarah Hamilton Fleischmann Bird Hall was my favorite. This was the old, original bird hall, which had nests and eggs in the glass cases, and stuffed birds suspended from the ceiling. How I adored that room. With its fusty smell and disheveled specimens, to me it was pure heaven. Wooden benches stood next to each oblong glass case, so I could sit or kneel and look down from the top into the display cases. Each nest was labeled with a faded card that reminded me of the illustrations in my Chester Reed field guide.

I knew the nests by heart. There were the soft, down-lined nests of the ducks, and the entrance to the kingfisher's tunnel with the cut-out of the mud nest at the end. But my favorites were the hummingbird nests — no larger than a quarter, perfectly molded, and placed in the most fantastic situations. One hummer chose to build her nest in the loop of a thick rope. The nest's blond fibers made a tiny cup sitting on the rope. Another nest was placed on the top of an orange.

I walked slowly around the whole bird hall, staring at the cases and the mounted birds. I learned what birds looked like that I never thought I'd get a chance to see on my own: the male magnificent frigatebird, with its distended red throat in nuptial display, the yellow and black orioles, and the fierce-billed hawks and eagles.

Later, when the bird habitat hall with excellent diorama paintings by Ray Strong was added, I loved those exhibits. This collection of local habitats with authentic background paintings featured locations recognizable in our region. I still carry those scenes in my mind wherever I go.

But back to my days of exploration in the 1950s. This was the era of Irma Cooke, otherwise known as Cookie, who was a famous educator at the museum. A few live birds in cages were cared for by museum staff. My favorite was the gray-mottled, fluffed-up western screech-owl, as it sat dozing during the day.

Then, I tiptoed into the museum library with the wooden book cases lining the walls. Still much the same now as it was then, it has a fireplace and a big painting of Max Fleischmann, the original benefactor of the museum. But I was on my way to the Mammal Hall.

Each exhibit in that spacious hall was familiar. I lingered before the one where the young mountain lions were sparring in front of a rock cavern. And what about that enormous stuffed grizzly bear? So scary, so wild. And the weasel, and the opossum. To me, they were as alive as could be. They weren't stuffed animals, but old friends.

Outside, I crossed the wooden bridge to check out the creek. If it was summer, I jumped from rock to rock, or caught tadpoles. In winter I watched the roiling waters engulf the boulders. After winter rainstorms, the boulders in the creek rolled shoulder to shoulder, making an ominous sound.

Once, Ellen and I brought Jane along. She was still young, but we must've persuaded her to either walk or ride her bike down the hill with us. We were at Rocky Nook Park, along a stretch of Mission Creek. A series of winter storms had just come through, and we knew the creek would be a sight.

We got to the middle of the creek by scrambling over to a big rock, and we sat up there, fascinated by the swirling water. Suddenly, Jane slipped down the side and fell right into the creek. The waters were an angry chocolate color, and there was Jane, bobbing around in them. I was supposed to be in charge, but it was Ellen who pulled her out. We never told Mom and Dad about it, but we'd learned a lesson: respect for creeks flooding after a rain.

Birding at a Red Farmhouse

At the end of my junior year in high school, our family moved to a simpler, more casual home. Best of all, it had a sloping pasture in front of the house. Dad could have horses at last. Both Ellen and Jane were excellent horseback riders, too. But for me, horses got in my way. I wanted my feet on the ground so I could see more of what was happening, and go quietly.

This is where I first noticed the sounds of local birds. Nature became an even greater part of my life at our new home on Las Canoas Road.

I learned the scream of the red-shouldered hawk, and the guttural cooing of the band-tailed pigeons roosting in the eucalyptus trees across the road. I watched as a mockingbird mobbed and hassled our cat, dive-bombing the cat when it walked past the mockingbird's nest in the pittosporum hedge. I found a lesser goldfinch nest in the orchard and watched the progress from eggs to nestlings to adults.

I prowled the property with my binoculars to see what I could find. In spring, when the western kingbirds perched on the barbed-wire fence in back of the house, I added a new species to my list. Same with Say's phoebe in the winter. Red-tailed hawks and turkey vultures were old friends, soaring in the quiet sky. One day a California thrasher scurried across the terrace, its long brown tail held up at an angle.

More than any other bird sound, the bell-like staccato of the wrentit's song haunted me. Before I had any clue as to where the song was coming from, it was a companion to my days exploring our hillside. At last, I spied a family of wrentits that nested in the garden that spring. They liked the over-grown plumbago, with its blue flowers and sprawling branches. When I actually saw the male wrentit singing, observed its whole body shaking with each syllable, I was thrilled. Here was a bird that I'd heard so often, and I finally set eyes on it.

Occasionally, a gopher snake slithered across the terrace. In spring, the frogs calling from Rattlesnake Creek filled the twilight hours. A great horned owl pair resided nearby; I heard them hooting back and forth. In late summer, if you took an evening walk, you might see one of the juvenile great horneds perched up on a telephone wire right by the road. Just seeing that big shape, the cat-like silhouette of a great horned owl, gave me a shot of adrenaline, a special kind of excitement.

Birds were part of my upbringing, but I never considered myself a birder. Everyone in the family knew I loved birds, and that was that.

Furthermore, I never revealed to my close high-school friends that I liked birding. Anything that made you stand out, made you different: horrors. Remember, this was the 1950s. I was "nerdy" enough as it was with my good grades and my bookish family. I dared not share that I prowled around looking at birds, that would've been way too embarrassing. I was governed by my peers' opinion, by a desire to be like everybody else and what they thought was cool. And in that era, birding was definitely not cool.

But birding was just what I needed, because in many ways coming home to our rustic family house was a refuge for me. It was downtime all on my own, a chance to recharge. Those memories of getting in touch with birds, of sensing that I was part of a bigger natural world — which I knew about but others didn't — that was a talisman I carried into adulthood.

And it was a pursuit I would eventually return to and never leave.

3.

Out In The Wild

From the time we were young, my father brought us along on day hikes up the front country trails of the Santa Ynez Mountains. On the weekends, he took Ellen and me, or a friend, and one of our dogs. We knew the trails up Rattlesnake, Cold Spring, and Romero Canyons especially well.

The flowing creeks were my favorites. We climbed the steep gray rocks and skittered down the other side, watched tadpoles as they nosed up to the underwater tree roots, looked for newts in the deep pools, listened to the rushing water up ahead. In this dry country, I clung to the promise of the streams, long before I realized they were a magnet for birds.

Dad longed to go backpacking. And our mother — as firm as she was about anything — was adamant that sleeping on the ground was not for her. Dad didn't question that, so his daughters were his chosen companions.

The no-frills policy extended to backpacking endeavors. Gear was army surplus, and food supplies were meager. Ellen and I were hungry most of the time.

Here is my account of a hike down-creek to the one-room Manzana schoolhouse. The schoolhouse was restored, with the help of my Grandfather Easton and others, and is now designated as an Historic Landmark. But in the 1950s, it was a dilapidated log cabin.

(The original journal for this trip was a set of scrawled notes Dad made me jot down all those years ago.)

NATURE JOURNAL: JUNE 18, 1958
Hike to Manzana Schoolhouse

We start down the trail, which follows along Manzana Creek.

This time of year, shallow water barely covers the smooth stones; they're draped in algae; green tendrils float in the sluggish current.

Dad tells us we can't drink the creek water, it's not good. It's moving too slowly. We have to wait till we get to one of the springs along the way to fill up our canteens.

This just makes me thirstier. The metallic taste of the warm liquid in my old-fashioned canteen doesn't quench my longing for water.

Ellen and I know better than to complain.

The day grows hotter. No breeze here.

I've brought the binoculars, though, and I'm identifying a few birds.

A black phoebe perches on a twig, flicks its tail, sallies out to catch a fly. I spot a yellow warbler, a bright flash of yellow against the green of the cottonwood trees. And over there is a nest high up in a willow, a little wad of fibers suspended from a fork in the tree.

I wonder if it's last year's, maybe of a warbling vireo?

In my notebook, I write the names of the trees we see:
live oak, alder, cottonwood, willow, bay. And the birds.
I don't know their calls yet, but I can identify some of
them by sight: a western flycatcher and a song sparrow.

Dad starts to relax. He's telling stories, adventures of
the old days on the Sisquoc Ranch.

Nobody can give the hot, dry backcountry such a
sense of mystery and dignity as my dad. His reverence
for nature, his respect for animals, trees and flowers
shines through in his stories.

We girls sigh. We've heard it all before . . . but at the
same time it is just what we need to hear.

The lesson we learn when we go hiking in the
backcountry with Dad is: respect for the natural world.

With a rattlesnake, caution is part of the respect.
Watch where you put your feet. Never step over a log
without knowing what's on the other side of it, says Dad.

At last we come to a swimming hole, strip off our
clothes and jump in. Heaven. Cool, dark water. No
slimy algae here.

Our toes feel fish nibbling them. Cliff swallows dip
and swerve flying to their nests built on an open rock
face above.

After spending the night at the confluence of
the Sisquoc River and Manzana Creek, we visit the
schoolhouse. The log cabin is one big empty room and
a blackboard. Dad explains that there used to be
nearly 100 people as part of a remote community of
homesteaders here.

I look out the dirty windowpane and notice a fruit
tree growing on the far hillside. A wooden ladder is still
propped against its trunk. How did the settlers survive?
Such harsh conditions, the long summers, the lack of water.

*It's hotter than hot, but we find another swimming
hole then catch ten rainbow trout. After lunch, fishing
again, ten more fish to take back to camp to cook.
In the evening, we walk over to an old hay field and
see a pair of western bluebirds nesting in the high hollow
of a sycamore.*

*The next day, the hike all the way back to the
trailhead is hard, unbearably hot. Canyon flies hover
around our faces driving us crazy. We stop again to
cool off in the deepest pool. Finally, we trudge into the
parking lot at NIRA campground. As always, Dad has
saved oranges as a treat to be eaten at the car; we stand
around savoring the sweet juice of the fruit as it dribbles
down our chin.*

Lucky — that's what Ellen and I are.

Days at Zaca Laderas

In 1952, the Sisquoc Ranch was sold.

By this time, after years of managing and then being part owner of
the Sisquoc Ranch, Grandfather Easton had decided to buy some land
of his own in the Santa Ynez Valley. He owned Zaca Mesa ranch, which
is now a winery off Foxen Canyon Road, and another piece of property,
Zaca Laderas, off Figueroa Mountain Road.

Zaca Laderas, also called Sycamore Canyon Ranch, was a swath of
rangeland stretching along the foothills of the San Rafael Mountains.
You could hike from the ranch straight up and over Zaca Peak, if you
made up your mind to do it. (I did once, but that's another story . . .)

I looked forward to the days when we were invited to come up
to Zaca Laderas. The ranch had a wide central valley where barley and
alfalfa were grown, but most of it was oak savannah, with steep canyons
and one or two creeks that only flowed after spring rains.

One day we were walking along when Dad stopped, put a finger to his lips, and pointed straight ahead into the distance. At first, I saw nothing but the wild oats and the coast live oaks that dotted the hillsides. When Dad described where it was, I gasped. A mountain lion.

The big cat hadn't caught wind of us yet. It was sitting with its back to us, staring intently at the ground. A large, pale beige lion leaning forward in pure concentration, it was sitting by a gopher hole, or perhaps a ground squirrel burrow, watching and waiting for prey. For a long time, the mountain lion didn't move.

It was about 200 yards away — pretty far — but we could see it clearly. Slowly, while we stood watching and holding our breath, the enormous cat turned, sensed us, saw us, and slunk away, its long thin tail curving behind it.

I haven't seen a mountain lion since that day, despite years in the backcountry and all my birding experiences. But the lions are everywhere; they make themselves invisible and hunt mostly at night to avoid humans.

Zaca Laderas was a working cattle ranch. Being a gentleman farmer was not part of my grandfather's psyche. He took ranching seriously, as did my father. When we girls were visiting, we were taught that you don't chase the cows (they need to be fattened for sale). You don't walk through the middle of a cultivated field. You leave every gate the way you find it, whether open or closed.

Later, I watched birds at Zaca Laderas. I have an early journal describing a red-tailed hawk nest I located high in a spreading valley oak. In order to observe the nest, I sat down in the middle of a cultivated barley field, completely concealed by the golden spikey heads. Here I waited for hours. I saw one of the adult birds bring a rodent to the edge of the nest, then watched fascinated as the three nestlings fought over it, stabbing the rat and tearing at it ravenously. The largest youngster grabbed the prey and gulped it down, a long tail sticking up out of its gullet.

While sitting waiting for the red-tailed hawks, I made a list of all the bird species I could hear around me. There were thirteen in all, beginning with the yellow-billed magpies, and ending with the red-winged blackbirds, which nested in the tall mustard on the far hillside.

Condors
and the Backcountry

Grandfather Easton began to take a part in saving the California Condor back in the 1930s. At that time, there was tremendous concern about successful firefighting techniques, which led to the building of graded dirt roads throughout the backcountry. During the Depression years, members of the Civilian Conservation Corps (CCC) were put to work constructing these roads, the first of which was known as the Buckhorn Road. It ran up and over Big Pine Mountain, connecting the Santa Ynez Valley to the Cuyama Valley.

When Grandfather Easton (known as Bob Easton Sr.) learned that a second road was contemplated to run from Manzana Creek (near NIRA, the National Industrial Recovery Act Campground) up and over Hurricane Deck and along the Sisquoc River, he was determined to stop it. Already he was concerned about the California Condor. He saw the depredations of egg collectors on the condor population, and he believed that this rare species needed to be protected.

Intervention on the part of an administrator of the National Audubon Society was a welcome development. But the Audubon official was anxious to know just how many condors were in the area. Grandfather needed to prove to everyone that condors did indeed still survive in this remote country.

Hence the famous story was told, and well-documented by Ray Ford in his article in *Noticias* (Vol. XXXII, No. 4), entitled "Saving The Condor: Robert E. Easton's Fight to Create the Sisquoc Condor Sanctuary," about the day my grandfather and his father lured the condors in.

Later in my life, when I was hiking the backcountry as an adult, I wrote this journal entry.

NATURE JOURNAL: JUNE 19, 1984
Hike to Sierra Madre Ridge

We park in the middle of a dusty oil field in the Cuyama Valley. This is the base of the Rocky Ridge trail. Dad and I are backpacking up the north side of the Sierra Madre ridge to reach Montgomery Potrero (a Spanish word meaning grasslands surrounded by chaparral or forest).

Although it's 4 o'clock in the afternoon, the temperature is toasty. I'd forgotten how hard it is to be hiking such a steep trail with a pack on my back.

A woozy feeling comes over me; I think I'm going to faint. I sit down, leaning my pack against the steep bank. We both take a break, me with an energy bar, and Dad lost in memories of the past.

He starts telling me about the time 50 years ago when he and Grandfather Easton, accompanied by neighboring ranch owner Eugene Johnston and his son, Lamar, hatched a plan to lure condors to Montgomery Potrero.

When Dad describes how they rode up this trail with a dead horse — bait to be laid out at a strategic point to attract the condors — I cringe.

Dad starts off by saying, "I was about 19, and my father had suggested that the only way to actually census the remaining condors in the area was to set a sort of trap for them. Hence, the dead horse."

He continues: "Lamar and I had prepared a blind a few days before, so we could view and photograph the condors without disturbing them. As the observers rode up onto Montgomery Potrero, they stared in amazement at the circling mass of ravens, turkey vultures, and the large forms of condors among them. The bait had worked. And the news of the California Condor sighting spread throughout the ornithological world."

I conjure what it was like: the group of men, my Dad among them, staring at these giant condors.

I am excited approaching Montgomery Potrero, because it was here, too, that Grandfather, then manager of the Sisquoc Ranch that owned 40 acres of Montgomery Potrero, would make his deal with the Forest Service: they could have an easement through the potrero for a fire road there, in return for not cutting a road through the middle of the Sisquoc watershed.

If that road had been built in 1934, it would have passed within a half mile of the Sisquoc Falls, where up to 21 condors had been observed bathing and preening.

And so the first condor sanctuary was established, the U.S. Forest Service agreed to stop the road construction, and, much later, it was protected for the future as part of the San Rafael Wilderness: all efforts in which Grandfather and Dad were leaders.

Feeling better at last, I shoulder my pack and push on. Higher and higher we climb, the sun going down over the rim of Montgomery Potrero, as we crest the hill in back of the enormous sandstone rock.

This famous rock, known as "The House of the Sun," looms over the surrounding grasslands.

If you scramble up the front of the rock, and squeeze through a narrow opening, you find yourself inside a high cave overlooking the whole San Rafael range with Big Pine Mountain in the distance. And on the back of the pale sandstone wall is a large pinwheel-shaped rendering of a sun. The reddish pigment of the painting, perhaps the work of a Chumash shaman ages ago, is still vivid.

Research at the Santa Barbara Museum of Natural
History suggests that this was the site of S'apiksi, a
recognized Chumash gathering place for worship
and daily life.

*I'm hungry, the stars are coming out, and we
decide to set up camp with our little propane stove
right here. Dad, being a purist, would hike with hardly
any food, if I were willing. But I crave a cup of coffee
in the morning, and an instant hot meal at night.*

*We eat under the big golden cup oak with its
spreading branches (long since dead) and fall into our
sleeping bags. The night is still. Coyotes bark down in
the canyon, a petulant, wild sound.*

*A barn owl shrieks as it starts its nightly prowl.
Then a great horned owl hoots from the top of the
water tank down the hillside.*

*Morning comes early. The sun rises behind distant
Mount Pinos and creeps slowly over our sleeping bags.
The bags are damp from the dew. I'm freezing, so I put
Dad's sweater on over my legs by sticking them into
the arms.*

*I'm anxious to begin birding the potrero. At Black
Willow Spring, a tiny seep of water draws in birds and
I sit there quietly.*

*My list from here includes California quail, both
black and Say's phoebes (a couple of pairs each),
western kingbird, house and Bewick's wrens, many
lark sparrows, many Brewer's blackbirds and brown-
headed cowbirds, and the specialty: the Lawrence's
goldfinches that arrive in a family group with juveniles.
Their black faces and mustard-colored wings suit their
backcountry habitats. I'd recognize their tinkling bell
call anywhere.*

After birding, we walk east along the dirt track known as the Sierra Madre Road. Now I understand what a disaster for the forest this would be if it were paved and open to tourists. If not for Dad and Grandfather, who knew?

The next potrero is called Pine Corral. Golden grasses are studded with weird sandstone formations. These rocks, looking like whales, gargoyles, and giant lizards, stand tall above a sea of wild oats. We pause, rest, stow our packs, and explore. Dad remembers which caves in the rocks have the best Chumash paintings. We go from one to the other searching for the hidden drawings.

Tonight we camp at Cherry Orchard Spring. A trickle of water runs down the hillside near a fantasy rock formation known as the Indian Princess. More birding for me at dusk. I hear the mournful call of poorwills in the distance and a swirling mass of cliff swallows swoops around the spring.

Next day, we move on to Salisbury Potrero. Fred Reyes, from one of the oldest ranching families in Cuyama, has a "line cabin" here where the cowboys can live for part of the year when they bring the cattle up to feed on grass in spring and summer. It's a cozy wood cabin, very small.

From Salisbury, the Bull Ridge trail heads straight down the side of Lion Canyon.

This canyon, with its sheer rock face, was picked as the first place to release captive-bred condors in Santa Barbara County. Had I known then that all the wild condors would be captured in 1987, bred in zoos, then released in Lion Canyon, I might've paid more attention to the precipitous terrain. The way the

steep canyon opens out into the flat Cuyama Valley miles below makes you feel you could set your wings, catch the rising air currents, and soar.
Instead, we tramp down the stony trail headed for home.

* * *

Nearly ten years later, in December 1993 at this same Lion Canyon, Dad, Ellen, and I joined officials and biologists from the condor recovery crew, including condor ornithologist Jan Hamber from the Museum of Natural History, as five zoo-bred birds made their debut into the wild in Santa Barbara County. The ungainly condors hopped from their cages, and perched on the rocks below us. The great birds took clumsy practice flights from one ledge to another. Would they know what to do? We watched and waited. Everyone was silent. Some people had tears in their eyes, I know I did.

Nobody knew better than Jan Hamber and my father just what a challenge it had been to preserve the California Condor. In the 1980s, the wild population had dwindled so rapidly that extinction threatened. By capturing the few remaining wild condors and putting them into a zoo-based recovery program, agencies and biologists were taking a huge chance: the cost was enormous, the program was controversial, and there were challenges nobody could foresee. Therefore, to get to a point where zoo-raised condors were re-introduced back into their wild habitat — well, we didn't know what would happen. After life in a zoo, could the birds navigate the updrafts, and find their way to a food source?

At last, one by one, the condors flapped their enormous wings and soared free into the sky above Lion Canyon. What an emotional moment for all of us who had hoped for the success of the program.

But it was only a first step. The condors were still being fed in an organized manner, with carcasses provided at certain locations. As Jan Hamber says: "Endangered species work is not for the faint of heart."

* * *

Fourteen Years Later: Santa Barbara Museum of Natural History Museum Field Trip, 1998

"Why don't we take people up to see a California condor?" This was part of a museum effort known as "Avian Adventures" and I, being on the Board of Trustees at the time, helped advise the committee. Since we were determined to make new friends and raise funds for the museum, we thought it would be a winner to take participants to see our newly-introduced California condors. For a modest fee, the folks would get a beautiful picnic lunch, lectures by the curators, and, we hoped, the chance to view a California condor.

On a clear October day, accompanied by Jan, Paul Collins, and Krista Fahy from the museum staff; and Robert Mesta, from the Department of Fish and Wildlife, we set off. Following the dirt U. S. Forest Service Road as it wound its way up Santa Barbara Canyon, our group was transported in a caravan of all-wheel-drive, high clearance vehicles.

I was a nervous wreck, wondering if the condors would appear, worrying about the logistics of the picnic to follow, all the usual concerns. The first disaster had come and gone: we couldn't use the restrooms at the nearest Forest Service station, so we had to drive to the hamlet of Ventucopa along Highway 33, where the wonderful roadhouse owners there opened their doors and let us use their facilities. What a great country place with a long bar and nice people.

Onward and upward, we finally found ourselves bumping and lurching along the dirt road that would put us atop the Sierra Madre ridge. That's where the action was, and where the condors would be coming in to feed. In these early days of the condor release program, the birds were being fed by Condor Recovery Team staff, and calf carcasses were delivered to the temporary headquarters above Lion Canyon nearby.

The sky was deep blue, cloudless, and we could see for miles. As we climbed up the road, we saw off to our right two large, dark birds: condors circling overhead with a couple of smaller ravens harassing them. At last, at last, condors flying free.

Arriving at the top of the ridge, we pulled over by a grassy area. Nearby, condors surrounded the carcass of a calf. One of the field biologists in the program was there to meet us, and he explained how the birds fed and how long they'd been there.

The enormous, rather ungainly condors, most with pale pink heads because they were immatures, hopped around what looked like a pile of bones. All had radio transmitters protruding from numbered wing tags, some green, some red, with white letters and numbers on each. Every bird had a Native American name, too.

The condors tugged and fussed at the white bones. Their wings flared up in a threat display. They pulled and tore at the carcass, looking like giant black turkeys. We watched from the road, a phalanx of scopes set up, everyone squinting through the lenses. I was completely happy, mission accomplished.

Gradually the birds stopped feeding and ambled away from the carcass. Through the scope we saw a pink bulge in their necks. They'd eaten plenty and the crops in their necks were full.

I was puzzled when one condor, then another, waddled up the grassy slope and stood there. Finally, I understood. They were getting ready to launch out over the canyon.

One at a time, each condor ran in bouncing hops down the slope, gave those long wings a couple of flaps, and they were gone, gliding out over the purple smudge of the distant chaparral. Three of them took off like this, then soared ever higher. They were riding a pyramid of hot air, way, way up. Enormous wings guided the birds with the slightest of movements. And they disappeared, perhaps to travel who knows how far.

After that, nobody could quite believe what they'd seen. I sure couldn't. I'd never been that close to condors for that length of time. It was the Pleistocene era, recreated up here on this wild ridge.

The day wasn't over yet, however. We drove the vehicles to Montgomery Potrero, right to the same place I'd camped with Dad in 1984. I looked up and saw "The House of the Sun" pictograph in the sandstone rock. And these fortunate people on the field trip could share in the wisdom that Jan Timbrook, Museum Curator of Anthropology, had to tell about the Chumash who once settled here.

Meanwhile, the staff had set up a big folding table with a spread of cold cuts, potato salad, fruit, rolls, and delicious wine. Everyone pitched in to help. The participants were impressed, awed by the whole place. This is how unforgettable a field trip can be. I was flying higher than a condor that day.

* * *

Jump forward with me to the present. I wish my grandfather and father could see the latest California Condor Recovery Program statistics on the re-introduced populations. As of 2019 there are 337 wild free-flying California condors in Arizona, Big Sur, Southern California, and Baja. Of those, 99 are found in Southern California. In addition, in various zoos, the captive population includes 50 breeding pairs.

Best of all I just learned that, in one of the canyons of the Sierra Madre Mountains, near the ridge upon which we stood that day on the museum trip, a pair of condors recently nested and fledged a chick in the wild. The great birds have found their way back to the Santa Barbara backcountry, the place where it all started in 1934 when my grandfather saw that action needed to be taken to protect the California condor.

4.

College, Marriage, and Birding Again

After high school, I went off to the University of Colorado with my high school friend, Ginger Verdin Beebe. I liked the outdoor feeling, the beautiful Rocky Mountains, the town of Boulder. The lifestyle there attracted a number of top professors, and my major, European History, lured several of them.

I discovered that I enjoyed studying history, arranging facts, and memorizing dates. Those were the days when "Western Civilization" was still required as a basic freshman course. That was my favorite class. I determined I wanted to pursue a History major. Since I already liked teaching, I eventually enrolled in the practice teacher program and wound up as a student teacher in one of the local high schools near Boulder during my senior year.

One summer, my parents urged me to sign up for a program overseas. Based in Vermont, an outfit called The Experiment in International Living was popular. They organized groups of students to go to various countries for summer home stays with a family. Immediately, I chose

Great Britain. With all my reading background and my knowledge of history, it was a good fit.

The young women I was with were just like me: first time away from home, eager to learn, anxious to see the world. I admired our leader, who was a graduate student at a U.S. university, and who had the perfect touch for this sort of adventure. We spent some time at an orientation course in Vermont, then flew all night in one of those rickety World War II "Flying Tiger" airplanes. The students were going wild, nobody slept. When we landed briefly in Newfoundland to refuel for the long journey, I was excited to go outside although it was dark and cold.

Most other participants had already received letters from their "English family," all except me. Here we were in cavernous St. Pancreas Station in downtown London, and I had no idea where I was going to be staying all summer.

At the last minute, our leader walked up to me with a small envelope. I was sitting on the bench, exhausted and freezing in my cotton dress, watching other girls being claimed. And out of the blue came this welcoming note from what I would start calling my "English mother," and with whose family I ended up having a lifetime of friendship.

Iola Symonds, a tiny, capable, well-educated woman, was a war widow, who had since married her second husband Tom. He had been a prisoner of war in Japan, and now he was the step-father to Iola's children — Christopher and Jennifer. The parents thought that having "an American girl" would be entertaining for their young people for a summer.

I was so lucky. The family, who lived in Derbyshire, were wonderful to me. I was settled into an English vicarage, for the Rev. Symonds had an Anglican congregation. However, his main duty was as private chaplain to the Duke of Devonshire.

As it happened, this was significant, because then-President John F. Kennedy's sister, Kathleen, was married to the Duke's brother, until both she and her husband were tragically killed — he in the War and she in a plane accident. Kathleen was buried in the churchyard down the lane, and the Rev. Symonds preached whenever the family came to visit.

I quickly settled into a lovely upstairs room in the ancient vicarage. No central heating. I was always cold. But the countryside of green pastures and gray stone walls was like a feudal storybook. And down the winding lane was one of the most well-known country houses in Britain, Chatsworth House. Here, the Duke and Duchess maintained their own quarters, while turning over the remainder of the house to visitors. Chatsworth house was filled with rare paintings and antiques, even though in the early 1960s the whole country was still struggling with war deprivations.

My great thrill was an invitation to have lunch with the Duchess, who was obviously making an effort to be nice to Americans, President Kennedy having just visited his sister's gravesite nearby the previous year. I got togged out in my one good outfit, the aqua dyed-to-match cashmere sweater and skirt. When I arrived, the Duchess was wearing pants and gardening shoes; I felt horribly overdressed. Like all the English, she adored her dogs, and they were allowed to eat the lunch leftovers out of silver bowls under the table. I was shocked.

Eventually, we American girls took our English "sisters" on a hiking tour of the Lake District, as a thank you for the home stay. It was a beautiful rural district in northeast England, where we stayed in youth hostels, and hiked the pathways. I visited the house of Beatrix Potter, my childhood idol. I remember drinking blackberry wine in the pubs, and the pouring rain.

Years later, as our visits to England continued and I introduced my husband to my English family, I wandered the hedgerows and parklands of Chatsworth House looking for birds. I grew to know European birds well, and it all began with a lovely note from an Englishwoman who was a complete stranger.

I'd say the Experiment was well worth it!

Falling in Love

When I graduated from the University of Colorado, I returned to California. I was looking forward to being in the Bay Area, entering graduate school at the University of California at Berkeley. In order to teach in California, I needed to enroll in the graduate School of Education. The ghosts of both sets of grandparents were hovering above me somewhere as I walked along those Berkeley streets; I felt at home there.

Shortly afterward I met and fell in love with Gib Lentz. He was in his third year of law school at Berkeley. We hit it off immediately. We found we had the same set of values and interests. We loved learning, appreciated history, and had been raised in the same generation: 1950s upbringing with a 1960s sensibility.

Gib and I both loved books and reading; I'd met my match with a guy who knew a lot about literature, both modern and ancient, and yet was on top of the latest good fiction. This, and a reverence for anything English, or shall we also say European — for both of us had traveled abroad before we met — drew us together.

Gib was a practical, detail person, a man who could be a rudder to my personality, which was somewhat carefree and drifting at this point. I was casting about for a person with conservative morals yet who was interested in a social justice point of view.

I needed grounding, direction, purpose. I eventually wanted to settle down and have a family, and here was a person I could trust completely. That was the key ingredient — a trust that I had never felt before with anyone. I knew Gib had my back, and I yearned for that quality in a partner.

We decided we wanted to spend our lives together. At about this time, many of my friends were getting married, and, although I was only 22, I was excited about taking the plunge.

Of course, we hadn't the remotest idea of what marriage entailed. None of us did. But we were game; life was an adventure to be shared. Six months after we met, we were married at the Unitarian Church in Santa Barbara.

That summer, with $500 in the bank, we set off in my old purple Plymouth Valiant, a convertible that leaked during our first rainstorm, en route to Washington, D.C., where we lived for two years.

We both worked "on the Hill." I was in Senator Thomas Kuchel's office, and Gib was in the Administrative Office of the U.S Courts. And who was his boss? Warren Olney III, my relative, the grandson of my ancestor, Warren Olney.

Living in Washington, D.C., Gib and I felt we had our fingers on the pulse of the nation, and we enjoyed our sojourn there immensely. But we missed California and it was only a matter of time before we returned to the West.

I never looked at birds when we were on the East coast. Why? Was natural history something that I didn't have time for? I'm not sure. We were young professionals living in a basement apartment in Alexandria, Virginia, and most every weekend we explored some aspect of D. C.: a museum, a battlefield, historic sites — I don't even think I had binoculars.

The gap years.

Sacramento — Birding Again

By 1967, we were back in California and settled in Sacramento, where Gib had grown up. I had a newborn, our son Jonathan, and Gib was gone all day at his job in the Sacramento County District Attorney's office downtown.

The long summer in Sacramento stretched before me, with no air conditioning in our small rental house. We had just moved in, so I had few friends.

I dutifully cleaned the house, cooked all the meals, went to the local Safeway once a week, and spent hours pushing my baby in a stroller around the big, shady residential area known as Land Park.

Fortunately, our house had a large backyard, which contained three paper birch trees with white trunks and drooping branches. Those birch trees saved me. Tall and skinny, these trees with heart-shaped leaves attracted sticky aphids that the birds loved. When I saw all the birds outside, I wanted to find out what was going on. I put the baby down for a nap, and picked up my binoculars.

Grabbing my old edition of Roger Tory Peterson's "Field Guide to Western Birds" (1941), I thumbed through it. Oh wow. Here was the page with the colorful warblers, grosbeaks, tanagers, and orioles. The bird drawings, with arrows indicating the key aspect of the bird to identify it, were especially helpful. The only problem was that the pictures were in a back section of the guide, away from the description of the bird itself.

This was soon rectified, in 1966, by the publication of the popular "Golden Guide to the Birds of North America," by Chandler S. Robbins, Bertel Bruun, and Herbert Zim. When I purchased the Golden Guide, I learned how birding could be easier, because the text was designed to be on the same page as the bird's illustration. It was a bestseller among birders.

With the help of the Golden Guide and the excellent text in the Peterson's guide, I noticed what was happening in my backyard. I didn't have a bird feeder, but during spring migration, birds stopped off in my garden. I saw my first western tanager: "Lovely crimson-headed, with yellow body, black wings, yellow wing-bars, perched on wire catching bees in twilight evening!" I wrote in an early field note.

One day on a whim I bought a spiral notebook titled "Birder's Life List and Diary." It had the bird species listed in taxonomic order with a space for date, location, and remarks. I began to organize my bird sightings and write them down.

New birders often ask why the birds in most field guides aren't arranged alphabetically. I had to learn about the term "taxonomic" or, as they say these days, "phylogenetic" order. The majority of books in the natural sciences follow an order, which traces the evolutionary history of the organisms they're discussing. In the case of birds, it is an ancestral time line that begins with the oldest forms and ends with those most recently evolved. Thus, in a current field guide, you will find the geese and ducks listed first and the tanagers and orioles toward the end.

The sequence of families is closely studied by members of an important committee of the American Ornithologists Society (formerly the American Ornithologists Union). Periodically, the AOS Check-List Committee reviews recent experiments that shed light upon the evolutionary relationships of birds. Thus, the terms "taxonomic" or "phylogenetic" order refer to this sequence, and field guides are organized according to the most recent published findings of the Check-List Committee.

I knew nothing of this; all I wanted was to put a name to these fabulous birds I was seeing. Was that a "pileolated" warbler or was it now called a "Wilson's warbler"? I wrote this in my notebook of those years. And, "An olive-sided flycatcher — or was it a kingbird? With a large, tufted head, long bill, white down middle of breast and on throat, the white separating the darker sides; couldn't see back; perched on dead limb of birch tree; largeness impressive yet flycatcher habits."

I can't remember the first pair of binoculars I got in Sacramento; they weren't very good. But when I put them to my eyes to spot a bird, the excitement and satisfaction of birdwatching came over me once more. It was so much fun. The thrill seeped right back in, as I recalled all the birds I'd figured out on my own back in Santa Barbara. I felt that familiar pull, that fascination with these beautiful creatures right outside in my backyard.

That winter, I went on my first field trip sponsored by the Sacramento Audubon Society. I was a passenger in a car with total strangers. And they *knew about birds*. I hung on every word, and learned so much.

We carpooled down to the area called Thornton, a bleak place surrounded by brown, agricultural fields in the Sacramento Valley south of town. It was a bitter cold day, with a thick ground-fog hanging over the river.

I didn't care; it was paradise to me.

I watched sandhill cranes for the first time, observed the pairs "dance" as they sought to impress each other before the return journey north to breed. I saw northern harriers, American pipits, white-tailed kites hovering, and huge, white tundra swans, with smaller white snow geese. The brown fields were white with birds. All were new to me.

Pretty soon Gib began to help me by spotting the birds. He was always better at seeing movement in the trees. Alas, he just couldn't figure out why I loved birds. We were so different in that way. He preferred to look at nature from inside a window, while I wanted to be out there in it. However, right from the beginning, he was always supportive of my birding interests.

I began to write down the new birds I'd seen, keeping a record of my firsts.

Just the other day, I came across a thick stack of 3 x 5 cards on which I'd typed out on my college Smith-Corona typewriter detailed information about each of the new bird species I'd discovered and was able to identify. The cards, arranged alphabetically, expressed my desire to put an orderly system on my sightings. I knew nothing about field notes or nature journals, but I sensed the importance of each new bird I saw and I wanted to describe it.

There's something satisfying and delightful about chronicling bird sightings. The sense that the moment must be put down for posterity was always with me. I simply transferred it to birding, to all the dates, locations, and habitats where I'd seen a bird. The urge to write it down came naturally to me.

By this time, both Gib and I were determined to relocate to Santa Barbara. I missed my family and my home land. We said good-bye to Sacramento.

Birding Memories in Santa Barbara, 1969-1978

These were some of the happiest years of my life.

I was settled in my beloved Santa Barbara; back to the land I loved. I could hike the trails, revisit all the childhood haunts. Gib and I climbed to the summit of La Cumbre Peak. We hiked from my parents' house on Las Canoas Road, cutting through the Botanic Garden, then up the Tunnel trail. When we returned, it was dark and we hiked by the light of the moon.

I was home again, with the smells, the light, the mountains, the chaparral.

Our daughter Jenny was born shortly after we arrived in 1969, and I felt blessed to have these young ones and this perfect life.

Downtown Santa Barbara seemed little changed from the 1950s. Ott's Hardware Store on lower State Street was still there, with its creaky wooden floors and that smell of mothballs around the woolen goods. You could find almost anything at Ott's. And just around the corner was The Children's Shop, where Mom used to buy our clothes and now I could shop here for *my* children's clothes and toys.

A favorite haunt was Osborne's Books, founded in 1926, with another of those noisy wooden floors. Our mom adored Osborne's because of the tiny lending library in the back corner of the store. Here, you could "rent" some of the newer titles for a small fee; my mother, a constant reader, was one of their best customers.

And there was Andera's for ladies' clothes with the pneumatic "tube" that the salesgirl would put your money into, and it went whirring along a pipe that ran down to the basement where the change was counted out, and the receipt printed up, and then "whoosh" here came the little metal tube back up to the counter. The salesgirl opened it up, and gave you your change.

The Blue Onion drive-in where we used to hang out in high school was now a restaurant named The Fig Tree.

At Christmas, the tall pine by the old YMCA building was lit up, just as it still is, and there were Christmas trees all up and down the middle of State Street, as I recall.

I loved the familiar streets, the beach, the Botanic Garden, the Museum of Natural History, and I was able to share them with my own young family.

The big new developments were out to the west: La Cumbre Plaza, once a lemon orchard, was the first big mall across from Kelly's Corner.

And the orchards that used to line Hope Avenue? Gone, with houses in their place.

Much of the area between Santa Barbara and Goleta had recently been built. I didn't recognize all the new tract houses that stretched to Winchester Canyon. The old walnut, citrus, and avocado orchards had been replaced with modern, affordable houses.

UCSB was growing like crazy; Isla Vista was full of what many would come to call hippies. The burning of the Bank of America building occurred shortly after we moved in to our first house. It was all part of the anti-Vietnam War movement.

Meanwhile around this time, the Santa Barbara Audubon Society, which had been pretty much defunct since after World War II, was reorganized by a group of committed environmentalists, especially Ken and Margaret Millar, who were close friends of my parents.

Both Millars were writers: he was best known as Ross MacDonald, who wrote mysteries that took place in a mythical town similar to Santa Barbara.

One of the finest descriptions of Santa Barbara's bird life can be found in Margaret Millar's marvelous "The Birds and the Beasts Were There," first published in 1967, then reissued by Capra Press in 1991.

Also involved in Santa Barbara Audubon were condor biologist Jan Hamber, Fifi Webster, Joy Parkinson, Waldo Abbott, and T. Nelson Metcalf. It was an informal group, but they organized field trips, had a newsletter, and at one point, when Brad Schram was president of the Audubon Board, I participated as membership chair.

It was the wonderful, free-wheeling 1970s. I look back on that decade as one where advances were made in preserving the environment that have been unequalled since, an example being the California Environmental Quality Act. And this environmental awareness everywhere was instrumental in attracting more people to birdwatching.

Birding on My Own
and in Class

When I first got back to town I wasn't tuned into other birders, because I had young children.

Gib would often babysit the children on a Sunday morning while I dashed out and went birding. I relied on those moments of peace and quiet, and the happiness of studying birds in my Santa Barbara.

One of my favorite destinations was Goleta Slough. Back then, you could walk around the airport property — no fences — and observe birds as they swam among the watery channels. I loved it out there. I would sit on a bank beside one of the tidal inlets for hours, binoculars in hand. In this way I managed to identify the eared grebe and the pied-billed grebe, saw 16 American avocets one day, puzzled over a cinnamon teal, and discovered my first marsh wren. And all the time, the planes were flying in and out overhead. The birds didn't mind; there wasn't much air traffic in those days.

Another special spot was Rattlesnake Canyon. I hiked up the creek early, before the trail got busy, and sat on a boulder beneath the tall sycamores. In spring, when the sweet smell of ceanothus wafted down from the chaparral hillside, I took my binoculars up there. The sound of a house wren warbling away could be heard above the running creek. Most of the common birds were familiar to me by then, but during one visit I had a surprise.

A northern pygmy-owl, known for its small size and appetite for songbirds, happened to be sitting camouflaged in one of the sycamores. It took me forever to locate it, but I followed the chatter of the smaller birds and the scolds of a couple of scrub-jays.

At last, practically overhead, I got a view of a tiny owl perched, its yellow eyes glaring at me. The pygmy-owl was the size of a sparrow and it had a long tail. My heart skipped a beat: could this be the owl that was famous for preying on other birds, and whose presence had set off a mob scene among them? When the owl turned its head,

I glimpsed a pair of fake eyes, part of a feather pattern on the back of its neck to confuse attackers.

Like all these discoveries, there was no warning, no announcement, just me watching and the birds living out their lives.

I raced home, came rushing into the house, and snatched my Peterson field guide. I was right, it was a northern pygmy-owl!

"Birds of the Pacific States" by Ralph Hoffmann

Two more milestones drew me deeper into birding.

I acquired a copy of what remains my favorite field guide to Western birds, Ralph Hoffmann's "Birds of the Pacific States," published in 1927.

Hoffmann was a schoolmaster from the East, where he'd already written "A Guide to the Birds of New England and Upper New York." He had relocated to Santa Barbara in 1921 to teach natural history at the Cate School. In 1925, he was selected to replace William Leon Dawson (another famous ornithologist and author) as head of our own Santa Barbara Museum of Natural History.

Hoffman wasn't just a schoolmaster, he was a brilliant field ornithologist, and he was keeping track of unusual bird sightings as soon as he arrived in Santa Barbara. In addition, he was a keen botanist. Tragically, Ralph Hoffman died in 1932 when he fell from a steep cliff while collecting plants on San Miguel Island off the Santa Barbara coast.

What was it about Ralph Hoffmann's book that made me read it over and over again? It was the writing. The descriptions of bird behavior, the way he placed you in the habitat where you were likely to find that particular bird, and his excellent interpretations of bird sounds spoke to me like no other field guide.

Hoffmann was writing about bird habitats that I could find right here in Santa Barbara; when he described a salt marsh, or a hike in the chaparral, he was there beside me.

Ralph Hoffmann's secret was that he wrote straight from his own experiences in nature. The book was more than a field guide, in fact, it was a companion that I could come home to after a day out birding, open it to the page I wanted, and say "That's it! That's the bird I saw!" or "Yes, it sounded just like that!"

The black-and-white drawings are good and the few colored plates are charming. But they aren't why you should grab any used copy of this book you can get your hands on. Trust me, it's the wonderful prose.

My second birding milestone was signing up for the Santa Barbara City College Continuing Education class, "Birds of the Santa Barbara Region." As early as 1972, I remember taking Jenny over to my next door neighbor's house to be watched, so I could go to the bird class for a couple of hours once a week. My friend looked at me, "You are going to do *what*???" But she agreed to keep my little 3-year-old.

At last, I was out in the field with other birders. My first teacher was Les Cooke, who seemed ancient to me at the time, but was probably about my age now, and he taught me to listen for the birds. He knew all the calls. I learned where to go birding, too, because we went to different habitats in class. At some point, Les retired and we had a woman teacher, Ann Terry, beginning in about 1977.

The fun of it was meeting other people with whom I could go birding: my two best birding buddies of those days were Jean Okuye and Kathy Schewel. They both ended up moving away from Santa Barbara, but we got together for birding trips later.

Taking Off — Birding Santa Barbara in the late 1970s

And so I went out birding whenever I possibly could, arranged around the day of a suburban housewife: picking up children at schools, cooking meals, volunteer work. Gib and I had moved to a modest house in Montecito by early 1976.

Often, I took the family out on natural history excursions — the Botanic Garden, the Museum of Natural History, a boat trip organized by the local Audubon Chapter.

One day Carol Goodell called up, wondering what a stunning rust, white, and black bird was that had come hopping across her patio. I rushed over, explained about the rufous-sided towhee (now spotted towhee) and urged her to get a field guide. Soon she was hooked on birding, too, and has been a faithful friend and birding buddy. However, she owned Memaw's, a gift store on Coast Village Road, for many years, which left her with less time for birding.

My constant birding companion from the day we met in October of 1980 was Karen Bridgers. We found each other while wandering around the empty parking lot of the Elks Club off Kellogg Avenue in Goleta. We were two young mothers with kids in school, toting binoculars and peering up at the trees. Our goal was a summer tanager, which had been reported on the Rare Bird Alert — a life bird (meaning we'd never seen one before anywhere) for both of us. We found it, too.

Birding news was transmitted by calling a local "hotline" phone number. One number was for reporting a rare bird if you'd seen one, the other was the one you called to hear a recorded message of recently sighted interesting birds. It was changed weekly by some patient Santa Barbara Audubon Society volunteer. Eventually, that volunteer was Karen Bridgers. She had a journalism background, and she also wrote a weekly column about birds in the *Santa Barbara News-Press*.

Karen got interested in birds because she had a busy feeder set up in her backyard in Goleta. During the winter of 1979, Karen happened to attract to her feeder three rarities: a white-throated sparrow, a Harris's sparrow, and a brown thrasher! All of these birds are out-of-range and not expected in Santa Barbara. Once she agreed to permit birders to come into her living room and stare out the window at the sought-after birds, she was totally hooked. She saw how exciting birding could be.

As for me, I took my binoculars whenever Gib and I went on short trips to nearby spots: Morro Bay (the peregrine falcon on Morro Rock), Carmel (my first wandering tattler at Point Lobos State Park), Point

Reyes Seashore (my first black scoter), the Sonoma coast (my first harlequin duck). Every summer we took the family to Rock Creek in the Eastern Sierra and then discovered Mammoth Lakes. I was in heaven learning the new montane bird species, devouring every scrap of knowledge I could get. The first edition of David Gaines' book, "Birds of Yosemite and the East Slope," was my constant companion. I was dying to learn about birds wherever I found myself.

In addition, it was these early visits to the Eastern Sierra that got me enthused about flowering plants. I was excited about the variety of wildflowers I managed to identify, whether walking along the road at Rock Creek or hiking Little Lakes Valley out of Mosquito Flat trailhead. We did a lot of hiking with Jonathan and Jenny, up to Mono Pass and Morgan Pass, and the ten-mile round trip to Lake Ediza was one of my favorites.

One day in 1976, I talked Gib into our first-ever birding vacation. We went to Southeast Arizona, one of the premier birding spots in the West. Gib's folks offered to keep the children, and off we went.

I will never forget that trip, which I've described in my book "Great Birding Trips of the West."

The trip stoked my passion for birds. I was bursting with new knowledge, new birds, and the thrill of exploring a new part of the West.

ABOVE: *Grandfather Easton and Dad at Sisquoc Ranch, early 1930s.*

MIDDLE: *At Tunnell House, Sisquoc Ranch: (l to r) me, Elizabeth Stevenson, Ellen Easton, Nov. 2011.*

Sisquoc River as it looked on jeep ride, Nov. 2011.

The villa outside Florence, Italy, where Mom spent her childhood in the 1920s and '30s.

*Grandfather Faust ("Max Brand")
holding me, his first grandchild, 1942*

*Mom and Dad holding me (Dad in
Army uniform), Santa Barbara, 1943.*

Our home on the Riviera in Santa Barbara, 1951-59.

Three Easton girls l to r: Ellen, Katherine, and me, 1948.

Me and Katherine on Miramar beach, Santa Barbara, 1949.

Me and Katherine playing dress-up, 1953.

Peabody, Goleta School Spelling Bee Contestants Qualify for Semi-Finals

-1952-

Dorene Sexton, Karen Day in Area Spell-Off

Carpinteria Union School held its semi-final today in the News-Press Spelling Bee to qualify contestants for the finals April 23.

Meanwhile, other contestants qualified for semi-finals to be held in Santa Barbara soon.

Karen Day won at Peabody and Dorene Sexton at Goleta Union to enter the West Santa Barbara semi-finals at La Cumbre Junior High School at 7:30 p.m. tomorrow night. The school is on Modoc Road.

Karen is 11, in the sixth grade, and is the daughter of Mr. and Mrs. Thomas Day, 3504 Foothill Rd. Art and arithmetic are her favorite school subjects, and playing the piano and swimming her out-of-school specialties.

Dorene is 11, in the sixth grade, and is the daughter of Mr. and Mrs. Eugene Sexton, 1150 N. Fairview Ave., Goleta. She is an active member of the Goleta 4-H Club, likes baseball, basketball, volleyball and swimming.

Another contestant for the East Santa Barbara semi-finals, to be held a week from tomorrow at Santa Barbara Junior High, has been qualified. She is Joan Easton of Jefferson School. She is 10, in the sixth grade, and is the daughter of Mr. and Mrs. Robert Easton, 1919 Las Tunas Rd. Her favorite school subjects are reading and social studies, and after school she plays baseball and collects stamps, among other things.

JOAN EASTON, who qualified for the semi-finals in the News-Press spelling bee, from Jefferson School.

Spelling Bee finalist from Jefferson Elementary School, 1952.

Sarah H. Fleischmann Bird Hall - Santa Barbara Museum of Natural History, 1950s.

55

Our home on Las Canoas Rd., ("the red farmhouse") where we moved in 1960.

Four Easton girls (l to r: Jane, Ellen, Katherine, me) with Mom and Dad in foreground at Zaca Laderas Ranch, 1974.

Mom and Dad, late 1980s.

Our wedding day, 1965.

MIDDLE: *The Lentz family (l to r: Jenny, Jonathan, me and Gib), Montecito, 1997.*

BOTTOM: *Grandma with Alex and Annabel, 2016.*

5

A Birding Revolution

Let's step back and take a look at what was happening in the larger world of birding in North America. A birding revolution, of which California was one of the leaders, was spreading throughout the continent.

A birding revolution? Indeed, throughout the 1960s and 1970s, new concepts about bird migration and new methods of figuring out bird identification were creating what field ornithologists in hindsight consider a revolution in the way birds are observed. You might compare it to what's occurred in recent years when it comes to citizen science, technology, and eBird. It was a fundamental change that altered the birding scene forever.

Ornithology is a vast and varied subject for scientific study. Formerly, many outstanding biologists with science degrees had chosen to remain in the laboratory specializing in the physiology or taxonomy of birds. These ornithologists were not particularly interested in field skills; most did not consider themselves "birders." They had research projects and other obligations to attend to.

But ornithology is an area of science that includes an army of amateur hobbyists, some with science degrees, some not, many with field skills, some less so.

We may qualify here that the revolution I refer to pertains to those birders and/or biologists who were exclusively interested in field study of birds outdoors: migration patterns, identification, status and distribution.

An uneasy truce existed between these two groups. The scientists with degrees were perhaps looking askance at some of these new-found geniuses with their field skills, and vice versa. The population I'm talking about is the group of high-level birders who were taking birding over the top. They may or may not have had a biology degree — most didn't — but they were bent on contributing to science in a way that bird observers had not done before.

In Southern California, it all started with Guy McCaskie. He was born in Scotland, and was an excellent birder before he ever landed on California's shores in 1957. He first lived in Northern California, where he met Rich Stallcup in Marin County. (More about Rich later, for he was another birder non-pareil, a truly gifted human being.)

Guy brought with him a whole new idea about birdwatching: the locating of rare or out-of-range birds that nobody every dreamed could be seen in California. He and Rich Stallcup teamed up, and they began looking for birds in the most unlikely places.

Guy's approach was as follows. First, you educate yourself using all the known bird literature that pertains to California. Then thoroughly study the status and distribution of all of the common birds. What dates were species likely to arrive in California in spring, when were they likely to depart in fall? Where did they breed? Where were they common, fairly common, rare, or super rare?

The groundbreaking reference on this information is "The Distribution of the Birds of California" by Joseph Grinnell and Alden H. Miller (1944). It was that long ago, and it is still astonishingly accurate.

Until Kimball Garrett and Jon Dunn published "The Birds of Southern California: Status and Distribution" in 1981, nothing similarly focused on the demographics of bird populations had been written. These books aren't field guides, but they contain important information about the bird species in an area. They describe birds' home ranges, breeding habitats, and species' abundance. They also tell you if that bird has visited Southern California from elsewhere, how frequently, and what time of year you can expect to see it.

Till then, most of us ordinary birders had gone on organized field trips, with the emphasis on what we could expect to find at a particular location in that season, because we knew these habitats contained those species.

For example, in spring we would travel to the Santa Ynez Valley to see lazuli buntings and blue grosbeaks singing in fields of yellow mustard. In fall, we might go to Goleta Beach to refresh our identification of shorebirds as they fed on the sandy shore. And in winter, there were always lots of ducks to look at in the harbor or at Devereux Slough.

The pursuit of birds by both professional ornithologists and birders had been limited to what we could expect to find if we knew the common birds that frequented a particular habitat, and if we visited at the proper seasons. Not much of an element of surprise in this kind of birding. You went to places to see predictably present birds. No element of the unexpected, or the active chase to find a rare bird.

But here came Guy and Rich and they'd studied up, were pretty adventurous, too. Let me quote Guy from a wonderful article about him in *American Birds* (Vol. 46, No. 2, pg 207):

"I can remember very well, one of the earlier times that Rich Stallcup was with me. We'd gone to Grinnell and Miller and studied what was around and then studied all of the recent publications and we concluded that the first of October was the time to see a Tropical Kingbird on the coast of California. Why, there were three records in California! They were all right around the first of October! We were scheduled to lead the Golden Gate Audubon Society on the first of October and when people arrived they said, 'Well, what are we going to see?' And we said, 'We're going to look for Tropical Kingbirds.'

"The most remarkable thing was we found a Tropical Kingbird. That was totally remarkable. They just absolutely couldn't believe that we had, at the start of the trip said, 'We're going to look for Tropical Kingbird and we found one.'"

(Tropical Kingbird is a rare but regular vagrant to the coast, a beautiful big flycatcher with a yellow belly, something you would never expect to see on an October field trip in those days.)

Later, Guy moved to the San Diego area, where he graduated from the engineering school at San Diego State University. San Diego at that time was another wide open frontier for birding, whether it was in the Tijuana River Valley toward the border, or offshore on a boat. And it was close to the deserts too. At the same time, he kept in close touch with Rich up in Point Reyes, even becoming instrumental in the establishment of Point Reyes Bird Observatory in 1965, California's first bird observatory.

Chasing Vagrants

You'd think with the amount of research that has gone into bird migration, scientists would completely understand the secrets of bird navigation. Now that we can tag birds with satellite tracking devices, we know more than ever before. Still, migration remains a complex subject.

After the summer nesting season, certain species of birds migrate long distances to find their way to wintering grounds, where food is abundant and the climate warmer. The position of the sun in the sky, the layout of the constellations at night, a magnetic sense of direction, and patterns of polarized light in the evening sky all appear to play a part in guiding a bird's route. What we do know is that once the first journey is successfully completed to a safe wintering spot, the bird will generally return to that location year after year.

Taking into consideration the length of the migrants' journeys, and the weather events such as wind, fog, and low pressure systems they might encounter, you can see why a young bird would be at risk of losing its way. And that's exactly what birders were discovering. It was the immature birds that, especially off the coast of northern and southern

California, were appearing at certain spots, if you knew where to look.

We've since learned that most juvenile birds have a built-in compass and clock to tell them how far to fly and for how long. However, several aspects of a young migrant's journey make it a perilous one. And if the bird drifts off course, or becomes misoriented due to a faulty inherent clock, it could end up in a place it shouldn't be.

At some point in its journey a young bird should have turned right, but perhaps it turned left instead. For example, reaching the Pacific coast on its southward journey, it may have overshot and flown out to sea. If it redirected itself, the bird would beat its way back to the nearest isolated clump of vegetation it could find that stood out along that coast. And there it would take shelter and refuel.

The proper term for migrant birds that become disoriented is "vagrants." Vagrants are not normally found along our coast during migration. They belong elsewhere, on another route. Consequently, vagrants bring with them an aura of the unexpected and with that, the thrill of the new. They aren't part of our everyday bird scene, they're different, and, often, rare. It's enough to get a birder's blood pumping. The chase is on.

Guy and Rich (and others such as Dave DeSante on the Farallon Islands) discovered these so-called "vagrant traps" along the California coast. The vagrant traps consisted of trees or water, mini-habitats isolated among inhospitable areas along the coast. Western migrant landbirds were concentrated here, especially in fall; and together with the regular migrants were these out-of-range species known as vagrants.

Why Young Birds Get Off Course

These immature vagrants aren't exactly lost, because their misorientation is not random. Vagrancy in numerous species appears to be rather predictable. And the two most common patterns are "mirror-image" misorientation, and "reverse migration" misorientation.

In cases of mirror-image misorientation, east and west are transposed. For example, during fall migration, instead of orienting themselves to fly east and then southeast, the birds fly west, and then southwest. Mirror-image misorientation means the bird is oriented in its migratory path at the same angle toward the southwest as it should be toward the southeast. This may explain the appearance of so many Eastern North American species as vagrants on our coast. For example, a young bird like a blackpoll warbler, which is born in the north woods of Canada, would ordinarily migrate east toward the Atlantic seacoast, then southeast to spend the winter in South America. But if the blackpoll warbler was born with a malfunctioning compass, it would migrate west and then southwest, potentially ending up at a clump of willows along the California coast somewhere.

Another form of misorientation is "reverse migration," wherein a young bird migrates roughly in the opposite direction to that which is normal, going north instead of south, or east instead of west.

More recently, researchers examining the phenomenon of Eastern vagrants landing on the California coast came up with the following: if you estimated the population of these species, with emphasis on the Eastern warblers, you could see a correlation between the size of the population and the numbers of vagrants. It's reasonable that if the breeding population of a bird is in the millions, it will have more immatures in the gene pool to go astray in migration. And that's what they found. The populations of American redstart, black-and-white warbler, blackpoll warbler, northern waterthrush, and Tennessee warbler are among the largest in North America, and in turn these species are the most frequently seen as vagrants in coastal California.

Vagrancy can also be viewed as an advantage: it is a good way for a species to increase its range, or to colonize new territory. Therefore, although some birds do indeed become lost, vagrancy may be a way of adapting to new conditions. When habitat loss or climate change makes a prior range unsuitable, these "lost" birds become scouts.

Status and Distribution
of Birds

Discovering vagrants along the California coast was only a part of what Guy and his new disciples taught us. Even more important was an appreciation of the status and distribution of birds.

You might ask, for the average birder, who cares? Once you've seen a bird, and identified it, what's the point? If you're on a sandy beach, a mountain meadow, or a desert wash, a bird is a bird, right?

No, because that's not enough information. If I've seen and identified a boring American crow in Santa Barbara, should I pay attention if the black bird I see flying high above the Sierra Nevada is an American crow? Yes I should, because it's probably not a crow. If I know the American crow's status and distribution, I know that it would be downright *rare* cruising the heights of the Sierra. Indeed, a common raven would be much more likely.

I should know when a bird "doesn't belong" in the place I'm birding, because that makes it noteworthy, makes it rare, and makes it an important event to be added to scientific literature. For example, a California towhee, one of the most common birds on the California coast, is a rarity in the Mojave Desert. One year, a verdin, a tiny desert dweller of a bird, was found in Santa Barbara County. If you'd seen a verdin in Palm Springs, no big deal. That's where they typically live. But one hopping around chaparral at the base of San Marcos Pass? That's a first record for our county and something special.

Here's an example from personal experience. On October 18, 1978, an extremely rare white wagtail was found at Devereux Slough in Goleta. It happened that Gib and I had just returned from a trip to England, where wagtails were all over the place! So I thought, and I wrote this in my journal if you can believe it, that I would rather drive to McGrath State Beach and look for a pectoral sandpiper than go to Devereux. Hadn't I just seen a ton of wagtails, because they were so common in England?

A third state record of a totally out-of-range bird! Because I didn't understand the importance of status and distribution, I nearly missed seeing one of the rarest birds ever to hit Santa Barbara County. Thank goodness, I turned around, drove back to Goleta, and got the wagtail. Next day it was gone. That's how it is with fall vagrants — if you don't chase them immediately, you miss them.

The lesson? Wagtail is a common species in England, but on the coast of California it is a mega-rarity. That's what we mean by distribution. What is the frequency (status) with which you are going to see a wagtail, of any kind, in California? The answer is extremely rarely.

Furthermore, Guy posited that in spring time, birds migrating north from Central America were forced to cross miles and miles of the Sonora, Mojave, and Great Basin deserts to get to breeding grounds. Where could they stop? The concentrating effect of an oasis in the desert is similar to that of vagrant traps on the coast.

Birders began to visit Death Valley in late spring, around Memorial Day weekend. They knew this was the time when lost Eastern species would likely be migrating north. Stories were told of birders sleeping on the golf course at Furnace Creek Ranch in Death Valley, waking up to spot an ovenbird (mostly found east of the Rockies) walking underneath a date palm next to them. At certain ranch houses surrounded by cottonwood trees in the desert, you might look up to see a hooded warbler flitting among the green leaves or a prothonotary warbler sipping from a leaky faucet.

The birds spy these green oases and drop down. If a birder knows this, he or she is bound to locate a rare bird in the middle of nowhere.

To quote Jon Dunn about Guy McCaskie finding rarities: "It was intoxicating to be in the field with him. Seeing numbers of rarities was reward enough, but there was a zeal and enthusiasm to Guy's birding that formed a permanent impression." These comments echo through the decades from the well-known birders in California. As South Coast Regional Editor for the magazine *Audubon Field Notes,* (now *North American Birds*) Guy's sightings of Eastern warblers and other rarities were unparalleled.

And the new (mostly young, mostly male) birders of the 1960s and 1970s were drawn to this man with his brusque demeanor. Guy didn't suffer fools, that's for sure, but was helpful to every birder he deemed serious in their quest. Through his leadership and example, he defined the standards for critical field observation. In those days, there were very few photographs of birds being taken. Documenting and recording bird sightings was serious business. Any hint of a birder who didn't know status and distribution of a bird in his or her area, or any sloppiness in writing up field notes, just wouldn't do. How could you claim to have really studied a given bird carefully, unless you knew it was rare or out of season *at the time of the sighting*?

Furthermore, Guy's rigorous methods of seeking vagrants and documenting bird sightings influenced a whole future generation of birders in what Don Roberson, a top Monterey birder, calls a "Renaissance" in California birding.

California's vagrant possibilities were endless. If you had to drive all night to see a blue jay (an Eastern species) at first light in Arcata, and then turn around and drive back to San Diego the next day to see a Sprague's pipit, so what? This was a tight fraternity of intense, excellent birders and they crashed on each other's floors in sleeping bags, or drove 500 miles in a day — all to see that special rarity that had never alighted in California before.

The establishment of the the California Bird Records Committee in 1970 was an important step toward creating a formal list of birds that had been sighted in our state. The records committee was the last word on whether or not any particular species had been properly documented by the observer so that it could go into the record. California was the first state to establish such a group, which served as a template for other states. All these developments can be traced to McCaskie's excitement at finding the next rare bird, and his obsession with accurate field notes.

Santa Barbara's Birding Scene, 1970s and early 1980s

At the time, I had no idea about this revolution in birding. I was a complete novice. I had no clue about science as a body of literature based on accurately recorded facts, and didn't know a thing about documentation, writing up field notes, or the status and distribution of birds.

I was simply going out birdwatching and trying to identify the species I found.

All around me, the birding revolution was taking place in Santa Barbara, too, but most local birders didn't realize what was going on. Looking back, some of us would recognize that this new way of understanding bird migration, and looking for vagrants, was the beginning of what could be called "modern birding."

Locally, Guy's approach to birding had its followers. Louis Bevier, Paul Lehman, Brad Schram, and Richard Webster were the top birders. They were joined by Jon Dunn when he moved to town. In addition, Jon's childhood birding friend, Kimball Garrett, now the Collections Manager of Ornithology at the Natural History Museum of Los Angeles County, frequently came up to Santa Barbara for birding.

Brad Schram was the elder statesman of the group, the voice of reason. He was a grad student in anthropology at UCSB, married with two youngsters. Nevertheless, he was in touch with Guy, and managed to go out birding regularly around the UCSB campus.

That's how he met young Paul Lehman, who came as an undergrad to UCSB from the New York area, where he'd been watching birds since the age of nine. Coming from the East gave him an advantage, because if you're chasing out-of-range warblers, they're most likely to originate from the eastern portion of the U.S.

In one of the early Peterson field guides, there was a page called "Confusing Fall Warblers." It had plates picturing pale, faintly-marked warblers, which all looked the same to me. I avoided that page. These are exactly how many of the Eastern warblers look when they get lost and come to California.

But Paul Lehman, a real whiz-kid when it came to birding, was urging Brad to go out and look for these immature Eastern warblers in places around the UCSB campus and in Goleta — right here.

Recall that vagrant traps are locations where migrating birds stop to rest and refuel. And if common birds were using these places, the new wisdom said that if you went there and looked through the common migrants, you would find rare vagrants.

So here was this cocky kid from New York, bright as hell, riding around UCSB on his bike finding birds. Paul wasn't going to sit around passively and hang out with little old ladies in tennis shoes. He was looking for rare birds, and by that he meant these vagrants. Paul was persuasive and assertive. Some thought he was arrogant.

A few local birders who'd been at it for decades were uncomfortable. "How can this kid come in and tell us how and where we should be birding?" grumbled some of the old-timers.

Soon, Paul talked Brad Schram into coming birding with him — and Brad, who'd been basically schooled in the old-fashioned methods, started to be swept up by this new, more proactive way of looking for birds. And, he had a car so he took Paul with him.

Another birder who had a car was Louis Bevier, still a high-schooler at this time. Louis grew up in Santa Barbara, and he was an all-out gifted person at walking around and finding birds. He would amble along a street, as he did one day in 1979 in Montecito, and look up in a pine tree and there would be a Grace's warbler! The wagtail at Devereux Slough flew right over Louis in the fall of 1978, and of course he knew how rare it was — and that was the key. Later, when he entered UCSB, he was Paul's roommate in Isla Vista.

So now we have Brad, Paul, Louis, and we'll add Richard Webster, whom I didn't know as well because most of the time he was at Harvard as an undergrad, and then he moved away. But he'd grown up in Santa Barbara, and his mother, Fifi Webster, was active in the local Audubon chapter. Richard was super-intelligent, and terribly quick at finding birds in the field. He played a major role in the early 1970s, working with Nelson Metcalf at the Museum of Natural History and acting as a bridge between this new way of birding and the more traditional study of birds that had been going on for years

Where did these birders go to chase vagrants?

In those days, there were a number of vagrant traps, and they were given regular coverage by the birders who knew what they were doing. They included the student vegetable garden near Devereux Slough; a row of tamarisk trees in a field east of Storke Road (the field is now a housing development called Storke Ranch); and North Goleta creeks that flowed to the ocean, such as San Jose, Atascadero, and Maria Ygnacio. But the best places were up and down the coast: Gaviota State Beach, Refugio State Beach, El Capitan State Beach, and Carpinteria Creek. Any of these places, due to their proximity to the coast and the fact that they provided shelter, water, and food for migrant birds, were fall hotspots for vagrants.

A quick aside: tamarisk is a bushy tree that was introduced into Southern California from Asia, often planted as a row of windbreaks in agricultural fields. The tamarisk has long, scale-like leaves, and deep roots. The species is no longer planted, but a few old stands remain. Migrant landbirds, seeing stands of tamarisk near the coast, are attracted to them because of an insect, a tiny leafhopper that often infests the trees. For this reason, Gaviota State Beach, which was planted with rows of tamarisk trees, was the hottest birding place for vagrants in the late 1970s and early 1980s. After that, most tamarisk trees were cut down.

I remember chasing vagrants with Karen Bridgers, as we dodged barking dogs and wandering toddlers from one end of the campground to the other. Here we were, in jeans and floppy birding hats, our binoculars focused solely on the ugly tamarisk trees and the colorful Eastern warblers that visited them. While we stared at the birds, the campers couldn't figure out what we were up to, then shook their heads when we told them.

Skipping forward to the mid-'90s and onward, birders discovered that stands of river red gum eucalyptus, which can host another pest called the lerp psyllid, attracted migrating birds. Eucalyptus groves located near the coast, which are infested with the psyllid, lure birds to feed on the sugary capsules formed by the larval stage of the insect.

Gradually, I, too, began to understand there was a whole other world of more serious birding out there. Sure, it was fun to chase rare birds and be the first to put them on the hotline, but it was more than that. And when I enrolled in the Santa Barbara City College Continuing Education bird class, which was then being taught by Paul Lehman, I recognized that Paul was birding at a significantly higher level than anyone I'd ever been with in the field. I saw the rigorous standards that he employed when it came to describing birds we had seen. Paul was also a geography major at UCSB, and his insights into the weather and topography of our region were concepts I'd been thinking about, but never learned.

I had to write everything down. I filled notebooks and journals with the new facts. This stuff was just so exciting. Here was a group of people who were not only watching birds, but going out searching for them, and recording what they saw. Why? Because nobody else had. There was still so much to be discovered about Santa Barbara County.

Rare Birds and Listing

If I am honest, in looking back over these early years of my birding in Santa Barbara, I would say that I was in over my head. I was around at a time when super-rarities were being found by super-birders. I, who was still struggling with identification of the more common birds, did I really deserve to have all these gorgeous rarities just fall into my lap? It seemed like eating dessert before you've digested the main meal.

For example, in perusing my field notes from the year 1982, I am astounded at the vagrants that arrived in our county that year.

It started when our daughter, Jenny, who was studying at her desk, looked out the window one rainy day that winter. She called me into her room, pointing to a strange bird she'd seen feeding on our front lawn. I ran to get my binoculars, and then I went crazy. It was a brown thrasher, an Eastern bird that reminds you of a mockingbird, except it's rusty brown on the back, has a pale yellow eye, and lots of streaking down the front.

That was my "county" brown thrasher, and it had landed right in front of me. I ran for the phone to let my friends know, but most of them had already seen a brown thrasher in the county. Notoriously shy and hard to see, that bird used to be a lot more common as a vagrant.

All the dazzling birds I saw in 1982 were originally found by other birders. They included yellow-billed loon, Mongolian plover, broad-winged hawk, broad-billed hummingbird, white-eyed vireo, yellow-green vireo, yellow-billed cuckoo, bay-breasted warbler, black-throated blue warbler, worm-eating warbler, Canada warbler, blackburnian warbler, golden-winged warbler, painted redstart, and hepatic tanager.

These were all life birds for me. I'd never seen them before. And it was important to keep track of each of them, to list them, to write up a description of the birds I saw, and to fill my notebooks with the excitement I felt each time my binoculars focused on one of these new birds.

Birders keep track of the new birds they see, name them and put them on a list. Most people I know have a life list, a California state list, and a Santa Barbara county list. There are also year-listers, a dedicated group that tries to see as many birds as they can within a year in a particular area. Elaborate computer-generated programs will help you organize your lists. But especially for those of us who aren't world travelers, our local county list has become significant. When you make a list of all the birds you've seen in the county, whether or not they're life birds, that's your county list. Some birders keep track of the birds they've seen for each of the many counties in California, but mine is only for Santa Barbara.

Due to Santa Barbara's location near the coast, and its tendency to attract vagrants, you can imagine the total number of species of birds seen and identified in our county is greater than that of many states. At this writing, the official Santa Barbara County List stands at 503 species of birds throughout its ornithological history.

Today's serious birders are always making lists. Every time they go out in the field, they count numbers of birds and enter them somewhere, either into eBird (a listing app available for smartphones), in a notebook, or on their computers. However, for a person who is genuinely engaged in birding, your list is only the tip of the iceberg. The list is shorthand for what was occurring in the bird world that day. The more details and photos you add, along with special behavior you notice, and the more accurately you describe your exact location — those are the extras that make a list truly valuable.

Among the good birders that I was getting to know, locating vagrants was just one aspect of birding. These excellent birders were studying common birds, too. They were trying to identify subspecies, geographic ranges, population cycles, and breeding behaviors.

Finding rarities is thrilling, but it's not everyday birding.

6

Adventures in Learning

I couldn't get enough of birding, and I had the best teachers. Jon Dunn, whom I would meet on a Yosemite trip, had moved to Santa Barbara. He and Paul Lehman shared an apartment off Turnpike Road near Goleta. It may have been small, but it was Bird Central for all of Santa Barbara during the 1980s.

The birding community consisted of a bunch of birders who went out regularly. The telephone was the chief means of getting in touch about a rare or unusual bird being seen. For up-to-the-minute information, you had to get a phone call from somebody who had found the bird, or who was passing on information from someone else who had found the bird.

Since there were no cellphones, if you had just seen a super bird, you'd look for a payphone as a way to relay the information. We wrote notes to each other, leaving them under rocks near a site or on the windshield of a fellow birder's car.

This small group of really active birders numbered about 20 or so. If you weren't hooked into this group, you were out of the loop. And sometimes there were hurt feelings because one or two folks might not have gotten the message in time to "chase" the bird in question. If you didn't go out and follow up on the phone message by attempting to look at the rare bird, eventually you ended up not being called. No wonder I was always racing out the door to see if I could find these birds, all of which were new to me.

One of the ways to be in the loop was to sign up for Paul's birding class, the same one I'd enrolled in (and would eventually teach.) He took the class to locations where he thought there might be interesting birds. Indeed, Paul was simply going birding and the rest of us followed wherever he chose to explore.

Not only was I learning birds, I was discovering new locations. The Cuyama Valley, the Carrizo Plain, the estuaries of the Santa Ynez, the Santa Maria, and the Santa Clara Rivers were all new to me. And the mountains. I'd never been to the San Rafael Mountains for serious birding. I'd only been hiking with Dad on the most accessible trails. And East Camino Cielo, that was a birding spot, along with the Santa Ynez and Santa Maria Valleys. Everywhere I went I looked at the landscape through new eyes — what birds were there, how many, and when they could be found.

Paul was focused on understanding Santa Barbara County bird distribution because he had settled upon a title for his Master's thesis: "The Birds of Santa Barbara County, California."

(The thesis was published in book form, an effort spearheaded by Mark Holmgren at UCSB's Vertebrate Museum, in 1994. Some of us called it the bible.

It still is, and you can find an annually updated version online at http://www.sbcobirding.com/lehmanbosbc.html).

Jon Dunn was also working on a project. He had been hired as chief consultant by the National Geographic Society for a new type of field guide, "The Birds of North America." Published in 1983, the "NGS" guide was considered the new standard reference for intermediate birders in the field, and eventually seven editions were published over the next thirty years.

For these reasons, both Jon and Paul wanted to spend lots of time in the field studying birds. In Jon's case, he was writing the text for his field guide, working with a team of artists and other birders, many of them back East. He was looking critically at birds, their plumage subtleties, and the fine points of their songs and calls.

Paul, on the other hand, was learning more about what was going on with the status and distribution of birds in Santa Barbara County.

I was an unabashed groupie, lapping up every scrap of knowledge I could get from these experts. Every time I went birding with Paul or Jon, I came home and filled my notebooks with all that I'd learned that day. I wrote in longhand in a small 3-ring binder that had lined paper.

Looking back, I realize Paul and Jon had become mentors, perhaps unwittingly. As a new birder I soaked up the facts about birds that, in some cases, were new to them too, as they worked on their own projects. Their expertise with birds was unmatched. I was lucky enough to be in the right place at the right time.

The Language of Birds

Learning to recognize the sounds, including bird calls and songs, was paramount. I had underestimated the importance of vocalizations.

It is one thing to become familiar with the dominant spring song of a bird species, usually given by the male. But I was to find out that the sounds birds make in fall and winter are just as crucial; they can help you pick out that "different" bird sound that doesn't belong. During fall and winter, when the birds aren't singing their territorial songs, they vocalize with a smaller sub-set of notes unique to each species.

Truly, when you begin to focus on bird sounds, you'll find you will learn some calls that you can recognize more easily if you set them to syllables, or even make up a corny descriptive phrase.

Don't be embarrassed. Anything that will set that sound apart is helpful. So your brain, the next time it hears the "pop" of a Bewick's wren or the "chimp" of a song sparrow, can think, "Oh YES!" Each "pop" or "chimp" note may have slight variations, but if you've got the most common one memorized, the similarity is easy enough to recognize.

And now, with all the excellent websites that feature bird vocalizations, you never have to carry around tapes, the way we used to.

I was fortunate to have keen ears, which made up for my poor eyesight. My nearsightedness was a deterrent. I was always looking through one set of lenses — my glasses — and then through another — my binoculars. Getting quickly "onto" a bird, raising your binoculars and focusing on the bird you want, that was hard for me. But I did the best I could, and I began increasingly to rely on their sounds to locate birds.

Looking through my old journals, I see that I had more notes to myself about bird vocalizations than any other subject. Many of the field guides in those days lacked good descriptions of bird sounds. However, the experience of being out in the field and listening to birds sing and call was still considered the best way to recognize vocalizations.

Interestingly, in the book "The Nature Fix," by Florence Williams (2017), she mentions that human brains are surprisingly similar to the parts of birds' brains that hear, process, and make language. Humans share more genes governing speech with songbirds than we do with primates. Humans and birds co-evolved these language centers, both using the same ancient neural hardware (Williams, p. 99).

And I was learning the language of birds. It was an adrenaline rush all its own, to recognize birds by their sounds. I embraced it totally.

While I was playing tennis or walking a tree-lined street downtown or standing at a party outdoors, if I was able to pick out a bird call, I was tuned into this other, newer, more exciting world. Birds spoke a language that could be learned. And it was another interaction with nature, in a way I'd never known existed. I loved languages, and I was compelled by this secret universe, revealed by simply listening to the sounds of birds.

And soon enough the term "birdwatcher" was switched out to "birder." Over the years, people have asked me, what's the difference? Frankly, there's none, and I use the terms interchangeably. But "birder" was originally meant to describe one of these new, younger-generation birdwatchers — those who went out actively seeking birds and were skilled at it, not those just passively watching whatever bird happened to plop into their backyard.

I didn't care what I was called, but the term birder definitely had a ring to it. I started using it more frequently.

The birding universe was a fresh view of the world, one where I felt I could be outside as much as I wanted, and focus on birds. Gripped by the thrill of the chase, by the idea that I could get better and better at identifying birds, and by the fact that these good local birders were serving up rarities nearly every other day for me to add to my life list, I couldn't help myself. It was all so much fun.

My First Professional Bird Tour

Another way to interact with other birders and be instructed by top guides was to take a birding tour. The 1980s saw the rise of the professional bird tour. There had been various small nature-oriented travel tours in existence, but when Will Russell, Rich Stallcup, and Davis Finch founded the tour group called Wings in the late 1970s, it was one of the first of what became the big three. VENT (Victor Emmanuel Nature Tours) was already in operation, and Field Guides was established a few years later.

Today, numerous bird tour oufits run the gamut from small to large and from one area of expertise to another, but in the 1970s professional bird tour companies were a whole new idea. They capitalized on the time and money that serious birders were willing to spend to see birds, not only in North America but around the world. Birders who sign up to go on professional tours are usually intent on finding target birds. The pressure is on the leader and the tour company to locate certain sought-after species. The participants are world birders, and one of their hallmarks is a desire to keep copious lists of the birds they see, and to make sure each trip provides them with the birds they "must get."

This kind of competitiveness was celebrated in the movie "The Big Year" (2011) starring Steve Martin, Jack Black, and Owen Wilson. I thought it great fun, and it gave the general public an idea of what a certain kind of birding can be like.

But back to Wings, the tour company that I knew a bit about. It was started by Will Russell, who grew up in Maine. Will was a rarity himself: a birder who was a good businessman. He was smart enough to recognize who were the top bird guys in the West, and he hired them to lead tours.

One of the most inviting tours was called the Wings Weekend. The trips lasted no more than two or three days, cheaper than the standard two-week birding tours. They featured good birding destinations in the U.S.

Since my friends Jeanie and Kathy had moved out of town, we'd sworn that we'd get together annually for a birding reunion. We finally decided on a Wings Weekend in Yosemite in the fall of 1980. I asked Carol Goodell if she'd accompany me.

It was on this trip that I was introduced to Jon Dunn and Kimball Garrett, who were the leaders. My friendship with Jon and Kimball reinforced all that I was learning from Paul, and I was astounded at this new level of birding.

My journal from that trip:

 **NATURE JOURNAL: OCTOBER 13-16, 1980**
Yosemite National Park

A 4:45 a.m. start to our trip this morning, amid snow flurries and spectacular scenery as the first snowfall of the season blankets the Yosemite backcountry. We have a small group and two vans.

We're searching for the great gray owl, one of the rarest resident birds in California. I know we'll be incredibly lucky if we see this elusive species.

We head out and drive up Glacier Point Road. Winter has come early. I have on every piece of outerwear I brought, and I'm still shivering.

At our first stop, we follow the trail through the dark conifers down into Peregoy Meadow. When we come out into the meadow, the golden grasses are white. Two coyotes, their heads and shoulders dusted with frost, get up from their night resting spot, look at our group, yawn, and trot away. No sign of any owl, despite a couple of hours of tramping around.

From Peregoy Meadow, we drive on to Glacier Point. Skies look threatening. We walk gingerly down the Four Mile Trail part way, admiring the view of Yosemite Valley far below us. A distant flock of evening grosbeaks proves too far away to get a good look.

We eat lunch, snow blowing in our faces as we munch cold salami-and-cheese sandwiches at the picnic tables.

Next, we drive down to Chinquapin to search for mountain quail. It's snowing heavily by now, and all seems a Christmas land of snow-covered firs. At last, the "kip-kip" call of red crossbills. In undulating flight, a male alights for us at the top of a tall pine. Another life bird for me, as we get excellent views of the bill on this bird. The bill fits together in such a way that the red crossbill can insert it into the cone of a conifer and then pluck out the seed with its tongue.

We watch the Steller's jays' behavior. They fly up at a dangling sugar pine cone, knock the seeds loose, then fly down and catch the seed in mid-air as it is falling.

Next day, stormy weather closes Glacier Point Road. I feel the great gray owl slipping away.

Another montane meadow, Crane Flat, was one of our destinations for the owl. We tramp all over the spongy grasses, now lying in tired tufts. We see a Townsend's solitaire, such a lovely bird of the mountains that I was to get to know better at other locations, but I learn its bell-like single call.

Then, we find out that Tioga Pass has been closed for the season. This is beginning to be a disaster.

Finally, that night, the group splits up into those who want to go try for the great gray owl again, and those who don't. Obviously, my friends and I want to go.

Snow and rain had fallen intermittently, but by evening, we could get back up to Glacier Point Road and try once more in Peregoy Meadow for the owl. Fourteen intrepid birders, plus Jon and Kimball, trudge through the woods. Snow begins to fall faster as we approach the meadow again.

Dark pines and firs make ghostly silhouettes around the straw-colored grasses. A stream runs through the middle. All the birders pull their ponchos tighter as we huddle together, while Jon and Kimball skirt the perimeter searching and listening.

We move down into the Lower Meadow. Nothing but a flock of robins. Quiet. Quiet. Snow flakes falling.

By now it's 7 pm. The snow tapers off; it's getting dark.

Patiently the band of birders waits, and listens. Even if we only hear the great gray call, we'll be elated.

And then "Whoo, whoo, whoo" . . . a deep, measured booming issues from the woods. It's the great gray. It calls three times. Everyone hears it.

I feel the thrill of the owl's basso hoots as they echo across the frozen meadow. We stand waiting and watching for another hour, hoping the owl might fly so we could catch even a glimpse. But night settles in.

Hiking the mile up the hill out of Peregoy, we don't need flashlights. The snow has whitened the forest floor.

Afterwards back at the lodge, we go over the list of birds seen. Nobody is complaining. We know we can "count" the great gray owl on our life list, even if we didn't see it. And who would exchange the magic of standing in a meadow on that snowy night?

• • •

Six years later, on a trip with David Gaines (a top Sierra Nevada birder who was subsequently killed in a tragic car accident), I had the best possible views of a great gray owl during a Los Angeles Audubon Society field trip. This time, we were camped at Crane Flat. Immediately upon arrival, all of our group dashed across one of the busiest intersections in the park, where Tioga Road meets Highway 120 at a place called Chevron Meadows. It's named after the nearby gas station, which was filled with the sounds of car engines accelerating and tourists chatting.

We learned that this tall-grass meadow is a favorite of the great gray, due to the owl's ability to hear voles — those tiniest of rodents — as they move beneath the vegetation. Surrounded by dense forest, the meadow formed a clearing.

We approached cautiously, using the forest as cover. As we got to the edge of the trees, David said quietly, "There it is."

The owl was in plain sight — perched to look like an extension of a dead snag that stuck up from a felled log, a perfect camouflage.

We stared. So soon. So effortlessly. Our goal for the whole trip, the great gray owl, appeared in the first half hour.

The immense owl then attempted one hunting dive into the grass, and flew to a new spot atop a rotted-out tree trunk.

We crept back further into the woods, then walked over wet bracken and swampy grasses to find a better spot for viewing.

From this new vantage point, I watched the owl. Its gray dome-like head swiveled to one side, revealing the depth of feathers that form the neck, a thick layer like a heavy feather duster. The huge facial discs, set in its massive head, were each centered with a powerful yellow eye. The eyes seemed to catch the inner fire of an Arctic forebear and fling it back at the nearest prey, or at us — the observers, the disturbers. Should we even be here?

But I couldn't stop staring at the owl. I was intrigued by the white mustache markings at the base of the facial discs.

Soon the owl appeared to relax. It scratched the side of its head with a long stretch of feathered anklet. It turned from side to side and glowered out of those yellow eyes, then blinked several times.

So yes, I eventually saw the rare great gray owl on that later visit, but it lacked the thrill of my first bird trip to Yosemite. I will never forget standing in Peregoy Meadow with the snow coming down and the deep hooting. Not seeing the bird that first time made me appreciate it more. That's when I realized that birding for me is more than a quick, visual "got that one" moment. I crave the adventure of knowing the bird in its surroundings. Each sighting is a treasure to be handled carefully, written up, and remembered long after the experience has passed.

Memorial Day Madness 1983

It was called "Memorial Day Madness" by some of us. A spring ritual among many California birders went like this. You drive for hours to spend the long, hot Memorial Day weekend where the good Eastern vagrants are to be found . . . in the middle of the desert. Granted, birding for Eastern vagrants in spring is productive along the coast, but the desert is a lot better; the area at the extreme eastern border of California where it meets Nevada was a typical target.

I've described the reason for this, the fact that desert oases concentrate migrating birds in spring, some of which may suffer from an internal compass that has malfunctioned and brought them there, instead of to the East Coast where they belong. Thus, the potential for vagrant-chasing was excellent.

I had heard stories about all of the rare birds to be found out in the California deserts, and I was positively dying to go. I managed to persuade Jon Dunn to lead a group of us around a few of the desert "hot spots" for three days in late May of 1983, in return for expenses paid.

As usual, Jon was patient with our plans to bring loads of provisions, a camp stove, parkas and blankets. Way more than we needed. Most birders just threw a sleeping bag on the ground and ate granola bars for breakfast, lunch, and dinner.

When we finally got to Cottonwood Canyon, the acknowledged headquarters where birders indulging in "Memorial Day Madness" gathered, it was pitch black outside.

We set up camp in the dark, surrounded by boulders and sagebrush. I could hear a creek rushing nearby. A moon rose over the barren mountains that surrounded a wild, empty basin. As I lay in my sleeping bag, I could hardly wait for the next day's adventures.

At 5:30 a.m., the birding started, as we awoke to the sounds of Bullock's orioles and house wrens singing around camp. Our first destination was Oasis Ranch, which I'd heard of many times. Oasis was a large agricultural operation, but there were several rows of neglected old cottonwoods, some of which formed a famous line of trees known as "the diagonal." We walked all over this ranch, and I saw my first ovenbird. After that, on the way to the tiny town of Dyer, Nevada, we came upon a row of trees where two adult and one juvenile long-eared owl stood tall and skinny, hugging the central trunks of the trees. Well-streaked below, the owls matched the bark perfectly.

Next stop was Circle L Ranch — also in Nevada, surrounded by lush, irrigated fields and many locust trees. Our excitement mounted. The shade around the house attracted all sorts of birds: rose-breasted grosbeak, dusky flycatcher, Cassin's finch, indigo and lazuli buntings, to name a few. The large lake beyond the ranch was packed with waterbirds, including a Franklin's gull and American and least bitterns.

After the Circle L, we went to another ranch with yet another row of cottonwoods. We began to encounter bird enthusiasts from other parts of California, all searching these same locations. Most of them were young men in a state of dishevelment, exuding the aroma of the frenzied birder. While we women were happy to rest under a tree and enjoy the MacGillivray's warblers and an American redstart, these characters made round trips to Death Valley (90 miles away, temperature 110 degrees F.) following a rumor of some possible vagrant being there. Whew. Not for me . . .

At the end of the day, we drove exhausted but happy back to Cottonwood Canyon, stopping to watch the common nighthawks soaring and dipping in the twilight sky. We sat on boulders in the dust, sipping white wine out of plastic cups, then devoured the canned ravioli, beans, and stew warmed on the camp stove.

The next day turned out to be the most eventful of all. Word came in that Deep Springs had three good warblers: a Cape May, a chestnut-sided, and a hooded! We were off in a flash. Arriving at Deep Springs, which is a unique private college in the middle of nowhere, we walked down the broad entrance road lined with cottonwoods.

We spotted an aggregation of birders all staring gratefully up at a gorgeous male Cape May warbler; the sizes and shapes of the birders were almost as interesting to me as the birds. But they were definitely not as beautiful.

The morning we were scheduled to leave, I woke up to find birders bunked down wherever they could. One couple slept halfway underneath their car; another woman had pulled her motor home up to a spot underneath a cottonwood tree. Problem was, a yellow-billed cuckoo had chosen to appear in that tree at dawn. The motor home owner, issuing from her lodging in her nightgown, was just fine with the fact that everyone in the campground was staring at her. We birders were just checking out the first — the breakfast bird — of the day. Not a bad sighting when you haven't even gulped a cup of coffee yet.

After that, we packed up to get going for home. As we stopped by Deep Springs one more time, a steady trickle of cars pulled up, the occupants disgorged and ambled over to say hi to Jon Dunn. I whispered to my friends, "Who's that?" And, "Isn't that Rich Stallcup?" and so on and on. It was a roll call of every top California birder I'd ever heard of.

The next year, when a group of us went back to Cottonwood Canyon, an article I'd written had been published in *Birdwatcher's Digest*, a small magazine devoted to birding. I was confident that nobody I knew would read the article, or I probably would not have written it.

As we were sitting around that first night, trying to do our bird lists by flashlight, I noticed a stranger approaching. Hmmm. I wondered who he was, but we were all busy with our checklists. After awhile, this guy, and I wish I could describe him but it was dark, came over and spoke up in a friendly drawl:

"Hey, where are all the women? Where's the party?"

I was flabbergasted. This person had read my article. Oh no, now what? Had I given the wrong impression of Memorial Day Madness?

I enlisted some of my birding friends to explain that this wasn't a party scene. But what had I said in that article, prompting a total stranger to come all this way to find out?

Later that evening, I moved my sleeping bag much farther up the canyon.

First writing lesson: Once your words are floating around out there, *anybody* may read them. Make sure you know what you're saying. Being a novice birder is no excuse for being a naïve writer.

(Today, many of the places mentioned above are no longer possible to access.)

Building the
Ornithological Record

Although I treasured my explorations far afield, when fall arrived, I stuck close to home.

Carpinteria Creek became well-known as a fall vagrant trap. The creek itself is an important one, flowing across the coastal plain from the Santa Ynez Mountains behind Carpinteria to its outlet at Carpinteria State Beach.

For over twenty years, I birded "Carp Creek" with Karen Bridgers every fall. She and I slogged our way in black rubber boots — up and down the creek looking for rare birds. Sometimes we were successful, sometimes not, but we were keen to get out there. Karen was a true vagrant chaser; she had sharp eyes. I tagged along. Birding together time after time created a strong bond. We would ask each other if such-and-such a field mark was good or not, and "Did you see the red eye?" or "What about the flanks, were they yellowish or greenish?" Those kinds of questions that only a birding buddy can relate to.

But here we were, Karen and I, a couple of newbie birders, and we had blundered into a world of birding. We tried hard, but we were definitely inexperienced. And we made mistakes. Many of the mistakes we didn't confess to anyone; we'd call on the phone and giggle about them with each other.

Since he was in charge of keeping the list of bird sightings for our county, Paul Lehman was no-nonsense when it came to reporting a bird you'd seen. Accurate descriptions of birds had to be written up in detail, describing what you saw, why it was that species, and where it was found.

With his East Coast background, Paul knew the status and distribution of birds in all of North America, not just the West Coast. The rigorous birding standards I learned from him were a big influence. I could never duplicate his birding ability, but he was very generous with his knowledge.

Both Paul and Jon imbued in me a healthy skepticism about everything in the birding world that I didn't know for sure, or that I hadn't corroborated or witnessed. This was well before birders took digital photographs, so we were still dependent on word-of-mouth reports or written descriptions.

The importance of what goes into the scientific record — that was my first and biggest lesson. Ornithology is a set of building blocks based on what qualified observers have seen and contributed over decades. Once erroneous information gets passed down, it taints the literature. You can't make accurate statements about a body of knowledge if the building blocks are wobbly.

When Paul moved with his wife, Shawneen Finnegan, from Santa Barbara to Cape May, New Jersey, in 1994, and I became the County Coordinator keeping track of all the bird records for Santa Barbara County, Paul's methods stood me in good stead. Did so-and-so report a bird that was way too early or way too late, according to what records we already had? Then you better make sure that person had a good reputation, or you go see for yourself, go check out the location, see if you can re-find the bird.

To be honest, this was the most difficult job I ever undertook. Unlike some of the top birding experts, I wasn't proficient as a detail-oriented record keeper. Understanding intellectually that the scientific record comprises these individual sightings, I still had trouble organizing and categorizing. Was a bird seen in late November simply a tardy migrant on its way, or a winterer that was going to spend several months here?

Although I typed all of the bird records into the computer, those annoying 3 x 5 cards popped into my life again. In order to keep track of who'd seen what when, out came the card, and on it went the date, the species seen, and the initials of the birder who saw it. Four times a year, the quarterly reports went out for the season: Winter (December through February), Spring (March through May), Summer (June through July), and Fall (August through November). Due to the usual flurry of fall vagrants, the Fall Report was the most lengthy. It took me hours (often days) to arrange all of this information in a cohesive format on the computer to be sent along to the Regional Editor of *North American Birds*. I struggled.

The experience taught me about status and distribution; I had to be aware of what birds were being seen throughout the county, not just on the South Coast. Furthermore, it was up to me to cajole a photograph or a description out of the birder who saw that rarity. If the description was flakey, the record from your county might not withstand the scrutiny of Guy McCaskie. I took it seriously.

You had to have this sense of judging what was considered rare and what wasn't worth including. Thankfully, Paul had left us with his book (see first page of this chapter) and that helped me figure out the status of the bird. In addition, I compiled a list called "Birds of Local Interest," which included sightings that wouldn't be significant on a state-wide basis but would be interesting for our local scene.

When Dave Compton arrived in Santa Barbara in the early 1990s, we became friends. He was the perfect candidate for succeeding me as the County Coordinator: he had been a copy editor for a scientific publisher. In 2000, I was relieved to hand over the seasonal reports to him.

But I'd worked through the intricacies of bird records and how they contributed to ornithology. Everything we know about birds in this county can be attributed to scientists before us keeping careful records.

7.

Teaching For The Fun Of It

Time flew. I was asked to teach "Birds of the Santa Barbara Region (Beginning)," sponsored by Santa Barbara City College Continuing Education, on Monday mornings from 8:30-10:30.

I was terribly nervous, but what an opportunity.

I love teaching, always have. I especially like helping students understand more complex issues. I give them the big picture, then narrow it down to the particulars. My goal was to get students comfortable with recognizing the common birds of our region. Then, we could go into the fine points of identification, bird behavior, migration — everything I'd so recently learned myself.

Regardless, I was anxious before each class. When I got out of the car and set up my scope, called out the roster, and had to pretend I really knew what I was talking about, my mouth got dry, my hands were clammy and my heart pounded.

What if I made a mistake? What if I misidentified a common bird, a bird that I knew easily, but that, in the nervous rush of trying to call out the correct species name, I had screwed up?

Introducing Students to Birding

Over the many enriching years of teaching, I made errors, some small, some huge.

I found that teaching people to distinguish one bird from another was as much fun as going birding on my own, and even more rewarding. I loved sharing my enthusiasm for birds with interested adults. Year after year, I thrived on introducing new birders to the fun, excitement, and beauty of birds.

Teaching combined my love of people with that of birds, of being outside, of nature. It gave my own birding a seriousness and a purpose that I'd never had before. And, I even earned a little money.

Several years later I took on the "Birds of the Santa Barbara Region (Intermediate)" class, the one Paul Lehman used to teach. During the late 1980s and through the 1990s, I taught birding classes four mornings a week: at the Museum of Natural History, at the Botanic Garden, and at the two Continuing Education classes.

One morning while at home, I looked around the tidied-up kitchen and realized I'd forgotten to eat my own breakfast. I'd made three lunches — one for Gib and each of the kids — fixed breakfast for everyone else, cleaned up, then laughed and knew why I was still hungry.

I had energy for it all. Beginning during the fall quarter, and on through the winter and spring quarters, I'd be teaching away, having exciting birding days, sometimes discovering unusual birds in class, but mostly enjoying whatever species showed up.

I learned from my generous, intelligent, alert students. They asked great questions; they were a forgiving audience, wanting to be there, eager to learn. When I started teaching, I was much younger than many of the participants. Then, as I aged with my students, I learned to admire those who've gone down the aging-while-birding path before me.

All sorts of people found their way to the birding classes. Some had held powerful positions in their careers; others were accountants for big corporations; some were in publishing; some were teachers, well-known philanthropists, little-known poets, famous professors from UCSB and elsewhere, or photographers. There were a few biologists, lots of engineers (mechanical, electrical), and a few doctors. Many were newcomers to Santa Barbara.

The newcomers delighted me. I, who feel I own every corner of Santa Barbara — well, I'd met my match. These people had given up living elsewhere for a reason: they too treasured Santa Barbara. They relished every destination we visited in class. This was their new home now, and they owned it as much as I did, although maybe not for as many years.

In bird class, it doesn't matter what you do or did "in real life," as I called it. Here, we all want to learn about birds. We're held together by this over-arching interest — a bond that supersedes education, wealth, and age. I love that about teaching birding, because you meet on a certain level, and you don't have to delve deeply into personalities. You'll naturally gravitate to some students more than others, but you will always hold them all in deep respect. For they are here to attempt something that's not easy.

People assume that studying about birds will be a snap. And it is, if you are a dilettante, just wanting a tiny taste, a sampler. You can take the appetizer approach, or you can dive in deep — go for the full course meal. I have had lots of students do both. Whatever they take away, they have given me something in return. A sense of spreading the word — and it's a very big word we need to spread these days, with all the challenges to our planet.

How many times have I heard this: "You've made me so *aware!*" Have I? My heart jumps for joy.

"I used to walk right by that bird!" someone will say. Or "I never knew what bird was driving me crazy at 5 a.m. every morning, but I think it was a California towhee."

I adopted this teaching philosophy early on: you have to *tell* people what to get excited about. They don't know. For the most part, they aren't born naturalists.

Make your students notice the beauty, don't let them get away with not looking at the birds through the spotting scope. Explain to them the wonders of the bird world. How tiny shore birds migrate vast distances from the Arctic tundra to the tip of South America; how fragile and yet how strong these creatures are — flying thousands of miles without stopping, some across the vast ocean, only to be grounded in an instant by a late spring storm that slams into them, altering their course.

I taught the students about bird sounds. It is so easy to recognize the common songs. But if your hearing is poor, watch for movement. The wiggle of a green leaf, a vertical posture in a horizontal landscape, a treetop shaking on a windless day. Those are the clues I'd pick up on.

The spectrum of commitment to birding runs the gamut in class. And no matter where my students were going with this birding hobby, I would be with them in spirit. I treasure them. They've given me what I sought: self-esteem, pride, and immense pleasure.

And after every class I made notes and species lists, so I have exciting days of teaching all written down.

Here is a snippet of a journal written a long time ago.

NATURE JOURNAL: JANUARY 6, 1986
Bird Class at Rocky Nook Park

I rush up the steps into the classroom at the Museum of Natural History. Twenty-five friendly faces are seated around the table. I give my standard introductory lecture, followed by registration duties.

Finally, at about 10 a.m., we leave the building. I think to myself, we're too late to see any good birds, but I feel compelled to take everyone across the street to Rocky Nook Park and try for the rare hepatic tanager and summer tanager (found on the latest Christmas Bird Count).

It is a glorious morning. Yellow-and-black Townsend's warblers search the oak trees, a red-breasted sapsucker hitches its way up a tree trunk, Hutton's vireos and ruby-crowned kinglets cooperate by letting us compare these similar birds as they forage close by.

Suddenly, somebody says "I have an oriole!" A participant has found a male Bullock's oriole in a pine at the end of the parking lot. Yay! My heart pounds.

This is going so much better than I expected.

We walk slowly up through the north end of Rocky Nook Park. It's one of those days when every bird cooperates. What are the chances of us seeing the brick-red hepatic tanager? Zero and none. Remember, these are beginners!

But, as we're strolling along, another lady with good eyes calls me over.

"Is this bird red or am I crazy?" I put my binoculars up, and there it is!

I squeal in delight as I get everyone to see the rare hepatic tanager. This bird should be in Mexico for the winter, but instead it became one of the most famous birds to ever be found on a Santa Barbara Christmas Bird Count, and, it returned for twelve years to Rocky Nook Park every winter after that.

These beginners don't know how lucky they are.

But there's one more bird I have to find. And I hear it! The "pit-i-tuck" of the summer tanager. It's a lovely mustard yellow female right above the trail in an oak.

"Where, Joan, where?"

"Just look in the small oak and it's at 10 o'clock"

"Oooh, it's so pretty!"

"Now what is this again, Joan?"

"I thought tanagers had a red head." I explain about the difference between summer and western tanagers.

Finally, everyone gets a chance to see this elegant bird. My spirits are flying.

Most teaching days aren't this easy. Besides, I was hard on myself. I wanted to be a good birder so badly, to identify everything we saw correctly.

As the years went on, I realized that the students probably didn't care as much about birds as I do. Put it this way: the students are there for a variety of reasons, and it's not always bird identification. Some participants like the outdoor venues, some want to learn only a few common birds, some want to chat with friends.

But on certain days, you teach a class that makes your spirit sing. Maybe the students will catch some of my enthusiasm, maybe not, but for me, the thrill is sharing.

 NATURE JOURNAL: SEPTEMBER 27, 1993
Bird Class at Maria Ignacio Creek, Goleta

The sun bears down on our backs this warm day, so we head for the sandy floor of the creek bed and the cool willows.

Carol Goodell is assisting me with the Monday class today, and we need her spotting scope to be able to see the white-winged dove that flushed up to the utility wire and posed there for us, its beige coloring blending perfectly with the willow branches it just left.

A puddle in the creek surrounded by reeds is the birdiest spot. We stand awhile, watching bright yellow warblers come down to drink — yellow, Wilson's, and orange-crowned — migrants just passing through. I was looking away at the time, when suddenly a participant behind me yells: "Yellow-breasted chat!"

No way, that's a super hard bird to see. It's a dynamite bird: large, but secretive, skulky, with a bright yellow breast a black mask and a long gray tail. Its song is an unmistakable repertoire of different sounds one after the other.

*I believe my student . . . sort of . . . I don't want to
sound skeptical.*

*And then, the chat shows itself again, behind the
reeds, and creeps up a tall stem into the open for all 22
members of the class to see.*

*A collective gasp of surprise comes from the group of
birders as we watch.*

*I've never had the chance to show a chat to a crowd
like that!*

They love every minute of it.

I realized the tremendous high, the power I felt when I shared my
love of birds with students. To be so totally focused on the bird, on the
"out there" or "the other" was a new experience for most of these people.

I wanted them to feel the pleasure and the frustration of it: the
shapes, the silhouettes, the glancing wing flutter, the disappearing tail,
the mystery and the search. It keeps our hearts beating and obsesses our
minds. It ruins our legs from standing and our necks ache, our backs
protest. We keep on. How can we let go? How can we ever again resign
ourselves to a life without birds?

Birding must be part of our life. It must be in our travel plans and
our writing and our thoughts. We know we can never escape it.

We feel a kinship with those who also suffer and labor under the
same yoke. We alienate others and lose friends, strain our family relationships, and prevail where we were once meek. There's no satiation.
Once you've felt the adrenaline rush and the thrill of seeing that unexpected bird, you're hooked. You won't give it up.

If someone handed you a present, and said, with this gift you will
never be lonely, you will always enjoy great natural beauty, you will
contribute to the future of science in our country, and you will never be
bored, would you take it? Of course.

But birding offers even more than this. It offers adventure, challenges to the mind and eye, friendship with terrific people of all ages
and backgrounds, and best of all an antidote to all that worries you.
For when you're birding, the checkbook is out of sight; sadness and

disappointments are pushed to the back of your mind; failures look insignificant compared to a good day in the field.

These were the halcyon days: days of joy and gratitude for me in my own life by sharing them with bird classes.

Without a doubt, some of my favorite field trips were the ones at Carpinteria Salt Marsh, when we were allowed to walk out the west side of the marsh on Sandyland Road. In those early days of teaching, at least up through 2000, the Continuing Education classes were generously given permission to park outside the marsh along Santa Claus Lane, and to walk over the railroad tracks into the privately owned enclave known as Sandyland.

Ever since my childhood, when I'd been invited to go swimming at the simple beach cottages that used to occupy those private lots, I'd loved "Sandyland Slough" as we used to call it. If you had a house on the narrow peninsula that encloses the marsh on that side, it had the advantage of a view of the tidal wetlands on the one hand and the open beach on the other.

Luckily, beautiful Carpinteria Salt Marsh Reserve was created due to the forethought of the Sandyland homeowners and the stewardship of UCSB. For the birds, this is a major stop-over and wintering destination.

One fall day, the bird class witnessed a sight we'd never seen before.

 **NATURE JOURNAL: NOVEMBER 1, 1999**
Carpinteria Salt Marsh from Sandyland Road

Try finding a bird or anything on a misty morning with the fog so thick you can hardly see two feet in front of you. In that murky landscape, as I shoulder my scope and head out in front of a class of 25 birders, my heart sinks. I can't pick out shapes. The gray-brown pickleweed blends with the gray fog. Birds appear as blobs. A lump on an old stake is a northern harrier? A white-tailed kite? I'm about to panic.

As the fog slides slowly away, ten willets materialize with black-and-white wings flashing. At last, a recognizable species.

A snowy egret stands as a white beacon beside a small pool close by.

The lump perched on the post becomes an American kestrel. The fog is lifting.

As we walk slowly toward the mouth of the estuary, where the fresh sea water flows in on the tides, more and more birds pop into view. It's one of those days when shorebirds of all sizes emerge out of a gray background. Tall, long-billed curlews poke their heads above the pickle-weed, then hide preposterous decurved bills. Tiny least sandpipers scurry in the muddy channel right by the road.

Great blue herons pose like statues, but they're deadly serious. Like every other creature in the marsh this morning, they're hunting for breakfast.

A brown-and-white osprey takes off from a driftwood snag, then returns carrying a fish in its talons. The fish, caught lengthwise between the bright blue flesh of the osprey's feet, is quickly ripped apart morsel by morsel once the osprey lands. After each bite, the bird looks up to make sure there are no challenges to its prey.

But the thrill of the day occurs on the sand bar near the estuary's mouth.

A great blue heron fights to get something down its throat. I focus the spotting scope and see that a flat fish the size of a small salad plate is wedged between its upper and lower mandible. The heron's mouth is open wide; the struggle is agonizing to watch.

In between efforts to get this strange salad plate to go down, the great blue heron slowly steps to the water's edge and places the fish in the water, then shakes it vigorously. Time after time, the heron tries to gulp the fish down, but it won't go.

Silently, we watch. The heron never flinches in its desire to hold onto that halibut, and to swallow it whole. It's like watching a narrow pole — the heron's long neck — that has been popped out in the middle like a piece of silly putty or play dough. At last the bird is finally able to close its bill, with the fish safely wedged much farther down the throat.

A mysterious looking flat bulge in the great blue's neck is all that remains.

None of us has ever seen this before, although we'd observed herons catch gophers and mice. At Sandyland Slough that day, there was one less juvenile California halibut in the nursery. The marsh itself is well-known as a place where young halibuts stay until they grow big enough to tackle the open seas.

Breakfast in bird class. Can a morning get any better than this?

"Chance Favors the Prepared Mind"

Variously attributed to several famous scientists, this quote from Louis Pasteur became a standard-bearer for me. "Chance favors the prepared mind" refers to how observations relate to science and scientific discovery.

The prepared mind is one that knows what the possibilities are, a mindset that's especially useful in the study of biology. If you've really studied your field guide, prepared yourself by carefully going over images of a variety of birds in a particular genus, perhaps looked carefully at the status and distribution of a species so you'd know when it might appear in our area, then you're armed with the information that you'll need *when the opportunity arises.* The latter is the "chance" part.

I'd seen what the top birders could do with identification of rare birds, and I wanted to impart some of those skills to my students.

In the early 1990s, I witnessed an example of this when I saw Shawneen Finnegan pick out a garganey (a rare European duck) from a flock of blue-winged and cinnamon teal at a farm pond in the agricultural fields west of Santa Maria.

To me and the rest of us in the car that chilly November day, all the ducks looked the same. As the wind whipped at the water, a group of teal huddled together at the far corner of the pond.

It was Shawneen who thought she saw that one of the ducks looked different. We're talking subtleties that go from A to Z, which you and I would overlook.

With the wind blowing a gale, Shawneen stuck to her decision to get out of the car. She had her camera, and she slowly approached that collection of ducks — at times crouched on hands and knees — and snapped photo after photo of one that she knew didn't "fit."

Her experience showed me that *knowing beforehand* what that rare duck, the garganey, would look like was how she just "happened" to pick it out. That's the preparedness factor. All good birders already know what the different bird looks like, before it presents itself in the course of daily birdwatching.

Additionally, the more familiar birders are with the common birds, which is 90 percent of what birdwatching is about, the more skilled they are at observing the differences that go beyond what normal variations might occur within a species. Similar to the individual variation within human beings, a certain individual bird may be more brightly colorful than average, may have more or less dark pigment, may even appear larger or smaller than normal, but it is not a different species.

The knowledgeable birder ignores these variations, because he or she is looking for the crucial differences, those that carry a big wallop. In this case it was a patch of pale green instead of pale blue on the wing, bold white eyebrows, instead of a plain brown crown — subtleties that Shawneen picked up on the garganey. We were all looking at the same ducks, but the rest of us in the group did not possess the prepared mind. She did.

8.

The Christmas Bird Count: Part I Foray into Citizen Science

Today it's called "citizen science," a relatively new concept, but for birders it's been around since 1900. That's when Frank Chapman, a renowned East Coast ornithologist, wanted to establish an event around Christmas time that would take the place of the side hunt, an activity that involved going out and shooting whatever type of bird you fancied adding to the Christmas dinner.

Chapman's idea was that citizens would count the birds they see using binoculars rather than acquiring them with a rifle. It was all part of the new movement to conserve bird populations, and had everything to do with the eventual establishment of the National Audubon Society.

Over the last decade, sciences other than ornithology have discovered that the layperson, armed with camera and smartphone, can contribute mightily to our understanding of what's "out there." Several online list serves invite you to collect and photograph an organism, then send it to an expert who can identify it. But a case can be made that citizen science — harnessing the manpower of the non-scientist to help us record the planet's biodiversity — began first in the field of ornithology.

The Christmas Bird Count

Early in my birding career, I felt if there was one aspect of this avocation that I might contribute to, it was the annual Christmas Bird Count, or CBC. This winter count, which has taken place in Santa Barbara off and on since 1909, has become an important part of every birder's year. At first, I didn't know rare birds, but I could recognize a common species if it was present in winter, like a black-headed grosbeak or a hooded oriole. Although fairly easy to identify, these species are not likely to be found here in winter. This fact gives the average birder a chance to discover an unusual bird, perhaps because it hasn't migrated south, or it was lured to stay locally by snacking at a backyard feeder.

Because it's a winter census, communities located in the southern tier of states in the U.S. have an advantage. Birds spend the winter in warmer climates; they also tend to congregate along coasts. The result: places in California and Texas have higher numbers of birds than other locations during the winter.

For example, in 1989, during the Prudhoe Bay, Alaska, CBC the total number of species observed was one, the common raven. Fourteen ravens counted by three birders — that's all there was. The temperature was -25° F, a snow cover of 17 inches lay on the ground, and all water was frozen. Contrast that with our Santa Barbara results for 1989: a total of 205 species, 37,350 individual birds, and 110 observers. That put us at Number 2 behind Freeport, Texas, in the counts north of the Mexican border that year.

Understandably, a friendly rivalry grew up between Christmas Bird Counts in Texas and those in California. For several years back in the late 1970s and early 1980s, Santa Barbara was able to tally a large number of species found in the 24-hour period. We would come out ahead of Freeport, or Corpus Christi, Texas — the top contenders in that state. That made Santa Barbara number one in the country.

I began to take the CBC seriously, and I wanted to be involved. It wasn't so much about being number one, but I was drawn to the idea of a lot of birders combing the CBC areas; the planning that went into it; the personalities you had to work with — the excitement of the whole effort.

What pleased me was how it took me away from the general chaos leading up to Christmas: the commercialism, the endless gifts that people don't need. The concept of going out birding when everyone else was Christmas shopping and spending a ton of money, I loved it. I preferred to be discussing the whereabouts of wintering birds, compared to being part of the massive materialism that dominates the Christmas season.

Of the several CBC circles in Santa Barbara County, the largest and the oldest is the Santa Barbara one. Each circle has a center, and ours is at the corner of Cathedral Oaks Road and Highway 154, also called San Marcos Pass Road. Participants fan out in a 15-mile diameter. The perimeter of the circle is carefully mapped. Any bird seen outside the circle doesn't count.

As I mentioned above, the number of species observed is key. Yes, we count total number of birds, which is extremely important to establish scientific trends, but the thrill is to try to locate as many different species of birds as possible. Our record for Santa Barbara is 224 species, seen on the December 30, 2006 count, but any total of more than 200 is fantastic. Inclement weather strongly affects results, because the number will be much reduced if it's rainy or windy.

Who organizes the CBC? Volunteers — under the auspices of the Santa Barbara Audubon Society. If done properly, organizing and signing up folks to participate in the CBC is a huge task. But more on that later.

The first time I went on a CBC was with my friend Brian Rapp, who persuaded me to come for a half-day census of Montecito with Mary Erickson, an ornithologist at UCSB. That was on December 14, 1974. I have notes on the fact that I learned how to tell a Hutton's vireo from a ruby-crowned kinglet. I also remember stealthily approaching a house where we heard an odd-sounding bird vocalizing. The three of us were intrigued. Upon investigation, it turned out to be a bird in a *cage* that was hanging in somebody's patio.

There were other memorable counts too. Early on, our son, Jonathan, had expressed an interest in getting out birding, and that was something he and I shared. One year Ron Smith, a long-time friend and birding aficionado in the early days, agreed to take Jonathan and another boy out birding off and on.

In subsequent years, Jonathan and I always had a good time scheming about the Christmas Bird Count, sometimes going out looking for special birds. He knew how much it meant to me, and he was game to take part. He and Ron had continued their friendship, and later, when Jonathan was in town over Christmas, he'd make it a point to do the count with Ron, surveying a particular territory year after year. Sadly, Jonathan passed away in 2004.

For the 1980 CBC, Carol Goodell and I were assigned to cover a portion of Montecito. And, luckily for us, a well-known hotshot female birder was told to accompany us — Donna Dittman (now a staff ornithologist at Louisiana State University). A gifted birder, she'd driven down from Berkeley, because she knew Paul Lehman and wanted to help out with the CBC.

Donna was another of those birders for whom birds wanted to come out of the bushes and be counted. Not only could she imitate a northern pygmy-owl, which would bring in the warblers to investigate her imitation, but she knew all the bird sounds and which species made them.

Carol, Donna, and I wandered from Manning Park to Riven Rock to the Bass estate (now Casa del Herrero). Everywhere Donna went, she birded by ear. I will never forget one scene. We'd somehow gotten permission to visit a large private estate. The owners weren't there, but Donna discovered a trampoline on the property. She was tall, lanky, with long blond hair. And there she was, jumping up and down on the trampoline, and every time she heard a new bird she'd yell out "black-throated gray warbler," or "Townsend's warbler" or "American robin" at the top of each jump. Her hair flying, her feet propelling her high above the trampoline, she was birding and she wasn't even *looking at the birds.*

Carol and I sat there with our mouths open. I was jotting down the species Donna was shouting out; I saw how crucial it was to recognize bird calls.

I'm not sure if I went to the Count Compilation Dinner that year, but somehow I found out that a prothonotary warbler had been found at the corner of Roble Drive and La Marina in Hope Ranch. The next morning when I arrived at this spot, there were a group of 20 birders already there, staring at a brilliant yellow and blue-gray warbler from the East, totally out of range, that had been discovered the day before on the CBC.

By the fall of the next year, I was pumped up for the count, which was to be held on January 3, 1981. Each Christmas Count circle can decide the day within the period between December 16 and January 5 on which to make their census; once decided, there's no changing and the count proceeds, rain or shine.

I finally understood that if you scouted your area of the count before the actual count day, you might discover a special bird of some kind that you could then go back and count on the official date. Wintering birds don't move around as much as those in migration. In other words, a bird that is spending the winter in a garden in Montecito or along a creek in Goleta will tend to remain in that general area throughout the season. If you can learn its routine, its habits, and then return on count day and officially see it, you can maximize your time spent birding.

These are known as "stake out" birds. Is your bird best seen in the afternoon, or does it have to be looked for before dawn? Is it visiting a certain blooming bush at about 9 a.m.? When does it visit your feeder? Thus the phrase "an afternoon bird" or "a morning bird" might be used to describe your bird's appearances.

You can imagine how I eagerly glommed onto this sort of information. It was a whole new way of describing birds and their habits.

A few days before the count, I scouted my neighborhood in the suburb of Montecito, because that area was my assignment for count day. I walked over to nearby Lower Manning Park. A portion of Oak Creek winds through this park, and the surrounding coast live oaks and sycamores attract birds.

(Since we've adopted modern methods of measuring the count circle on the computer, Lower Manning Park is now considered outside the circle.)

That winter I spent hours hanging around Lower Manning Park. And I found an odd bird that I'd never seen before. It looked like a Hutton's vireo, a common, small olive-green bird, but this individual was gray above and white below, not like the Hutton's.

I raced home and scoured the guide books. I came to a page with a picture of a bird that matched my bird, but one that shouldn't be here: the "plumbeous" race of the solitary vireo (now split to become its own species, Plumbeous Vireo).

This vireo had no business being in Manning Park. It should have been spending the winter in Central America, like all the other solitary vireos. Moreover, even in spring and summer, it's a bird that breeds in the Rocky Mountains, not around here. A vagrant, that's what it was.

Bursting with pride, I called Paul and tried to describe the bird. I think he believed me, but when he and Jon Dunn came over to check it out before the count, the vireo was nowhere to be found. I was crushed. My claim to fame had turned to nothing.

With that as a background, here's my journal entry of the day.

NATURE JOURNAL, JANUARY 3, 1981
Christmas Bird Count

At 5 a.m., I open my eyes. I hear gentle rain falling outside. Oh no. It's got to stop.

It does.

I meet my group, which has been assigned to cover "eastern Montecito." The rendezvous is Oak Road, where the Grace's warbler has returned for its second year.

Into my beat-up blue VW bug, I squish the members of our team: a novice birder from Pasadena, and two guys from the Berkeley area. Total strangers, but they all seem nice.

Slowly, we bird along East and West Pepper Lane. We count hordes of yellow-rumped warblers, Bewick's wrens,

Townsend's warblers, and other common birds. As we call out the birds, one of us records them on a species list on a clipboard.

I am worried about my possible rare vireo. I know we have to hit Manning Park before 8 a.m. to avoid the crowds and begin our search. On the way, we stop at Upper Manning, nothing much of interest there, so we cross the street and go down the footpath into the oaks and sycamores by the creek.

It's quiet. Very quiet. My heart sinks as we locate nothing more than a flock of American goldfinches gathered above us high in the sycamores.

I move out onto the playing field so as to get a better view with the sun at my back.

There it is! My bird, methodically searching the branches and leaves for insects right on the tree in front of me.

I call softly to the two guys from Berkeley. They both corroborate a nice "plumbeous" solitary vireo. I am beyond thrilled to have been able to get my stake-out for the count.

I'll spare you the description of the vireo in my notes. Anyone else looking at this plain gray and white bird with white spectacles around the eyes would dub it one of the dullest birds they'd ever seen.

The rest of the morning is pretty routine, although stimulating and fun for me. We spot a brown creeper on Picacho Lane, find a black-throated gray warbler somewhere else. The yellow warbler in the oak tree behind the Upper Village is another stake-out that we had to get, so that was lucky.

Meeting at El Camino Pharmacy for lunch, we compare notes with other groups who have birded

Montecito. After that meeting, we communicate by payphone with Paul Lehman, who's manning the "western portion" of the count circle, and try to find out what's been seen or if any unusual species have been sighted.

However, the afternoon in Montecito is uneventful.

As I look at my journal summarizing the count totals for Montecito that year, I am astonished at the number of rare birds.

Birds of note:

Western tanager — 3

Solitary vireo — 1 (mine in Lower Manning)

Warbling vireo — 1

Northern oriole (now *Bullock's*) — 1 at Riven Rock

Grace's warbler — 1 in pines at Oak Road

Tennessee warbler — 1 south of the freeway

Yellow warbler — 1 behind San Ysidro Pharmacy

You might wonder how we recorded all of the species seen on the count in those days? Good old pen and paper. There was no digitized central database for the National Audubon Society, the way there is now. Various forms had to be filled out; $5 was collected from everyone, which in turn financed the printing of a thick tome — a special issue of the magazine American Birds. I loved looking through this magazine, because Santa Barbara was always in the top five counts in the nation, and usually in the top two in totals of species seen. Various charts showed the number of birders who participated in each count (our CBC was one of the largest).

9.

Christmas Bird Count: Part II
Compiling A Monster Effort

From 1994 onward, I found myself in charge of the Santa Barbara Christmas Bird Count, or CBC. By this time, the original hotshot birders had moved away, but we still had a fine corps of committed observers who were essential to our CBC.

Larry Ballard, Allyn Bissell, Karen Bridgers, Suzanne Barrymore, Jamie Chavez, Mike Collins, Fred Emerson, Krista Fahy, Carol Goodell, Jim Greaves, Joan and George Hardie, Brad Hines, Ron Hirst, Jim Hodgson, Mark Holmgren, Ken Hollinga, Jean Okuye, Paul Keller, Linda Lissy, Rob Lindsay, Patrick McNulty, Barbara Millett, Hugh Ranson, Gage Rickard, Teresa Rounds, John Storrer, Ron Smith, Nancy States, Guy Tingos, and Matt Victoria were local stalwarts.

From out of town, I could depend upon Brad Schram, Robb Hamilton, and Curtis Marantz to come help. Thankfully, Paul Lehman was a regular after he relocated from Cape May to San Diego, and Jon Dunn and Louis Bevier would show up whenever they were able. In the mid-1990s to the early 2000s, Jay Bishop, Dave Compton, Rebecca Coulter, Wes Fritz, Peter Gaede, Jeff Hanson, Marilyn Harding, Nick

Lethaby, David Levasheff, Peggy Kearns, David Kisner, Betsy Moles, Peter Schneekloth, and Wim Van Dam joined the hard-core birding community. More recently, John Callender, Eric Culbertson, Rob Denholtz, Glenn Kincaid, Bill Murdoch, Liz Muraoka, Libby Patten, and Conor and Julie Scotland were active CBC birders. Plus many more.

Throughout the years, numerous people have flowed in and out of the ranks of area birders. Some we'd call "meteors," because you'd see them out birding every day for a year or two, and then quite suddenly, they'd lose interest. That was hard for me to understand, but it's like any pastime — people come and go.

My goal was always to broaden the base of the number of folks involved. The more birders there are, the more wonderful birds will be found. Birds may be travelling through or stopping by, but if nobody identifies them, they might as well be invisible.

Chris Walden was my first assistant, and after Chris moved out of town, my invaluable helper was Joan Murdoch. Here we were — two Joans — always on our phones. Not cellphones in the early days, but lots and lots of phone calls and forms.

Then Bill Pollock appeared, and what a godsend he was. In 2005 we went digital, and Bill wrote a program with a spreadsheet tailored to our Santa Barbara CBC, with all its quirks and complexities. Gone were the days of counting columns and species totals, headaches and sleepless nights. I was learning how to delegate, and the count was getting more efficient than it had ever been.

From La Cumbre Peak to Gibraltar Reservoir, all the way to San Ysidro Road in Montecito on the east and Coronado Drive in Goleta on the west, the habitats to be covered were divided into nine sub-regions, including a boat that counted offshore in a four-mile arc. And the sub-regions were further parceled out into various groups of birders. In order to stay strictly within the circle, we had to be ruthless about which streets were "in" and which were now judged "out" of the plotted zone.

My Achilles heel was that I cared so much. I felt personally involved with every bird that was found or missed, every identification that was shaky or solid. It was as if the CBC was an organism. Sometimes it was a monster dragging me down with a thousand annoying problems; at other times, it was the force that lifted me to the top of the world. Conceivably, my approach was too holistic, not professional enough. But in the end, I wouldn't trade all the CBC experiences I had for anything — working with all those fabulous birders, and then getting to lead the "countdown" which was held at a potluck dinner.

CBC Compilation Countdown

You rarely find a group of birdwatchers together in a large room, eating, drinking, and talking. Birders are not known for their sociability. But at the compilation dinner, held in historic Fleischmann Auditorium, you'd see 250 people sitting at long tables, partaking of food, writing lists, and greeting acquaintances from years past. The auditorium is at the Santa Barbara Museum of Natural History, and there's no better place to hold the post-count get-together.

I remember standing up at the front of the room, looking out over all of the birders, some of whom were new to me, most of whom were familiar from long ago, and feeling tremendous camaraderie.

While I was up there with the microphone calling out the bird species as they appeared on the checklist in taxonomic order, birders would answer "Yes!" or "No!" in a loud chorus. That way we could get an initial, although preliminary, total of the number of species being reported.

Karen and I had an ongoing debate about how long the "Countdown" should be. She insisted that everyone was exhausted, often rain-soaked, and had long drives home ahead of them. "Speed it up, Joanie!" she would silently mouth to me from the back of the room, where she was keeping a running tally.

But I lingered over each surprise bird that was called out, marveled at those species we'd missed (but were there yesterday!), and puzzled over those that appeared in higher than expected numbers. And then, at the very end, we got the goodies. The rare finds — oh yes, there were always a few — and often they were enough to send us way over the top in the species totals. I could not contain my feelings, it was too emotional. These fabulous, crazy birders who really cared about something I cared about, had been up all night owling, had survived a windy boat trip, or sleet and rain in the mountains, or a dull day with few sightings — they were my heroes and I wanted to be sure each one was recognized. I even got in the habit of stamping my feet, jumping up and down, and various other antics to enliven the show.

When it was time to relinquish the reins, I was overjoyed that Rebecca Coulter and a team of excellent birders stepped up to the plate. These folks have harnessed the Internet and cellphones to their cause. Efficient, committed, and talented with birds and with computers, the Santa Barbara CBC Committee continues to lead our birding community through a fabulous count every year. I was so lucky to take part when I did, and now I have the fun of going birding to look forward to during the holidays, without any of the responsibility.

Women Birders and the CBC

I researched the Christmas Bird Counts in California held in 2019, to determine how many had women compilers.

Of 135 bird counts, 35 were headed by women. I didn't count those headed by couples, of which there were a few.

The number 35 was a big advance compared to when I got started, and when I took over from Paul.

When I first got hooked on birding, I noticed there were few women involved. Lots of women came to birding classes and wanted to get acquainted with the common birds. But only rarely would they or other women, especially those of my age, get bitten by the bug. They were content to be shown birds by a teacher, and to get out occasionally in small groups.

Few chose the necessarily rather solitary life of the observer. And some of the isolated creek beds and remote locations were too threatening for women to feel comfortable on their own.

I never felt this way. I was never afraid while birding. With my hat, hiking boots and clunky binoculars around my neck, I looked pretty outlandish. I relished my odd appearance, my mini-rebellion against the proprieties that many of my generation felt.

Furthermore, even in the days when I was a novice, experienced birders never made me feel ostracized because I was a woman. They might have considered my birding skills inferior to theirs, which was often true, but it wasn't a sexist attitude.

There is one story, however, that I like to tell on myself. It happened during one of the especially competitive CBCs back in the early 1980s, when I was just getting started. As usual, Paul had gathered a team of heavy-hitters from out-of-town, and one of them, who's now a highly respected biologist, was supposed to be birding in the Montecito area for the count. For some reason, he'd been told to call me to find out what his assigned patch was, and as we spoke, I made some remark about his helping me out with a tricky identification problem — clueless beginner that I was.

"Listen, lady, this isn't a bird class, and we don't have time for. . . etc., etc." That was the gist of it, and that's when I said to myself, "Oooh, I guess I didn't realize how competitive this CBC tally was."

I felt like a complete dope, of course, but I never forgot it. And, when I was in charge, I often wanted to say something dismissive to somebody who, like myself in those days, didn't quite understand how seriously we took all of this. But I bit my tongue.

When I took over the Santa Barbara Christmas Count, I didn't hear any whispers behind my back, any hint from my mostly male colleagues, that I might not be up to the job. (They may have thought it, of course.) The voice I did hear was the one inside me saying: you aren't good enough, you aren't ready for this responsibility, it's too much for you.

No question, there were fewer good female birders around when I got serious. Other than Elizabeth Copper, Donna Dittmann, Shawneen Finnegan, Debbie Shearwater, and a handful of others in California, I'd met none.

That was soon to change, both locally and nationally. The environmental sciences are now filling up with women who care about the future of our natural world. The idea that birding was a bastion of the white male of a certain class has grown stale. Newcomers are in the offing, and they're young, with a mix of boys and girls.

I bring this up when I think of Rebecca Coulter and her CBC Committee — many of them good women birders — and how times have changed for the better.

CBC Birding Techniques

One of the discoveries that occurred in tandem with the birding revolution in autumn vagrant chasing, was how to locate interesting birds *in winter*. Residential areas, where exotic shrubs and flowering trees grow, are excellent for birding in California's mild winter. In the past, the theory had been that you needed to get away from suburban habitats and go out in the wild to see birds.

But Santa Barbara, with lovely residential areas like Hope Ranch, Mission Canyon, the Riviera, and Montecito, has been planted with a variety of non-native trees, shrubs, and vines that bloom *in winter*. These lush plantings attract birds, which feed either on the nectar or the insects attracted to them.

Down in San Diego, birders were discovering the same phenomenon in certain neighborhoods with subtropical vegetation: if birds heading south to Mexico and Central America for the winter could find a ready food source here in Southern California, why make the journey? Why not remain right here?

You had to have an eye for sizing up neighborhoods. Paul Lehman was fearless at walking up driveways, or peering over fences into backyards, all because an orange-flowering cape honeysuckle (*Tecomaria capensis*) hedge was attracting a slew of hummingbirds, and one might be a Costa's or a broad-billed or some other winter rarity. Or a red-blossomed bottlebrush tree (*Melaleuca* sp.) grew in a front yard, and it might lure an oriole or a tanager. Normally, hooded and Bullock's orioles migrate south to Mexico and Central America, but if we looked in the right places, we might find one or two that had decided to winter in Santa Barbara.

Recently, Paul related a story about one of the first Christmas Bird Counts when this phenomenon became obvious. Kevin Aanerud, another top birder whom I never met, was standing in the western parking lot of the Biltmore Hotel on Dec. 31, 1977, when he discovered a MacGillivray's warbler, two Tennessee warblers, and a mixed flock of orioles that included orchard, hooded, and Bullock's. All of these birds should have been south of the border by December, yet here they were lounging around the Biltmore. Joking aside, the idea that birds would overwinter in these sorts of man-made habitats was pretty much unheard of before the birding revolution and the new ideas it generated.

One of the most reliable trees to look at in winter used to be the blue gum eucalyptus (*Eucalyptus globulus*). In late December or early January — which coincides with the Christmas Bird Count — the blue gums were popping with the yellowish-white blossoms favored by hordes of yellow-rumped warblers. If you looked long enough and got enough of an aching neck, you would definitely see a wintering rarity up in those eucalyptus trees, especially if you were a skilled birder. In recent years, however, the blue gums haven't bloomed as prolifically.

We've since discovered other non-native trees that attract birds: the tipu (*Tipuana tipu*), commonly planted as a street tree or in parks, is a lure for a variety of warblers. Coral trees (*Erythrina* sp.) with their bright red flowers can be a magnet for birds. The point is that wintering birds need food sources and a mild climate. If those requirements are filled, interesting bird species can be found just by walking down the streets in your neighborhood. If I see a flowering shrub, or notice that somebody has put up a hummingbird feeder — I stop and check it out. This technique for winter birding, sometimes termed "address birding," proved successful over the years, but before the 1970s, nobody took any notice of backyard plantings.

Another angle was to eyeball a neighborhood as you're driving by for mini-habitats. Sometimes I'd be birding with a friend and I'd slam on the brakes, stop the car, and get out.

Perhaps I had just seen a healthy stand of Monterey pines bordering someone's backyard, and I wanted to check them out for red-breasted or pygmy nuthatches. Mini habitats are those that mimic the preferred surroundings of a certain species. Mountain birds such as chickadees and nuthatches are found in pines, and planted pines will do nicely as a winter refuge. Similarly, a sapsucker, which is like a woodpecker, feeds on certain types of trees — especially pepper trees (*Schinus molle*), that have soft bark in which to drill their characteristic holes. The holes act as wells, bringing sap to the outer surface of the tree. The sap attracts insects, and the sapsucker will often return time and again to feed at these trees.

Winter Vagrants

So those were the tricks of the trade. We surveyed likely habitats that might harbor a lot of common wintering birds, but also an unexpected rarity or two, if we were lucky. Winter vagrants, those off-course wanderers, behave differently from those we see passing through in fall migration. In winter, there's no urgency. If the bird is finding sufficient sustenance and shelter, it may remain in that wintering location until spring migration beckons, usually sometime in March. Winter vagrants aren't here today and gone tomorrow, the way a fall vagrant would be.

Moreover, because of a bird's uncanny ability to home in on a specific location after migrating for thousands of miles, that wintering vagrant sometimes returns year after year to a particular spot. You can imagine how exciting it might be to find one of these rare visitors. It would be a great species to add to the Christmas Bird Count, and also other birders would have a chance to see the vagrant, photograph it, and get to know its habits because it would stick around.

Several outstanding examples of this phenomenon occurred during my novice birding years, and beyond. A Grace's warbler, which is a beautiful combo of yellow, black, and white plumage, returned for nine straight years to spend the winter in a row of pines that used to grow at the intersection of Oak Road and Hot Springs Road in Montecito. And the hepatic tanager, mentioned in Chapter 7, returned for twelve winters.

However, my all-time favorite tale features Hugh Ranson. One December day in 1993, Hugh, an excellent birder and photographer, was pushing his daughter in her stroller in the Riviera section of Santa Barbara. He happened to look up, and straight above him was a dark hawk soaring. It circled and glided, and he could pick out grayish bands on the tail. Hugh called Karen Bridgers immediately so she could get it on the hotline; he wanted other birders to see it. Hugh believed the mysterious hawk was a zone-tailed hawk, a species that had never been seen in Santa Barbara County before.

It was indeed a zone-tailed hawk. Once arrived there, I went running frantically around the parking lot of the Riviera Theater, with Karen by my side, as we sought to get a good view of this amazing bird. Finally, we had wonderful sightings. We could see the dark feathered head, so we knew the bird wasn't a turkey vulture. We could also see two of the grayish bands on the tail, from above as it banked and flew close by.

The zone-tailed hawk had charisma, no question. Karen and I ended up calling it "Zoney," and it returned to winter in the Goleta/Santa Barbara area for the next 13 years.

Zone-tailed hawks have large winter territories, so until we could figure out the hunting pattern of this individual, re-finding it every winter was an all-out event on the part of Santa Barbara birders. For many years, it chose a utility pole as a regular roosting spot up in the Goleta foothills on North Fairview Avenue. But some years, it was a terrible pain.

From a distance, a zone-tailed hawk looks remarkably like a turkey vulture, and it has used this similarity to its advantage. The reason? Most other birds do not consider turkey vultures a threat, because they feed on dead animals. But here comes the "camouflaged" Zoney, circling with the vultures, and boom, suddenly the hawk dives after an unsuspecting starling or dove, grabs it, and returns to one of the phone poles on Fairview to munch away.

In the end, the crows had his number, though. They knew he was a predator. So the mantra was: any dark hawk being mobbed by crows might be the Zoney, and all birders better have their heads up. On September 22, 1995, I wrote in my journal about how I was birding along the bike path at the end of Turnpike, when I saw a black silhouette slowly flapping away above me . . . and it was being mobbed by ten crows. I stopped. I saw the grayish-white tail band on the bird. My heart pounding, I raced to the car to see if I could get the bird in the spotting scope, but the hawk was flying toward Hope Ranch and soon disappeared.

And that's what happened every year: one day in early fall, a birder would be driving around and get a glimpse of the zone-tailed. Once relocated, we knew we had the Zoney as a visitor that winter, and we tended to rely on it for the Christmas Bird Count. Most years it was cooperative, but there were some difficult times locating that hawk. It needed to move around a lot so the birds it preyed upon didn't catch on to its habit of imitating turkey vultures. And each fall we'd ask ourselves, do you think the Zoney has died? We knew that there would come a year when it didn't appear . . . and that finally occurred in 2007.

10.

Mountain Birds:
My First Research Project

Paul Lehman and Jon Dunn insisted that if I really wanted to be taken seriously in the world of ornithology, I had to write a research paper. Naturally, I wanted to be taken seriously.

Here was a chance for an amateur, a casual birdwatcher like myself, to turn my hobby into a purpose. I'd been looking for a long-term project about montane birds that might further the knowledge of bird distribution in Southern California.

The result of their suggestion was the publication of my research paper, "Breeding Birds of Four Isolated Mountains in Southern California," in the journal *Western Birds,* Vol. 24, No. 4, 1993.

Perhaps it was those summer trips to the Eastern Sierra early on, or maybe it just runs in the blood: I am fascinated by the birds of the high country. I love mountain birds.

Growing up in the arid lowlands of Southern California, I longed for the cool conifers, the smell of pines in summer breezes, the view from the top of a peak. Knowing the lay of the land matches my love of the high spots. You can see where you've been, and how you got there. Up here, the bird life is different.

I know the chaparral birds, their calls, their habits. But it's the magic of the mountains that beckons my heart, that sings to me something new and yet old. A relict of a wetter past, a different climate, a climate that engendered these islands, these "sky islands" as they call them — isolated patches of montane habitat that cling to the summits of a few Southern California mountains.

Big Pine Mountain

In June 1981, Jan Hamber asked Paul and Jon if they'd help out on one of her California condor surveys. She and her husband, Hank, had set up routes and observation points in the backcountry. They were making important contributions to what we knew about condors —roosting and nesting sites — and just how few still remained in the backcountry. Jan and Hank were always looking for volunteers to put in some time condor-watching.

During 1981, the condors had a nest site near Big Pine Mountain, the highest peak in Santa Barbara County. That was the destination of the Hambers' trip.

Most birders aren't backpackers. Certainly Jon and Paul weren't, but they wanted to see what was up on this peak — no bird study had been conducted there in ages.

They returned with stories of a steep pine forest on the north slope of Big Pine, an area filled with birds you would expect to see in the high Sierra. There were breeding red-breasted sapsuckers, white-headed woodpeckers, dusky flycatchers, red-breasted nuthatches, golden-crowned kinglets, yellow-rumped warblers and fox sparrows — to name a few. It was important, groundbreaking news for those of us who cared about the avifauna of the county.

Birders tended to dismiss our backcountry watershed as a wasteland of chaparral. But on the cool north slopes of a few mountain ranges, which trend chiefly in a northwest/southeast direction, enough moisture collects to nourish a relict population of conifers.

These forests attract a small group of outliers, those species of birds that take a chance on breeding at the fringes of their normal ranges. The nearest area of any substantial montane breeders is in the Southern Sierra Nevada ranges, and at Mount Pinos in Ventura County. So the fact that some of the species had spread as far west as Big Pine was new information — and nobody had described it yet.

Although I'd heard about Big Pine from my Dad — and my sister, Jane, who had been up there on horseback with Dad and the local naturalist, Dick Smith — I never paid attention. Our backpacking trips had always been to the low country, which was the hot chaparral landscape that Dad loved. (We called him "the lizard.") But this Big Pine report was something special, and the whole idea grabbed me and took hold. I had to go and see for myself what it was like.

From my first visit up to this high mountain the following summer, I decided it was an area I wanted to study. I couldn't believe the miracle of seeing the white firs and the Jeffrey pines, the sugar pines with their long drooping cones, and the tall fire-scarred incense cedars — all right here in Santa Barbara County.

Island Biogeography

The thought of visiting Big Pine Mountain on a regular basis inspired me. But I needed a thesis, a reason for doing the research. What pattern was I looking for?

In the 1970s, ornithologists became interested in island biogeography. Although it originated as the study of true islands, it soon became popular as a way of examining islands of montane habitat surrounded by barren desert. Similarly, the mountains of Southern California are surrounded by chaparral. Only on the highest peaks do you encounter these small patches of coniferous forest habitat.

According to island biogeography, larger islands of habitat were predicted to have a greater variety of species, and larger populations of those species, than smaller islands. Moreover, islands closer to a source of potential colonization were predicted to have more species than distant islands.

The mountain ranges of the southern Sierra were the most likely source from which montane birds would spread. So if, beginning with Mount Pinos located southeast of the Sierra, I took four mountaintops in the Santa Barbara/Ventura area, where would they be?

In addition to Mount Pinos, I chose Pine Mountain, also in Ventura County, along with Big Pine Mountain and Figueroa Mountain in Santa Barbara County. I would compare the breeding bird data from each.

These were like four giant stepping stones of montane habitat — each lower in elevation and farther west than the one before. I wanted to survey the birds that inhabited them during breeding season (May 31-July 10).

Would the montane species drop out as my study areas got lower in elevation and were located farther west?

That was my hypothesis.

Once I'd chosen my study areas, I had to find out if there had been any ornithological research done there before. I learned quickly that all but Mount Pinos had been overlooked by birders in the past.

Mount Pinos (8,831 feet) has the largest area of montane habitat. It has a respectable ornithological past, having first been visited by the famous zoologist Joseph Grinnell in 1916. Moreover, I found that Los Angeles area birders had visited Pinos frequently. Not that we knew everything we could about Pinos, but it was the only mountain that had received any attention from birders. And it had a paved road with good campsites almost to the summit.

The next stepping stone, Pine Mountain, is a narrow forested ridge ending in Reyes Peak (7,510 feet). A rough road leads along the spine of this ridge, with several public campgrounds along the way. It's close enough to Santa Barbara to be surveyed in a day.

The most remote study area is on Big Pine Mountain (6,828 feet). From the south, a dirt Forest Service road winds for 25 miles through chaparral. Known as the Buckhorn Road, it eventually takes you to the north side of Big Pine, where it then becomes the Big Pine Road and heads on out to other areas, skirting the boundaries of the San Rafael Wilderness. Permission to drive a vehicle up there is not freely given.

The last mountain, Figueroa (4,528 feet) is an easy two-hour drive from Santa Barbara. Its lack of extensive habitat, and the fact that local birders visited frequently, made this mountain less exciting than the others. But Figueroa was a good contrast to Mount Pinos, in height, distance, and quantity of bird life.

Writing a Research Paper

I knew it would be difficult and time-consuming, but I looked forward to gathering all the new data, the field work and the discoveries.

I soon realized I'd need to rely on my birding friends for help, a cadre of dedicated birders upon whom I depended. How grateful I am to this day for their commitment to the project. Names that come to mind are Jay Bishop, Allyn Bissell, Paul Collins, Dave Compton, Chris and Rebecca Coulter, Peter Gaede, Greg Giloth, Ellen Easton, Wes Fritz, Joan and George Hardie, Jan Hamber, Brad Hines, Mark Holmgren, Cher Hollingsworth, David and Johanna Kisner, Barbara Millett, Betsy Moles, Florence Sanchez, John Schmitt, John Storrer, Guy Tingos, and T. Dion Warren.

I knew nothing about the logistics of accessing remote areas, gathering provisions and camping gear, censusing for owls at night, or compiling all the field notes. But nothing stopped me. I had backpacked with Dad early on, which gave me confidence.

Joan and George Hardie were essential to my efforts. George was a retired engineer who could fix anything; both were strong hikers, great birders, and experienced campers. I don't know how many times I sent them to Mount Pinos to listen for sooty grouse (formerly blue grouse, now extirpated there).

On each mountain, there were tantalizing gaps in knowledge. To fill them, I learned that you had to contact many people, and plead for field notes from a variety of birders who had visited any of the mountains.

Big Pine was the great unknown, because it was the most inaccessible, and had never been birded before. The only way to get Big Pine bird data into the literature was to compare it with these other mountains, which had received more attention.

I can't believe I went on all those surveys, raised a family, and still stayed married. Was I crazy? No, just starved for something to get my teeth into — something so exciting, so fulfilling that I just kept pushing forward until I had it finished.

I'll never forget the day when, after years of research, I was discussing this with another ornithologist and he said, "But Joan, this means nothing in the big picture. You have to compare your mountains with the breeding avifauna of other Southern California mountain ranges. What about the San Gabriels, the San Bernardinos, the San Jacintos? How does your data match up? And what about the Southern Sierra Nevada?"

I remember the sinking feeling in my stomach. I needed to dig further, find records of montane birds from those ranges. Granted, they'd all been explored, and the bird records were there, it's just that I had to piece it together to make a statement about my mountains that would compare to these other ranges.

Renewing my efforts, I spent the winter of 1992 creating charts that had nesting records for each of the boreal species on my mountains. Then I cross-referenced that data with figures I'd dug out pertaining to the major mountain ranges in Southern California.

Joseph Grinnell, in his seminal 1944 work with Alden Miller, "The Distribution of the Birds of California," had identified a suite of species that he labeled "boreal," meaning birds likely nesting above 5,000 feet. So I took those species as the focus of my paper. These were the ones

I would search for. But I couldn't just ignore the non-boreal birds, also present in large numbers. In the end, I had 108 species to deal with.

I spent hours in the Santa Barbara Museum of Natural History Library. The shelves there contain ornithological journals like "The Auk" and "The Condor," where you can find accounts of early observers. (Today most of this is online.)

I scrutinized past issues of *North American Birds*, the repository of all modern sightings. Records, records, and more records — they are the nuts and bolts on which you build your theories of status and distribution of bird species.

The actual writing of the research piece, however, turned out to be a grueling exercise in incorporating data into a readable document. The bulk of the text was a series of detailed accounts of each bird and its pattern of occurrence on the four peaks in summer.

I learned to write in a new way. Professional scientific writing means squeezing the excitement and hyperbole out of your style. No emotional musings, anecdotal descriptions, or exaggerations. When I got the hang of it, I found there was something pure and satisfying about writing a scientific article. If you concentrate on providing the simple research — competent observations meticulously documented — the big picture will emerge.

The observations needed to be made over a period of time, and mine was twelve years.

After the first draft was completed, I sent it out to six birders, two of whom were museum curators. The others were knowledgeable field ornithologists. When I got their comments and suggestions, it took me another year to have a final draft of the manuscript ready, complete with maps, photographs, and tables. At last, I sent off the manuscript — all sixty pages of it — to the journal *Western Birds*. The editor, Phil Unitt, was an esteemed ornithologist at the San Diego Museum of Natural History. After condensing and streamlining the manuscript, I was the proud author of a paper published in *Western Birds*.

My Conclusions

The original hypothesis for my research was that species would drop out as my study areas got lower in elevation and were located further west.

And I did find that the single most important factor in assessing "sky islands" was the extent of suitable habitat for a species.

Not surprisingly, we found the greatest number of montane species on Mount Pinos. It has the largest acreage of coniferous forest. Other variables, such as rainfall and elevation, contribute to the suitability of the habitat.

Mount Pinos is also closer to a source for populations to replenish — the Southern Sierra Nevada — than the other mountains in the study.

Generally, the number of montane species declined from east to west and from the highest mountain to the lowest, but the drop-off wasn't uniform.

For example, species such as the golden-crowned kinglet and red-breasted nuthatch were more dependent upon a moist forest habitat, and were more common on Big Pine Mountain than on arid Pine Mountain and Mount Pinos, despite the fact the latter mountains are higher and support more forest.

One of the species we were especially interested in was the flammulated owl. This tiny owl was not known to breed anywhere in Santa Barbara County before our surveys. In fact, the first time it was discovered, by noted biologist and artist John Schmitt, we weren't sure if the bird he had heard was just a one-off.

I will always remember the night we went back up to Big Pine to see if there really *was* a breeding population of flammulateds up there.

There was, and this added to the mystique of Big Pine for me — the fact that this highly migratory owl, which wintered in Mexico, had found conditions to its liking here.

Lessons Learned

Once I decided to do field work on Big Pine, I had to figure out a way to get up there. I had no official mission. The U. S. Forest Service was strict about who had a key to get through the various gates. I did not qualify.

During my earliest surveys, my father had been my loyal companion. Once, Jan and Hank Hamber gave us a ride up to Big Pine and dropped us off; then we backpacked out through the Santa Cruz watershed, and up over Little Pine Mountain out to Upper Oso Campground where we had left a car.

That was fabulous, but I needed to spend more time on the forested part of Big Pine.

To that end, twice Dad and I backpacked in via Santa Barbara Canyon — a 17-mile trip each way. My enthusiasm lightened the load. I could go for miles when the goal was birds on "my" mountain.

I carried an old Kelty backpack, a small one, and all of my stuff just got piled up, stacked in layers behind me higher than my head. The topmost item was a small wooden plant press, which I always brought with me. I pressed all the plants I collected on Big Pine.

Eventually, I convinced the Forest Service to give me a key for a two-night breeding bird census to be conducted annually on Big Pine Mountain with vehicle access. Before each census, I pored over the topographic map. We had divided the area to be surveyed into subsections, of which there were eight.

During the surveys, my colleagues and I censused the mountaintop by covering each subsection and making lists of birds and any breeding behavior.

Pencils and notebooks were the tools, no fancy phones with helpful lists. I can report that it took me hours and hours after the trip was over to collate the totals. I didn't care; I was making a contribution to the ornithological knowledge of our county and I was thrilled. My journal tells the tale of arriving "at a place I've wanted to be all year long."

NATURE JOURNAL: JUNE 18-20, 1999
Big Pine Mountain Trip

We've just completed the dusty drive up the Buckhorn Road. It's a graded dirt road, but last winter's rock slides have thrown down giant rocks. We take turns getting out of the car and heaving them off the road.

The chamise in bloom gives a white frosty look to the chaparral, lovely in large spreads over the hillsides.

Wildflowers brighten the roadsides, among the tall grasses that interfinger the chaparral. Deep yellow mariposa lilies lean from the steep banks, and the purple flowers of farewell-to-spring crowd the spaces in between. Toward Bluff Camp, we pass the famous stand of scarlet larkspur. Growing out of white limestone rocks in a shady patch, these delicate red flowers float in graduated whorls on long, thin stems. You see the deep crimson blossoms against the white limestone, seemingly without stems to hold them up.

At this spot I remember the old o.p. (observation point) where the Hambers used to set up their scopes. This view north to the cliffs of West Big Pine is perfect for condor watching. For several years, wild California condors nested in the crevices of the ragged sandstone columns that form West Big Pine.

Bluff Camp, where a Forest Service cabin is located, marks the start of the steepest part of the road. Washouts are common.

Finally, my old Subaru hatchback wheezes its way to the summit, following the Forest Service vehicle driven by Jan Hamber, the condor biologist whom I've known for years. John Schmitt is also along on this trip.

We round the corner and there it is: the coniferous forest — with tall evergreens on either side of the road.

*I'm here. I've arrived at a place I've wanted to be
all year long.*

*It takes awhile to relax. First I set up my old blue tent
— a task that assures you get absolutely and completely
filthy — then toss all the gear in a pile
into the middle of it.*

*Gradually, you feel yourself sinking into the mountain.
You worry about the weather, and all the surveying you
have to do. But after the first walk your mind settles into
the mountains — gets comfortable
with the thin, sweet air and the wind in the pines.*

*We're camped at the western edge of the forest on
a narrow shelf. Tall Jeffrey pines mix with white firs here.
The north side of the slope is so steep you'd roll forever
if you tripped and fell. The south side is a wall leading
upward to the summit of Big Pine.*

*I walk east along the dirt road that leads out of
the forest, binoculars ready. Here, on either side, an
impenetrable stand of tall shrubs creates a mass of green
leaves and spiny stems. A cloud of fragrance hangs above
it, everything is in bloom.*

*And then I hear the clear, rich song of the fox
sparrow. And another. And yet another. The whole thicket
is alive with fox sparrows! Brown and chunky with large
yellowish bills and spotted breasts, each male sings from
his own territory. Black-headed grosbeaks fly across the
road like orange and black meteors. A brilliant western
tanager, red head gleaming, perches nearby. Aha! I hear
the "slip-slop-slurp" of the tiny dusky flycatcher, one of
the "gnat kings," as Rich Stallcup famously called them.*

*Back at camp, the trunks of the trees harbor brown
creepers hitching their way up the bark. A white-headed
woodpecker and its mate fly over us to a nest hole in a*

big Jeffrey pine downslope. Steller's jays "yack-yack" at the campsite, scolding us.

And then it happens: John looks up, spots a soaring bird, yells "Condor!" and we all come rushing. As we watch, the condor slowly descends in circles and perches . . . at the top of a tall Jeffrey pine right above Jan's tent! The bird preens and rests there for the remainder of the day. At nightfall, the condor creeps along the branch closer to the trunk and sleeps there, huddled over and lying lengthwise along the branch all night long. What an amazing sight to see this huge bird reduced to a bundle of dark feathers, which blend in with the tufts of pine needles.

The condor's wing patch says R7 in big numerals. Jan later figures out its pedigree: it was sired by AC9, the last wild condor trapped in 1987, a favorite of hers. In 1995, R7 was released into Lion Canyon, a zoo-bred yearling, and now here he is, snoozing at the top of a tree over the tent of a person who's done more to save the California condor than anyone I know.

After dinner, we watch the sunset. If you stand and face north you see the ranges of the Sierra Madre, Caliente and Temblor mountains in purple links of color fast disappearing in the mist of evening. And to the west — down the Sisquoc — more folded ridges as the flanks of the San Rafaels dip down all the way toward the Sisquoc Ranch and Santa Maria. Like watching a sunset from the top of the world.

I love the paradox — the high mountain forest of green pines and firs juxtaposed with the yucca-studded slopes at lower elevations. I could look at this view forever.

These Southern California ranges aren't glamorous mountains. They have no snow-capped peaks, rushing streams, spires or deep lakes. What they do have is a spare quality of land existing at its limits. This montane stuff has no business here — too dry and hot for the conifers. And yet they persist and thrive on the very edges of their comfort zone. And with them they bring "their" birds, those species adventuresome and tough enough to make it at the limit of their range.

We begin the owling early. Along the nearly two-mile stretch of suitable habitat, we must stop, get out, and frequently use playback tapes to attract the owl species. Forget the visual. We just need to count the number of vocal responses.

The night is perfect, no wind. The afterglow of sunset holds the distant hills still purple. Darkness penetrates the deepest draws and silhouettes the trees against the rosy glow of post-sunset. Tree shapes become more fantastic as night falls. They seem like people, standing in peaceful judgment at our crass efforts with the tape recorder.

The whole forest lies quiet. But on the lower slopes of the mountain, the moon's white shadow is spreading. It will be bright in an hour; we won't need flashlights.

The moon brings out the owls, or so some experts say. Many responses, one of our best surveys ever, after which we collapse into our sleeping bags at midnight.

Zaca Fire Aftermath

Long after my paper was published, the devastating Zaca wildfire of 2007 on Big Pine Mountain changed the landscape I had censused. Like many modern forest fires, the blaze burned with high intensity in certain areas of the mountain. The summit, Alamar saddle, and the canyon leading down to Upper and Lower Bear — all patches where the fire burned hottest — became shrubfields after the first ten years.

Ceanothus and manzanita grew back more quickly than the tiny conifers; the shrubs had out-competed the young coulter pines, incense cedars, and white firs.

Fortunately, most of the forested parts of the north slope burned in a more mosaic fashion, leaving some good stands, and only partially destroying others.

Big Pine Mountain still possessed a good swath of forest, and I continued to help Peter Gaede and others survey, but it was different. At least one montane species, golden-crowned kinglet, hasn't returned to breed. Others such as red-breasted sapsucker and yellow-rumped warbler are scarce. More chaparral species found at lower elevations have gained a foothold, as the shrubfields march up the mountain.

Drought cycles, pressure for human access, and climate change have all had an effect on these sky islands of montane habitat atop our local mountains. The islands may soon disappear, but then again who can predict with certainty?

11.

From One End Of The Americas To The Other In Spring Migration

One spring afternoon, I got a call from my sister, Ellen. Since she'd moved back to Santa Barbara with her family, we'd become even closer.

Ellen had done something unique with her life. After raising four children, she had successfully opened an art gallery in her beautiful home. She named it The Easton Gallery, and displayed original art depicting many of the wild and scenic places in the surrounding Santa Barbara region.

Most of Ellen's artists were plein-air painters, that is, they painted while out in nature, using outdoor light and color to render their creative efforts. Some were members of "The Oak Group," a loose association of artists that became popular locally. The landscapes they painted were usually at locations you might drive to within a day. Ellen and I had many a fun excursion while she'd be scouting out a new place for her artists to paint, and I'd come along and go birding.

But that day Ellen had a bird question. It was early March, and she'd just noticed that the black-and-gold hooded oriole that previously nested in the palm tree near her house had returned.

Oh, I was pretty excited by that. It was definitely an earlier-than-usual arrival date for spring, and I knew that was important. Another one for the record books.

I've talked a lot about fall migration so far, but spring migration is a little more difficult to understand. Which birds return first in spring? When do our wintering birds leave, and where do they go? Which birds never nest here, but are just passing through?

The bulk of spring migration takes place in April and May, although some birds arrive beginning in February and early March. The species that choose to stop and nest in Santa Barbara are considered summer visitors, and will stay until September, while other migrants don't stop, but rather continue on farther north. Examples of the earliest birds to appear in spring are Pacific-slope flycatcher, warbling vireo, tree swallow, and hooded oriole.

The first migration map I ever saw was one that came as an insert with the monthly issue of *National Geographic* magazine. Once folded out, this oversized map illustrated migration flight paths of various species. I couldn't get enough of that map of the Western Hemisphere. It showed the routes of selected birds of prey, waterfowl, seabirds, and landbirds. Here were finely drawn plates of birds winging their way from one end of the Americas to the other.

Migration itself, this massive relocation of birds from one area of the hemisphere to the other, is actually a giant search for breeding success. The birds seek optimum nesting conditions, no matter how far or how different those nesting areas are from their wintering grounds.

For example, the sanderling, a small shorebird wintering on our beaches, departs when the spring snowmelt in the Arctic Circle uncovers acres of open tundra. By heading north to take advantage of the long daylight hours and the plethora of insect life (mosquitoes, midges, flies) on the tundra, the sanderling optimizes nesting success by relocating and changing its diet. Abandoning a diet of sand crabs and worms here, it flies thousands of miles to alien surroundings. Bigger territories, less crowding, more prey. It's that simple.

The Pacific loon, which winters in warm, saltwater bays off Baja California, flies north to nest on solitary lakes in northern Canada. How can a waterbird that breeds in freshwater adapt to a saltwater environment in the winter? The answer is, easily.

Take your ordinary cliff swallow, which spends the winter scooping insects in the skies over Argentina, then flies to North America in spring. Once here, the swallows have a whole fresh crop of insects swarming over lakes and reservoirs on long summer evenings. And if there aren't natural cliffs close by, they build their familiar mud nests under the eaves of our houses.

Spring Landbird Migration

On April 4, 2019, I wandered in the Santa Barbara Botanic Garden. Purple sage, blue ceanothus, and gold fremontia framed the upper meadow. Clouds hung low over the mountains. The air was still and cool.

Coast live oaks were full of yellow-rumped warblers. A few gave the feeble trill of their song, but most were feeding quietly, bulking up for spring migration.

I sat on a stone bench. Looking up, I knew there were lots of yellow-rumped warblers in the tree overhead, but I couldn't see them properly against the gray sky. Then I made that "pishing" squeak with my lips that birders resort to when they want birds to come closer.

As soon as they heard me, a sizeable flock of yellow-rumps came fluttering down, investigating the disturbance. I got my binoculars on a fresh yellow-black-and-white plumaged male. He looked almost surprised to find himself in such bright feathers, after those winter months of drab, dull gray. Soon he would depart our warm, safe Botanic Garden for the chilly forests of Western mountains.

Also, imagine the warbler's upcoming route: some of these yellow-rumps fly north as far as British Columbia and the Cascade Range to nest in summer. A few make an altitudinal rather than latitudinal migration, meaning that they choose to breed in the high mountains of our region. These birds will follow the spring thaw as it releases the snow from higher elevations, and then make their way to Mount Pinos, or to the Southern Sierra Nevada.

Perhaps a yellow-rump's migration would go like this. He would wait until the last cold front had passed, and any north wind with it. Then, soon after nightfall, he would begin flying north. On his own, he makes his way, flying below 2,000 feet, certainly not high. Our male yellow-rump may fly for 200 miles or more at one stretch, landing somewhere along the coast, or maybe choosing a route up the inland canyons. How he finds a suitable place to land in the dark hours of the morning is still a mystery. But it's safer for a small bird to fly at night: there are fewer predators, and the weather is calmer.

So his trip unfolds, guided by the various instinctual tools with which all birds are equipped. Navigating with a built-in compass, using the stars and sun as a guide, this yellow-rump steers unerringly for his natal home. Hopscotching up the Pacific states, the warbler may take a month to complete the journey to the forests of British Columbia. There, near where it was first hatched, this male will carve out a territory from which to attract a female. All the more reason not to linger too long on the way north. Male birds, driven by the desire to breed, arrive earlier than females, in order to claim territories and lure mates.

The Desert Route

Spring migration brings landbirds from South and Central America up through Mexico to California; of course, many of our migrants only winter as far south as Mexico. Flight paths through California that include the immediate coast, interior foothills, and interior mountains, may send birds right over our region in spring. Look up some spring afternoon and watch the turkey vultures as they make lazy circles in the sky on their way to northerly territories.

Watching birds in migration fills in the blanks about which species is going where, but it can be confusing. For example, if I see a Wilson's warbler in my backyard on our South Coast, it could be an individual that will nest locally in the willows up at Vandenberg Air Force Base, or it could be one of many that nests as far north as Alaska and Canada.

And the olive-sided flycatcher that spends the winter in Panama or the Andes Mountains of South America may stop off, but is it one that's headed for the Sierra Nevada, or might it nest locally, as do the ones I've seen up Cold Spring Canyon in Montecito?

In our region, two aspects come to mind when contrasting spring and fall migration on land: in spring the pace of migration is faster and frequently more concentrated inland; in fall the pace is more leisurely and tends to be more coastal. These are generalizations, but they help grasp the big picture. In spring, males in crisp breeding plumage race to northern nesting grounds. They first cross the deserts in Southern California, then follow inland foothills and mountains up the state. In contrast, fall birds' journeys are protracted, taking place over a longer period of time. Also, during fall migration a number of species choose to follow the Pacific coastline as a landmark on their trip south, rather than negotiating inland routes, although there are some species, especially hummingbirds, that prefer an inland route in fall.

In spring, species that have wintered in Central America, Mexico, and points south migrate across the deserts of Mexico and California. With increasing developments in the deserts, there are plenty of green lawns and well-watered gardens, not to speak of the numerous natural oases and blossoming native trees.

From the deserts, the birds fan out. Most will choose to travel up the foothills and ridges of California's Central Valley flying due north. Others fly to the coast. When they reach the Santa Barbara region, they might keep to the coast, flying in a westerly direction, due to the east-west orientation of the coastal plain here. Or, more frequently, the birds begin to re-direct by flying up the numerous north-south trending canyons that lead them over the Santa Ynez Mountains and thence to the Southern Coast Ranges and beyond.

A fascinating website found at http//www.Birdcast.info.com has harnessed the power of radar to show where the birds are migrating through the U.S. at night. Have a look!

Weather in Spring Migration

You may have heard about the great waves of landbirds that can be observed in springtime if migrants hit a weather front and drop down to take shelter, as happens in the Eastern part of the continent or along the Gulf coast. We don't have those fronts here, our weather being more benign, with spring storms that are not as fierce.

However, there are two significant weather conditions in our region that may create short-lived waves of migrants which stick around for a bit. The first is the presence of strong winds out of the north-northeast (north being best), and the second is a thick marine layer of fog or clouds.

Small birds will temporarily cease to migrate if they encounter strong winds. The longer the winds continue, the more birds you get arriving from the south, and the bigger the wave of birds stacked up waiting to move on. The winds are sometimes associated with a weak storm front that has left our region; rarely, rain accompanies these weak fronts, but wind usually follows them. When the wind abates, expect a surge of birds moving through. I learned to take the "temperature" of the bird world by walking outside the day after a wind event. My backyard would be full of birds if the wind had blown the night before, but if the wind had died down and it was calm all night, the backyard would be empty because the birds would've migrated onward.

Another rather mysterious phenomenon concerns the "morning flight" of birds flying into a strong northeast wind that's blown all night. For example, observers at dawn have noticed that a flood of Passerines can be seen moving up a canyon or funneling through a pass heading north over the Santa Ynez Mountains. The wind has drifted them off course, if it blows from the east, and the migrants are determined to re-direct themselves by going north over the mountains. It's believed some of these birds have started their journey at dawn or before. Birders on the watch at dawn describe multitudes of small migrants staying very low as they crest the passes at low points such as at Romero Saddle or up Refugio Canyon in the mountains behind Santa Barbara. Later in the morning the birds drop down to rest.

In addition to winds, the marine layer, otherwise known as "June gloom," can cause migrating landbirds to become confused. If a bird is flying above the fog, it can't see the landmarks along the coast. The same is true of high overcast or cloudy conditions. If a bird seeks to take off, it can't see the night sky well in cloudy conditions. Similar to the winds, the longer the spell of fog or high overcast persists, the more of an effect it has on the migrating landbirds. That's when I go out birding after several cloudy days and find a slew of migrants in bushes and trees waiting for the skies to clear so they can navigate their way north that night.

Wherever they find themselves after dawn, groups of warblers and flycatchers usually continue foraging in a northward direction. They've made their way up the drainages and they are not stopping. They're going north, headed toward the San Rafael Mountains, where they might come to Figueroa Mountain.

 **NATURE JOURNAL: MAY 2, 1982**
Figueroa Mountain

This is one of the best birding days I've ever had.
I am in a dream, a dream of birds everywhere.
A chilly day. I decide to have coffee and a muffin in the Figueroa Mountain Campground on the south-facing slope of the mountain at 8:45 a.m. Heavy marine layer covers the Santa Ynez Valley up to 3,500 feet on Figueroa. Emerging from the fog, I look back and out over the silhouettes of Zaca Peak and Grass Mountain.

Lupine and poppies spread a mantle of blue and orange where they scatter on sunny slopes.

I begin by taking a leisurely walk through the campground. I can't believe what I'm seeing. But I have to. It's happening. In every red-barked manzanita bush, in every green live oak, a western tanager calls, swoops down, then takes off flying up the hill. The majority are males with lovely yellow and black plumage, their red heads shining in the morning sun.

I start to make a rough count. I feel like an idiot. Nobody told me I'd have days like this in California; is this what they call a "fallout"? It happens when, for whatever reason, a mass of birds is halted in the midst of migration. We'd had a cold front pass through the day before. Could that explain it?

I have never seen so many western tanagers in my life. I know I saw (and heard) 150 tanagers. They are calling from every clump of vegetation. Their gentle "ththrrup, ththrrup" call. They aren't singing or slowing down now.

The tanagers are on a mission to get as quickly as they can to the Sierra Nevada or the Cascades, the mountain ranges that lie within flying distance of a route, peak-hopping up the middle of our state.

I am not sure if the tanagers spent the night on this sheltered side of Figueroa Mountain, or, more likely, just arrived at dawn after a night flight. Perhaps the weather had kept them grounded elsewhere until now. But today, in morning sunlight, they landed and began moving up the mountain.

They aren't alone! Masses of black-throated gray warblers, their tiny gray and white forms exploring every leaf surface, hang upside down in the pines. They examine the pale green tips of the oaks for insects.

I count a minimum of 50 black-throated grays in the campground, maybe more.

I am just learning the thin, wheezy song of the black-throated gray warbler. It's challenging to pick them out from the similar song of the Townsend's warblers, but the latter aren't singing as much. They may not be singing, but I have a total of 40 Townsend's!

Birds are everywhere. My numbers are estimates, but I've got nobody to help me count.

I feel my heart leap, my step quicken. How many days will I ever have seeing this many of these breathtakingly beautiful mountain birds? I love the mountain birds, but I never expected this.

And the tanagers are mixed with black-headed grosbeaks, the sparkling orange-and-black males, some singing, some not. All are moving through, following the ridgetops as they make their way north.

I'm lucky enough to have hit it just right. To witness this amazing journey that all birds make in the spring, but usually not all at once in these huge numbers.

Afterward, when I leave the campground, I come to the road that leads to Pino Alto Picnic Ground near the summit of Figueroa. The gate is closed; I must walk up. I park the car, then start slowly walking along the dirt track through the pines.

Once again, the trees are full of birds making their way up the mountain. Some of them are the same ones I saw in the campground below. I notice that wherever a little ravine or arroyo leads up the mountainside — a route where more oaks and pines grow — the birds simply follow it up and fly right over the road. Then, they resume their journey, following that same arroyo but on the other side of the road. Someone should put up a sign saying: "Migrants Crossing."

I am not used to counting such numbers. What if I'm wrong? I'm trying to be conservative, but I really have no idea exactly how many tanagers, black-throated gray, and Townsend's warblers I've seen. Have those flying across the road already been counted down below? It's insane.

At Pino Alto, the birds are fewer. The morning is wearing on, and the avian migrants have begun to shelter. They've refueled at the sunny campground, and now, once at the top of the mountain, they hunker down and wait for nightfall to continue their journey.

(Note: In subsequent years, I've experienced numbers of landbirds passing through in spring, but only upon rare occasions. You have to be at the right place at the right time.)

Seabirds in Spring Migration

As a novice birder, and well into the years when I was getting out more frequently, I hadn't realized how exciting watching the seabird migration from Goleta Point could be. Once I tried, I loved it.

Back in the 1980s, birders were still learning about the phenomenon of how seabirds moved in spring migration up the North American Pacific Coast. Beginning in early March and lasting through May, a large movement of seabirds can be observed flying offshore. Most have wintered in the sheltered lagoons of Baja California. Indeed, it is estimated that nearly the entire population of Pacific Loons spends the winter in Baja. (A carefully counted estimate at Point Piedras Blancas revealed approximately 456,000 birds passing northward in 1996.) The most common species that can be observed from coastal promontories as they fly north toward their breeding grounds in Canada and Alaska are loons, cormorants, brant, scoters, gulls, and terns.

Unlike landbirds, seabirds and many shorebirds migrate during the day. They aren't as affected by weather phenomena, although an onshore breeze can stir up the action, forcing the loons, Brant, and scoters to fly closer to shore.

My friends and I chose an afternoon once a week and headed out to Goleta Point to do a seawatch, especially during April. Carrying our scopes and backpacks, binoculars and clipboards, we would park and walk past the Campus Lagoon at UCSB. Once arrived at the Point, the trick was to get a seat on the old piece of cement foundation. Sitting on that, we could look through our scopes to the east, back toward the cliffs below Hope Ranch. And in this way, with the late afternoon sun illuminating the approaching flocks of seabirds, we got excellent views.

Here I was with the panorama of Goleta Bay to my left, the mountains over my shoulder, and only the blue Pacific stretching between me and the Channel Islands. Enchanting on a calm evening, it was excessively uncomfortable on a windy day. Afternoons at the point censusing birds became an annual ritual with many of us.

From 1999-2003, David Kisner and Santa Barbara Audubon Society organized an informal volunteer effort to census the spring seabird migration for several years. Not since Paul Lehman's studies in the 1970s had anybody taken this on. David handed out printed sheets on which to record our data, making it more fun and important. We were assigned slots to cover — certain afternoons usually — although we discovered that there were astonishing numbers of seabirds moving through at dawn. Loons, especially, could be seen by the thousands flying by in early morning. Still, I preferred the afternoon.

The configuration of the coastline, in an east-west direction from Los Angeles County to Point Conception, forces the seabirds to hug the coast, even if they want to stay on a northerly course. This is one of the reasons seabird viewing is excellent at Goleta Point. The birds are close in, some even turning inland at Goleta Bay, where they then right themselves and resume their journey westward. After they reach Point Conception, where the coastline reverts to a more northerly direction, seabirds are apt to pass by farther offshore.

On certain days at the Point, when the wind was howling and the sand was blowing, we moved down to the shelter of the beach directly below. Here, shielded from the ferocity of the wind, we set up our spotting scopes on the flat rocks and counted the loons hurtling by.

The Pacific loons flew low, close to the water, in loose, straggling groups of a hundred or more. As they passed, their black throat patches were visible first, then the soft gray of their napes, then the white speckling on their dark wings. Sometimes the loons came so close you could see their long necks pumping up and down with the effort of each strong wingbeat against the wind. Relentlessly, they were bound to battle their way north to glory. As the end of April approached, there was no stopping these beauties. Such is the miracle of life distributing itself among the resources of our planet.

Memorable days at the Point fill my notebooks. On April 7, 1997, another windy day forced us to watch from the beach below. Tugging and churning at the water, the wind whirled the birds about the sky. But it brought them in close, almost at eye level as we stood with our scopes.

Luckily for us, this day featured an extraordinary number of Bonaparte's gulls. One of the smallest gulls, Bonaparte's gulls fly like terns in a buoyant, lilting manner. Their stunning breeding plumage of coal black heads, pale gray wings, and white underparts make them one of the truly elegant gulls. These Bonapartes were going to Alaska and Canada. Starting their long migration, from coastal bays and estuaries to the south of us, the gulls traveled all that way to nest in the spruce trees of the boreal forests in the high Arctic. No other North American gull nests in *trees*!

Standing on the sandy rocks, with surf crashing nearby, we looked through our scopes east across Goleta Bay. Out of the blue, the gulls began to materialize: tiny white dots high in the sky in flocks of 100 or so. Like pieces of confetti, they came swirling and swooping toward us. One group flew low over the tops of the waves — a distant white line of small gulls — but most came wheeling and tilting over our heads. Forster's and royal terns were mixed with them.

I'd never seen Bonaparte's gulls migrating like this before. When they couldn't make it past the point, due to the force of the wind, they turned into the bay and settled down on the water. The choppy, dark sea was packed tightly with white gulls. That day, we counted over 500 of them going past the point, not including the ones resting in the bay.

But the phalarope migration described below is even more exceptional.

NATURE JOURNAL: APRIL 28, 1997
Goleta Point Seawatch

This morning in bird class as we scan the ocean from East Beach, we see hundreds and hundreds of tiny birds flying low over the water or just above the horizon. They circle around and around, sometimes alighting on the water. So distant, it's impossible to discern what species they are, the birds move steadily east to west. Right then, I determine I must go to Goleta Point that afternoon to find out what's happening.

At the Point, I am accompanied by Jay Bishop, Guy Tingos, and Joan Hardie. It's a calm day, thankfully, and the sea is smooth, glassy. A high overcast gives us gray clouds. I put on another jacket as we settle for the watch.

Then we spot them: a multitude of tiny shorebirds with darkish gray backs and white underparts. In clumps of individuals or straggling lines, huge numbers of "salt and pepper" bird dots are heading from left to right.

We've not seen anything like this before. It happens only rarely, when the phalaropes, which spend their winters at sea in the waters off Peru, chance to migrate close to the coast like this. The majority are red-necked phalaropes, with a few red phalaropes mixed in. It's an unusual phenomenon in seabird watching. We're overwhelmed.

Guy starts to organize us.

"Let's look in our scopes, and count how many birds are flying past us in a minute."

I squint through the lens and immediately feel totally confused. How can you count thousands and thousands of salt and pepper flakes?

"I'm getting close to a thousand birds per minute," Guy says.

"Oh," I caution, "That's impossible. I think it's more like 500 per minute."

But my colleagues overrule me. They unanimously agree they're seeing a thousand phalaropes per minute as they look through their scopes.

In clusters of individuals and long wavering lines, the masses and masses of dots keep coming in an endless stream as we scan beyond the kelp line.

From 4 to 5:30 p.m., we watch, mesmerized by the action. If our calculations are correct we saw 100,000 phalaropes that afternoon alone. And I'd first seen the flocks this morning, so all day they'd been steadily flying by. (The phalaropes were still passing through the following day; we may've seen most of the Western population of red-necked phalaropes as they migrated north.)

But back to the afternoon at the point: suddenly, we notice that one flock of the salt and pepper flakes flies higher than usual above the horizon. Then down they dip — way, way down. One of us yells "Jaeger!" Mayhem ensues.

A parasitic jaeger is chasing one of the phalaropes. The jaeger, a hefty super-charged seabird, looks like a big dark gull. It carves the pursued phalarope

*away from the hurrying flock, harassing it all the way
to shore. The stricken phalarope is headed straight
for us as we watch from the cliff. To see the jaeger
with thick, powerful wings pursue the phalarope is
traumatic. Closer and closer the phalarope comes. For
a second, I close my eyes.*

*And then, the jaeger wheels around, as if in
boredom or disgust, and flies slowly back out to sea.
The terrified phalarope zooms over our heads and
circles round, hoping to rejoin its flock.*

Saved . . . the phalarope escapes this time.

We birders are drained.

Guy McCaskie and Paul Lehman, in San Diego, 1974. (B. Schram)

MIDDLE LEFT: *Jon Dunn, Santa Barbara, 1980s.* (T. Dion Warren)

MIDDLE RIGHT: *Paul Lehman. 2005* (S. Finnegan)

BOTTOM LEFT: *Rich Stallcup on a pelagic trip off Northern California, 1979.* (D. Roberson)

Early days of teaching: bird class at Carpinteria Salt Marsh, 1986. (S. Malone, *SB News-Press*)

In Oklahoma on a trip with Karen Bridgers. (l to r) Karen Bridgers, Jeri McMahon, Helen Matelson, me, 1987.

Later days of teaching: bird class at Rancho Santa Barbara, Santa Ynez Valley, 2005.

"Memorial Day Madness" trip to the desert, (l to r) Joan Hardie, Jean Okuye, Kathy Schewell, me, 1983.

MIDDLE: *Dad and Jan Hamber at one of the condor releases in the 1990s.*

BOTTOM LEFT: *Birding at the rock formation known as "The Indian Princess", 1984*

BOTTOM RIGHT: *Admiring my beloved conifers, Big Pine Mountain, 1993.*

At Christmas Bird Count
compilation countdown
calling out species on the
list. (C. Coulter)

*Two former
Santa Barbara
CBC compilers
(me and Paul
Lehman) relaxing with
mouths full of goodies, 2016.*
(L. Muraoka)

*Sample of pages from
my nature journal
describing a day of
spring seawatching
at Goleta Point.*

Sunset view on Big Pine Mtn. looking west down the watershed of the Sisquoc River and out to the Santa Maria Valley. (W. Knowlton)

Aerial view of the "potreros", Sierra Madre Mountains. (B .Dewey)

1999 Big Pine survey crew of birders:
(l to r)back row: Jan Hamber, John Schmitt,
me, Dave Compton, Betsy Moles.
Front row: George Hardie, Guy Tingos.

Pressing plants, Lake Tahoe.

With sister Ellen hiking in the 1990s.

My tent on Big Pine Mtn.

TOP: *Cathy Rose and me, Eastern Sierra Nevada, 1990s.*

MIDDLE: *Botanizing during the super bloom, Carrizo Plain, 2017. (l to r) Joanne Rapp, Carole Halsted, me, Carol Goodell*

BOTTOM: *Field trip with Santa Ynez Valley Natural History Society, Mt. Pinos. (l to r) Larry Ballard, me, Brad Schram, 2015.* (J. Evarts).

TOP LEFT: *With daughter Jenny holding latest book before launch party, 2013.*

TOP RIGHT: *With Patti Jacquemain after receiving the Wilderness Spirit Award from the Wildling Museum of Art and Nature, 2018*

MIDDLE: *With Ellen and grandchildren at Cold Spring trailhead, 2016. (S. Couvillion)*

BOTTOM LEFT: *"The Velcro birder" with oxygen tank and paraphernalia for birding, including Bud on a leash, 2020.*

12.

Writing, Writing, Writing

Writing came naturally to me. I liked moving sentences around, describing things, putting it all down on paper. For years I kept diaries. In college, I was good at research papers, liked to rummage around in books — both old and new. Throughout my life, I've been a constant reader. Reading and writing go together, and birding lends itself to both.

Another of the bonds that brought Karen Bridgers and me together, besides our passion for birds, was writing. Karen was a bona fide journalist, and a skilled editor. During our birding years together, she was usually employed part time at home, working on various material for all sorts of projects. She never got paid enough, but she liked the independence.

In addition, both of us discovered we had a fondness for an English author, Vera Brittain, who had become popular at the time through a television series based on one of her books. We both read several of Brittain's books, including "Testament of Youth," "Testament of Friendship," and "Testament of Experience," the last published in 1957.

Vera Brittain was a feminist and unconventional for her time. Her best-known book was "Testament of Youth," which described the loss of her fiancé and her brother in World War I. She became a pacifist, having seen what war did to civilization, and was committed to that cause for the rest of her life.

We admired Brittain's independent ways. Although happily married, her career often kept her apart from her husband, who taught in the U.S. She refused to be identified solely by motherhood and housewife duties. We sympathized when she said she longed to write, to work, to pursue interests.

Vera Brittain was our shared heroine and a masterful writer. I have kept a page Karen gave me before she left Santa Barbara, with her favorite quotes. I had written mine down in a notebook that I kept beside my bed for years. (My dear Karen passed away in 2017 from a multitude of health issues.)

Karen and I, two intelligent women in our forties, were stay-at-home moms. We wanted to be good wives and mothers, but we were chafing at the bit. We didn't know any housewives who were birders in the sense that we were. Karen and I were different, and proud of it. We were both searching for our own selves, after spending the first half of our lives devoting all our energies toward family.

Eventually Karen suggested I try writing about my birding adventures. She'd had a few articles published in a small birding magazine located in the Midwest, called *Birdwatcher's Digest*. Since it was a relatively new publication, the editor there, Mary Bowers, was anxious to get authors from the West to broaden the magazine's appeal to birders on the Pacific coast.

Up to that point, I had filled my daily nature journals and notebooks with descriptions of birds and field trips. Everything went first into the journals. But with the excitement of birding, why not put it into written accounts that would appeal to others?

Almost like a continuation of teaching, I wanted to share the wonder of all I'd learned about birds with a reading public. I had articles published in the Los Angeles Audubon Society's newsletter *The Western Tanager*, *Birdwatcher's Digest*, and other birding magazines.

Most of the articles were about trips I'd taken. The travel format suited me. It provided a natural way to begin an account, describe the landscape and the birds, and finish with the end of the trip.

I wrote about seeing the wintering sandhill cranes in the Carrizo Plain, which had not yet been established as a National Monument. The tall, gray cranes came to the Carrizo Plain to feed in dry stubble fields, and they roosted at night in shallow Soda Lake, as a protection from nocturnal predators. After grazing all day on the cultivated slopes of the hills, the cranes then flew in at dusk to roost. I will never forget that sight of thousands of cranes flying in to land at the lake, with their throaty trumpeting calls, and the sun going down behind the cold, bare mountains. I had to write it, had to let others know of what I was discovering in the bird world.

I wrote about a trip I took with friends to see the sage grouse (now called greater sage-grouse) in the Eastern Sierra at Crowley Lake near Mammoth. You had to get out onto the sagebrush flats early while it was still dark and wait, sitting in your car so as not to miss the display. I was stunned at the performance of these male grouse, as they fanned their tails and danced in front of the homely females. The females, gathered on the mating ground, or lek, appeared uninterested at first. But eventually, one of the females would accept the attentions of one of the showiest males.

Imagine this drama being played out against a background of steep, snow-capped mountains on a freezing morning in March. I was determined to describe it, to share it.

I wrote articles about the Christmas Bird Count, visits to Carpinteria Salt Marsh, and other local birdwatching events for newspapers and magazines in Santa Barbara.

And then, I got a big break.

"Birdwatching:
A Guide for Beginners"

In fall 1984, Judith Young signed up for my Monday bird class. Judith was married to Noel Young, a close friend of my father's and well-known as the owner of Capra Press, a local publisher.

Judith was intrigued by birds and birdwatching. "Joan," she said. "Capra needs another book for this spring's catalog, and I think a beginning bird book would be just the thing. We'll write it together!"

I was flabbergasted. A real book? How would this work? What did I really know about birds? I still had misgivings about my birding ability.

But Judith was enthusiastic, positive, and encouraging. I don't know how we did it, but we wrote that book in six months. With publishers, there's always a deadline. Judith was calm as a cucumber. I was a nervous wreck.

The key ingredient was the computer. Judith had one of the early models down at Capra Press, and she knew how to use it. At our house, we had no computer.

But I sat at the card table in our sun room, a yellow legal tablet in front of me. I wrote in longhand. Forcing myself to sit there, hour after hour, I crossed out sentences, re-phrased, and re-wrote each page.

And the words spilled out.

Time flew when I wrote about birds. The book was a slender beginner's guide, but I tried to include everything I'd learned up to then about birds. When I had several pages finished, I'd rush them down to the old Fithian building on lower State Street, where Capra Press had its offices. Judith would transpose my words into the computer, which made book production fast and easy.

I supervised the black and white illustrations, drawn beautifully by Karen Foster. At the time, she lived in a house up at the San Marcos Trout Club, and I made many trips back and forth. She wasn't a birder, but she loved nature, and we had fun working together.

Judith wrote several of the chapters, and I wrote the rest. I found it challenging working with another person, who was bound to write differently than I did, but at the same time it was excellent practice. I learned so much about writing.

My first autograph party was at Chaucer's bookstore. The owner, Mahri Kerley, having been a friend of the family, was a devoted supporter, and remains so. We sold 120 copies at the autograph party. Everyone was there, many of my loyal friends, many bird class participants, Audubon members, and even longtime friends of my parents. People were incredibly kind and caring. I wanted to send everyone a thank you note, because they came for me, I assumed, and not due to the merits of the book.

That first book opened a door to the world of writing for me. I realized that my *words*, my very own arrangements of ideas, of a way to enjoy birding, could be seen, read, and absorbed by other eyes far away.

Articles in magazines were fun, but a book was the real thing. I couldn't wait to write another.

"Great Birding Trips of the West"

After Capra Press published "Birdwatching: A Guide for Beginners," Noel and Judith Young wanted me to embark on further birding adventures and write about them.

"Do it yourself" bird travel books had begun to hit the shelves of local bookstores. Particularly if we were exploring for birds within the U.S., many of us felt we didn't need a professional bird tour guide, because we could use books to figure out how to find the specialty birds of a region by following directions.

I wanted to emulate some of these authors. I decided to put my own creative touch to a suite of selected birding trips around the West. Noel Young gave the book a title: "Great Birding Trips of the West." At last, I would get a chance to travel to places I'd always wanted to go birding.

In the summer of 1986, I planned how I could complete a travel bird book and stay within my budget. Travel by plane to destinations west of the Rockies was still inexpensive. I'd already been to Southeast Arizona, so that was one chapter. Other ideas followed: I was dying to go to the Colorado Rockies and the Pawnee Grasslands of Nebraska. The San Juan Islands of northwest Washington were another destination I thought would be good to explore.

Gib agreed to accompany me on all of my research travels. This was our first long birding trip together, and it wasn't easy. I was rather proud that I had a formal contract to write a book about my birdfinding adventures, but Gib was the one who had to do most of the driving. And birds in themselves meant little to him.

He did it all for me. He knew how much I loved it. At the same time, I was sad that he couldn't share in the joy of seeing these marvelous birds. But he was always quick at getting on the birds, much quicker than I was.

I recall the hours and hours I spent studying maps to get directions right, and taking notes from people who knew where to find specialty birds. What a contrast to today's world, when all of this information is available on a laptop or smartphone.

I didn't want this to be just a book full of "Turn right at the second stoplight, go .2 of a mile and come to a green space . . ." I did not want it to be just lists of directions to birding destinations. So I decided to include in each chapter a general introduction, a description of the habitats and the birds found there, a close-up description of a target bird found in the region, a short selection from my nature journal written at the time, and finally, directions for getting from one birding spot to another.

It was a crazy amount of detailed work.

In the event, I was struggling with getting accurate distance measurements, as we dashed around in the rental car.

"Hold it —STOP! Let's get a speedometer reading here!" I yelled. And "Wait a minute, we were supposed to turn LEFT back there at the stop sign. Can you please go into this driveway, turn around and head north instead of south?"

"I can't just stop in the middle of the road!" Gib huffed. "This is a state highway, there's no shoulder, and there's a guy on my tail."

By the end of the day, we were not fond of each other.

Furthermore, once arrived at the destination, we still had to find what we were looking for. And this is where Gib was an enormous help.

As soon as we got to Rocky Mountain National Park in Colorado, we attempted to find a white-tailed ptarmigan, one of the unique birds of the West. Ptarmigans are in a special family of quail-like birds suited for alpine climates. In winter, their white plumage blends with the snow-covered mountains, but in summer they molt into a coat of mottled brown, perfect camouflage on a hillside of rocks and wildflowers.

One beautiful morning in the park, we drove way up to a special spot along Trail Ridge Road. I had the map on my lap.

We parked the car and began hiking over the alpine meadows. We were searching for a bird that looks "more like a rock than a rock" as one of the local authorities had advised me. When I'd given up hope, Gib saw a shape that didn't belong, a head sticking up above the carpet of wildflowers, an immoveable lump that turned into a white-tailed ptarmigan. I wasn't surprised that he found it first.

The search had taken us a couple of hours. We were exhausted.

And then, driving back down the mountain, on a whim we stopped at a pull-out where groups of tourists were parked. As we walked along a short trail, surrounded by mobs of people including families with children, a female ptarmigan and her brood of chicks foraged tamely nearby. Completely oblivious to the crowds, here were the ptarmigans, the ones we had hiked for hours to see, the ones we'd risen at dawn to find. That's when I had to laugh. Ironically, birds are where you find them . . . often not far from humans.

It took me three years to write "Great Birding Trips of the West." Writing exact directions for a wide range of birding places, navigating unfamiliar territory once we arrived, and handling last-minute disasters, were all part of the mix. A hail storm was so severe it dented our rental car. Another time, we found a high-rise building being constructed on a lot formerly home to rufous-winged sparrows. An angry farmer kicked us off a place that used to be ideal for seeing vagrants on the California coast.

I didn't care. I had boundless energy and more. To be honest, when I'm on a project I become intense, driven, uptight. And my husband was there for me. That meant a lot; I never forgot it.

Soon afterward, Gib decided to purchase a computer for his law office, and simultaneously we got one for use at home. I've forgotten the brand, but it was somewhat of a dud. Like so many old-fashioned computers, it was a huge machine. And I had to learn "DOS," the computer operating system that was outdated almost as soon as it was painstakingly learned.

I forced myself to do it. I couldn't possibly write a book without using a computer. I, the most technical idiot in the world, taught myself how to operate that darned slow, clunky computer.

After that hurdle, drawing rough maps for the book seemed easy. I knew we needed maps, and I liked the idea of translating my directions onto a map. Then, I took my sketches to an artist whom Capra Press suggested. She knew how to put them on the computer and make them look good.

"Great Birding Trips of the West" sold well. I concentrated on the California market, since there are more birders traveling in California than anywhere I can think of. Long out of print now, the book was a success in its own small way.

Costa Rican Adventure

One of the best articles I wrote for *Birdwatcher's Digest* described my trip to Costa Rica, a first venture to the tropics.

I had a birthday coming up, and Carol Goodell insisted on using her contacts in that beautiful country to organize a birding trip. We were accompanied by two other friends from Santa Barbara — Carole Halsted and Joanne Rapp — plus our Costa Rican guide, Marco Saborio.

In 1992, parts of Costa Rica were untouched by tourism. I couldn't get over the green of the burgeoning rainforest around us, and the alien sounds of tropical birds. As we drove along a deserted coastal road in our van, I looked at the thick soil that had become a slushy mess of red mud, and marveled at our sturdy four-wheel-drive van.

But then we came to the Rio Uvita, a river that had turned into an ugly torrent due to recent rains. There was no way we could cross in that van. Marco assured us it was nothing to be alarmed about. Plan B was to cross on horses.

So we returned to the hamlet of Uvita, where nine horses were waiting to take us and our luggage across the river. Again, we approached the river, this time on horseback, and the water appeared even deeper and swifter. But the horses plunged in sure-footedly.

We were on our way.

That ride on horseback to the ranch (*finca*) owned by Carol's friend was unforgettable. I kept reining in the horse to get a better look at the birds. I saw my first laughing falcon, the *guaco*. A small and snappy falcon, the *guaco* is pale beige with a black-bandit mask. It preys exclusively on forest snakes, killing them by biting off the reptile's head, then flying to a perch to devour the remains.

At last we arrived at the ranch where we were to spend several days. Like a Swiss chalet made of tropical woods, the house was perched on a grassy clearing above the sea, and the view up and down the coast was spectacular.

Life at the ranch quickly settled into a delightful rhythm. Up at 5 a.m. with the skies clearing and a mound of pink clouds puffing over the ocean . . . the harsh chittering of orange-chinned parakeets outside our windows, the eerie wail of the howler monkeys coming from the creek. I took a pre-breakfast bird walk, prefaced by a thorough dousing of "the sulphur sock" around my waist and ankles to stave off pesky chiggers. (A seasoned birder told me this trick: you get some loose sulphur from a pharmacist and put it in an old sock. Once dabbed around vulnerable spots, it repels biting insects.)

The big flycatchers were vocal at dawn. The great kiskadee, the social flycatcher, and the gray-capped flycatcher sat on wires or fences and welcomed the morning in repetitive, bossy voices. The tanagers were quieter, showing themselves as nuggets of yellow or chartreuse, blue or buff. The euphonias were navy blue and yellow.

162

Everywhere I looked, the birds were new — my head was spinning, my ears confused.

The first time a chestnut-mandibled toucan landed in the cecropia tree nearby, I gasped at this extraordinary creature: the bird was using its gigantic yellow-and-maroon bill so dexterously to feed on the tiny seed pods. The shapes and colors of the birds were bizarre, like nothing I'd ever seen — except in the zoo.

In addition, I learned about our own North American birds. Costa Rica is a major wintering area for Baltimore orioles and chestnut-sided warblers, both breeders in the eastern U. S. One evening, I was enjoying the tropical sunset while looking out from the porch, when I saw flecks of orange and black bouncing around in the tree below. Grabbing the binoculars, I was surprised to see this was a gang of Baltimore orioles. There were males and females, old and young — and all were consuming fruits while they chattered to each other. I counted fifty birds in this one tree.

Later, I was to see many chestnut-sided warblers as we continued our travels around Costa Rica. The whole experience increased my understanding of migration. I saw that habitat conditions on a species' wintering grounds are as important as the conditions where it breeds. The world is tied together for birders, because we know the distances that migration spans for so many species. Globalization is nothing new to birds.

Dr. Alexander Skutch

I had a hunch Carol and Marco had planned a surprise for me to celebrate my birthday, but I had no idea what it was. When the day came, they announced they'd arranged for an interview with the famous ornithologist, botanist, and author Dr. Alexander Skutch. A resident of Costa Rica for many years, Dr. Skutch has made huge contributions to our knowledge of Central America. He wrote more than thirty books and countless articles on tropical natural history, but was best known for his work as an ornithologist. To my mind, Skutch had the rare ability to write accurate science in a beautiful and understandable way.

No formal gate or sign marked the humble entrance of Los Cusingos, the farm and nature preserve of Skutch and his wife, Pamela. As we approached, we went round to the side of the house, where the sound of a typewriter tapping came through the open window. I glimpsed an elderly gentleman with white hair neatly combed, his shoulders stooped as he sat before an old-fashioned typewriter, in concentration. His back was to us, and he was writing, writing, writing. For a minute, as we paused regarding this famous man — who seemed unaware of our presence — a sense of awe filled everyone. We exchanged glances, tears in our eyes.

Skutch was easy to talk to. Although by then in his late 80s, he was sharp. His bushy eyebrows rose and fell as he spoke. High cheekbones gave his face a strong look, though his body was frail.

We began with the ritual of watching the feeder, a rustic wooden platform with several bananas laid out for the birds. Our group sat on the open veranda with our feet dangling over the edge and saw one life bird after another come to dine on the bananas. The speckled tanager, a striking blend of chartreuse and blue, was a bird you can't imagine actually exists in the wild. Same with the silver-throated tanager and the green honeycreeper. After each bird, I had to restrain myself from jumping up and down and shouting "I can't believe I'm here" again and again.

Skutch autographed my field guide when we went to his study. The room was sparsely furnished with a large desk, a wooden armoire and shelves full of books and professional journals around the walls. The wood floor was bare and clean. A lopsided kerosene lamp stood on the desk with a Maine scene drawn on the lampshade. The elegance and simplicity of the house reminded me of New England thousands of miles away.

Two of my favorite books by Skutch had just been reissued by the University Press of Florida: "The Imperative Call" and "A Naturalist in Costa Rica." Both describe his adventures birding in Central America in the 1930s and 1940s.

We had a good conversation. He described how an informal census he took every fall on the number of North American migrants he sees for a certain period had dwindled to about one-third of those tallied ten years before. He blamed deforestation in the tropics, and loss of habitat in North America.

There's a moving short essay titled "The Appreciative Mind," from his book "A Birdwatcher's Adventures in Tropical America," in which Skutch shares with us the feelings he had on a sparkling morning in Costa Rica. The forest is awakening and the birds are everywhere in the treetops above him. A rain has just washed the plants with freshness. He describes the brilliant plumages of tropical birds and their melodious calls. He says that even with the hardships scientists such as he had to undergo to observe and identify birds in their native haunts, these moments make it worthwhile. He portrays the intensity of an experience birdwatching in the forest as felt by one deeply in touch with nature and birds.

"Despite their fragility, the rare moments when we respond with fullest feeling to nature's glory, when we are glad to be alive and grateful for the privilege of living on so favored a planet, are infinitely precious . . . "

As we continued our conversation, I understood what he meant by the appreciative mind. People like myself and my friends on the trip, plus thousands of other birders, have chosen an appreciation of birds as the link between us and the natural world. When we're immersed in the act of observing or studying a bird, whether it be a new species in a foreign land or a sparrow on a fence at home, a path of understanding is formed. Instead of remaining locked within the confines of our ordinary lives, we become linked to an object of beauty or of special interest in nature. An appreciation of birds is the first step in such treasured moments. Those moments, for Skutch and for many of us, are a product of the appreciative mind.

Two aspects of my Costa Rican trip were harbingers of the future: a love of travel and a desire to continue writing about birds. I wanted to write. I preferred non-fiction.

Research was my muse. If I could find the facts I was hunting for, I could write. And I was looking for science to give me the black-and-white answers that would fit neatly into whatever I was describing. Comfortable writing non-fiction, grounded in whatever science I could teach myself or learn from others, all I needed was a new project.

But that would have to wait.

13.

In Love With The "Wind Birds"

One day in 1967 I picked up *The New Yorker* magazine and an article caught my eye: *The Wind Birds* by Peter Matthiessen, later published as a book.

"The restlessness of shorebirds, their kinship with the distance and swift seasons, the wistful signal of their voices down the long coastlines of the world make them, for me, the most affecting of wild creatures. I think of them as birds of the wind, as 'wind birds.'" (Matthiessen, page 16, in "The Wind Birds," 1973).

I wasn't familiar with shorebirds, so I almost didn't read the article. Shorebirds were foreign to me. I was the listener on the land. My birding experiences had been with songbirds in the woodlands. Growing up, I swam at the beach all summer, and walked there at low tide on winter days. Why hadn't I paid attention to shorebirds before?

By the time I finished reading Matthiessen's lyrical portrait of shorebirds — their migrations, their breeding behaviors, their visits to the author's house at Sagaponack on Long Island — I was mesmerized. It was their long-winged shapes, their mythical migrations from Tierra del Fuego to the Arctic Circle, their ability to fly long distances that got to me. The author had a way of making the science of shorebird study into a mysterious treasure hunt, one that I could follow. The essay didn't concern itself with the detailed examination of shorebird plumages and identification, but sparked my imagination, my wonder. I wanted to focus on shorebirds for the first time.

As it turned out, I'd have to wait till the 1970s and my move back to Santa Barbara to act on this. Plus, I'd need a detailed field guide, a spotting scope, and a commitment to shorebird study. Figuring out shorebirds on your own is daunting; I knew I needed help.

Most ardent birders, both then and now, are adept at identifying shorebirds. Anyone who got started birding in Western Europe is mad for shorebirds, or "waders" as the British call them. You won't find a Brit who doesn't know his waders backward and forward. The routine in Great Britain for watching shorebirds was that you don full-on foul-weather gear, shoulder your spotting scope, and head for the nearest estuary. There you sit for hours and hours in a blind. Most of the blinds I've been in are well-built cabins on stilts, with seats to rest on and openings through which you can view the birds. The weather is misty or rainy and a blind is perfect.

In Southern California, we don't have blinds, it seldom rains, and our coastal wetlands have almost disappeared. Ninety percent of the salt marshes and mudflats have been lost to development caused by human encroachment. Those that remain have been set aside after hard-fought conservation battles.

On the south coast of Santa Barbara County, few good places remain to study shorebirds. Devereux Slough, a part of UCSB's Coal Oil Point Preserve, is the best, but it usually dries up by summer and fall. Carpinteria Salt Marsh Nature Park and UCSB's Carpinteria Salt Marsh Reserve are both excellent, but the birds are often far away.

A bright spot on the horizon is the recent restoration of UCSB's North Campus Open Space, formerly Ocean Meadows Golf Course. The wetlands here will no doubt lure many shorebirds, due to the mixture of freshwater from upland creeks mixing with the brackish water of Devereux Slough.

But in the 1980s and 1990s, most of us felt as though the South Coast didn't offer much in the way of shorebirding. And that left me two choices: drive north to the Santa Ynez River Estuary that's in Santa Barbara County, or drive south to the Santa Clara River Estuary in Ventura County. I ended up choosing the shorter route from my house, which took me to the Santa Clara River Estuary, adjacent to McGrath State Beach near Ventura.

In our region, where a river meets the ocean, the river's mouth is usually blocked by a sand berm many months of the year. If winter rains increase the freshwater flow of the river, the berm may be temporarily breached. Afterward, the sand blockage at the mouth forms once more, leaving a large lagoon of deep water on the landward side. For shorebirds and the birders who love them, you want drained mudflats for stopovers in fall migration, not a big lagoon.

At the Santa Clara River estuary, the sand berm blocked off the ocean completely by summer. But, if the lagoon started flooding the nearby campground, the authorities would get a bulldozer out to breech the berm. At least once or twice, the rumor was that in the twilight hours, a group of birders had gotten together to help dig out the sand berm. However it was done, piercing the sand berm let the river rush out to sea. What remained were the muddy channels where migrating shorebirds could forage.

My introduction to birding at the mouth of the Santa Clara River began in summer 1982, when I chased my first rare shorebird. The bird, a Mongolian plover (*Charadrius mongolus*, now called lesser sand plover), should have been migrating south along the coast of Asia, but instead here it was on the coast of California. Probably due to misorientation, this tiny plover might have flown all the way from its nesting grounds on the plains of northeast Siberia. I was desperate to see it.

As soon as I arrived at the Surfer's Mound section of the beach near Ventura Harbor, I spotted the birders. Only a few had gotten the word, but they had scopes and cameras. It was a lovely summer evening, the sun setting in the west, and before us lay an expanse of soft white sand that made up the berm. We could see the wide sandbars and pools of the riverbed to the north, while to the south the breakers roared. As we walked toward where the plover was roosting, I saw we'd need to cross a narrow channel of turbulent water flowing to the sea. The birders were taking off their shoes and clothes, tossing their boots on the sand, and jumping in. One guy fell over, but we grabbed him. I remember my jeans being wet to the waist, as we made a human chain to cross the outflow, and eventually scrambled up the other bank. By this time more birders had arrived — albeit a small group compared to what this news would have drawn had it been on the Internet today.

This beautiful plover, seen in the soft evening light, was a small shorebird with a dark gray head and back, and contrasting pure white throat and underparts. Imprinted on its white forehead was a curious "medallion," made up of a black horizontal line slightly bisected by another vertical line. Think of a "T" shape, with the bird's eyes on either side, and the long part pointing to the bill. But the stunner was the thick band across the upper chest — a deep cinnamon rust color. The experts pronounced it a female. To me it was one of the most incredible shorebirds I'd ever seen.

After this, shorebirds were my focus in late summer and fall. I examined field guides trying to make sense of shorebird families. Shorebirds, those birds you see spending the winter on Southern California beaches, are largely of two main bird families: the plovers (*Charadriiadae*) and the sandpipers (*Scolopacidae*). It was easier if you sorted them by leg length, particularly the sandpipers. Being the probers and drillers of the mudflats, sandpipers take advantage of their bills to mine the wet sand. Their bills and their legs come in a variety of lengths for this reason. Taller sandpipers wade into the deeper water, while the tiniest sandpipers (otherwise known as "peep" when they're too far away to identify), resort to shallow pools.

In addition, I learned that the age of the shorebird was crucial to identifying it. Take the western sandpiper, one of my favorites. In spring breeding plumage, this little sandpiper exhibits an exquisite blend of rust, gray, and black feathers. In non-breeding plumage, which is how these western sandpipers are going to look from fall through winter, they are a flat symphony of gray and white. Gone are the vivid rusts and crisp blacks.

But what about the juvenile, the young western sandpiper that's just hatched, that's flocked to the vast estuaries of the Alaskan rivers near where it was born, and sets off alone on its way south? These juvenile westerns are fresh and crisp in their own new set of feathers. They look different from both the breeding and non-breeding versions of the adults. Aha! One more plumage to learn.

The reason for knowing these three plumages of the western sandpiper is important. You are basically scanning the sandpipers for that rarity, the semipalmated sandpiper that belongs on the East Coast. Here on the West Coast, the semipalmated is a prize. And if you could pick one out from the flocks of peep, which are guaranteed to be made up of the common western and least sandpipers, you have proved yourself one of the shorebird cognoscenti.

To say that this was a challenge for me is an understatement.

So when I discovered that in half an hour I could drive to a place that had natural shorebird habitat, the Santa Clara River Estuary, I was ecstatic. I walked out into the riverbed and studied shorebirds to my heart's content.

 **NATURE JOURNAL: AUGUST 1, 1989**
Santa Clara River Estuary, Ventura County

We're parked on the wide median beside the bridge that spans the Santa Clara River. Accompanied by two excellent birders, Shawneen Finnegan and Barbara Millett, I know the drill. Unload the rubber boots from the back of the car, take off your casual shoes, struggle to get the boots on, heave a scope onto your shoulder. Grab your hat, your binocs, and quickly scan the mudflats far below. Looks like a great day with masses of shorebirds.

We scoot down the bank and follow the well-worn path through the thick willows bordering the river's edge.

Weaving in and out of the willows, we eventually come to the river bank. Today it's steep, and the channel we have to cross over is a foot deep. One by one we step into the water, but it doesn't come over our boots.

On this summer's day, when the sun is high and filtered through an ocean haze, when I walk slogging through the rich ooze with my boots protecting me from the puddles, the seabreeze in my hair, the smell of mud and saltwater mingling with the foggy odor of a typical beach day, I am in heaven.

The joy I feel when I'm trudging along the mudflats fills me with confidence that I can understand the "wind birds" after all.

The estuary is a world filled with the hoarse croaks of the terns and the cries of the gulls overhead, the wild questing calls of the plovers, and the seeps and eeks of the many sandpipers hurrying from one food morsel to another along the damp sand.

When we climb back out of the first deep channel, toward the middle of the riverbed, the footing is firmer. All of us are scared of quicksand, so we test each step before we take it. Every flock of shorebirds is worth a scan. Stop, set up the scope, close one eye, peer through the scope to see what's there.

Each puddle is crowded with groups of western and least sandpipers. I can now tell a juvenile western from an adult. Young ones are lovely with their fresh feathering, rufous highlights, and snow-white underparts.

Wonder of wonders, I discover I can at last distinguish the juvenile semipalmated sandpiper from the juvenile western sandpiper. I never thought I'd be able to, but today, I succeed!

As we approach the mixed flocks of shorebirds, those that are hiding their heads under a wing open one eye.

The smallest ones scurry away a bit, but they're still not frightened. The larger sandpipers, like the willet and the greater yellowlegs, raise both wings over their backs in a stretching movement (like a nervous yawn), as if to prove that they're still OK with our approach, but they're watching us. Marbled godwits and whimbrels shuffle off to get into the center of the flock, just in case.

In truth, we have a myriad of fearless shorebirds at our feet, so close we can see them clearly even without binoculars. These birds are hungry, already well along on their journey from Alaska. They're layering on the fat, enough to propel them southward from one estuary to another along the West Coast.

We count close to 500 westerns, 200 leasts, plus the treasured two semipalmated sandpipers.

And the list goes on. From Wilson's phalarope, to avocet to short and long-billed dowitchers, every common variety of shorebird you could find in August is somewhere on these mudflats.

We watch them at the smorgasbord as they devour the crustaceans, the worms, and the minuscule biofilm of diatoms that lies camouflaged on the surface of the mud. This is the nourishment that keeps the birds going, and gives them strength for the next leg of their journey tonight.

Tired but thrilled, we tramp back out over the rivulets and mudflats toward the edge of the river and home. Three hours have passed in a minute. When I'm in the world of an estuary, time flies.

One spot that was good for shorebird watching was the Goleta sewage treatment plant near the Santa Barbara airport. In summer, the settling ponds were full of gooey mud to support the weight of all but the heaviest shorebirds that flocked there to feast on flies. Birders were allowed to park, sign the registry in the office, and then walk around the dikes that separated the ponds. Even without a scope, you could get close to shorebirds and examine fine plumage details.

When I first started looking at shorebirds, I often ended up at the sewage treatment plant. I was determined to ignore the surroundings. The powerful odor of sewage was intensified by an onshore breeze. But there I was, with my scope and my field guide, trying to get good looks at the shorebirds that landed on the surface of these icky ponds. I concentrated on the juvenile westerns, hoping to pick out a semipalmated.

At that point, Jon Dunn usually showed up to give me a detailed lecture, and I knew I was in trouble. Instantly, he'd pick out the nuance that made that plumper shorebird with a straight, short bill a rare semipalmated, and the one that I had targeted was just another western, with its tapered bill and sleeker body shape. But somehow, Jon's suggestions always made sense, once he was there to calmly point out the subtleties.

Eventually I tried to get my friends to come with me and look at shorebirds at the treatment plant. That is, my birding friends. Everybody else turned away with a "Joan, I'm sorry, but you're crazy" look on their face.

But for me, the Goleta sewage treatment plant has a top place in my shorebird memories.

It was the summer of 1999, and I'd had a particularly sad day. My father was quite ill; I hadn't been birding in weeks. I usually reach for my birds to pull me up and out, to get my mind in another place, to take me away.

I called David Kisner, a graduate student in biology at UCSB. He had been assisting me with the bird classes, and he lived in Goleta. I swung by and picked him up, knowing that he would be the one carrying the heavy spotting scope, and we would get excellent looks at shorebirds.

 NATURE JOURNAL: AUGUST 10, 1999
Goleta Sanitary District

Here we are on a summer evening, walking slowly around the three settling ponds. Black ooze gurgles up in bubbles; in several areas, floating mats of mud (or something!) have formed over the watery sludge underneath. One pond supports grasses and tall weeds growing in it. Fun to try to pick out the birds as they hide behind the vegetation.

Baby black-necked stilts wobble around on long legs, their parents screaming frantically at us.

As soon as I look through the scope, I realize how long it's been since I studied shorebirds. I search through the scattered flocks, trying to sort the western from the least sandpipers, a bit overwhelmed. David agrees, so we walk slowly and examine each bird closely.

As we approach the back pond, David points to a bright red plump sandpiper, which we both assume was the red knot (yes, that's the name of a sandpiper) that had been reported here earlier today.

What I see through the scope is a deep reddish-brown sandpiper, with what appears to be a drooping, downward-curved bill. Instantly, the bird flies, we hope not far. By walking over to the west side of the ponds, we've got the evening light at our back. Every shorebird stands out now.

Suddenly, my mind does a flip. "David, that bird had a decurved, drooping bill!" Knots have straight bills. What the heck? Thumb through the book. Something's wrong!

The mystery bird appears out of nowhere again, flies in, settles in front of us. Perfect view, great light.

"And this bird has black legs, Joan," says David. "Knots have greenish-yellow legs."

"Oh, that's just because its been in the mud," I say dismissively. "Besides, if its not a knot, what can it be?"

"Joan, it's a Curlew Sandpiper!" David laughs in that definitive way he has. Like, here's a math problem and I just solved it.

"What? Impossible," says I, the record keeper,

recalling that we'd only had one previous county curlew sandpiper, in Santa Maria in September 1984, a juvenile.

Very few August records exist of an adult curlew sandpiper. And indeed, this gorgeous bird was an adult just beginning to lose its bright breeding plumage before attaining its somber wintering outfit.

Curlew Sandpiper! A second county record! I can't believe it, but we start calling our birding friends so they can come and take a quick look, before the plant closes. We need photos badly.

Karen and several other birders show up.

"Joanie," Karen Bridgers says in her matter-of-fact voice that I love, "That bird has a down-curved bill!" Triumphant, we grin at each other. "And look at that rump, it's pure white," she continues. We pull out all the books and start reading the appropriate descriptions of a Curlew Sandpiper. Everything fits.

Soon, other birders arrive. Joan Hardie gets down on her hands and knees and crawls the distance over those sharp pebbles in order to get close enough to take photos. To me, they're the most beautiful photos in the world. For years, the best shot was framed and proudly displayed at the front desk of the Goleta Sanitary District offices. They are so birder-friendly there.

When I started reading up on the curlew sandpiper, I learned it breeds on the tundra of Arctic Siberia, then winters all over the place, including Africa, Malaysia, Australia, and New Zealand. A tiny breeding range, and an enormous wintering range. What brought the curlew sandpiper to Santa Barbara? It wasn't a juvenile, so it had successfully migrated before. However, this is what makes shorebird watching so thrilling. Finding the unexpected treasure, just quietly sitting there in the middle of a sewage pond, thousands of miles from where it nested. It should be in an estuary in Malaysia en route to Australia.

Below is an excerpt from my notebook describing a more recent shorebird adventure.

 NATURE JOURNAL: SEPTEMBER 12, 2018
Ocean Beach County Park, Santa Ynez River Estuary

One fall day I was walking my dog, Happy, when an alert came on my phone. I knew right then I was cancelling my plans and heading for Lompoc no matter what!

You see, the day before, a good friend, Brad Hines, a Lompoc birder, reported that he saw a weird-looking godwit.

Even if you're not a birder, you might remember the godwit that commonly winters on our beaches, the marbled godwit. It's a tall shorebird with a long slightly turned up straight bill. The bill is pink at the base, the bird itself a warm cinnamon.

I wasn't at ease with godwits. I'd seen a Hudsonian godwit once before, and a bar-tailed godwit, but either would be super rare for Santa Barbara County. And I was working on my county list like a crazed person that year.

I leave Santa Barbara, driving mindlessly fast, cursing the road work with the "flagger ahead" signs, passing the slow trucks when I can. I am sure Brad Hines has that bird tied down there just waiting for me . . .

Toward 11 a.m. I arrive at Ocean Beach County Park, a patch of parking lot with a nice viewing platform located at the mouth of the Santa Ynez River, west of Lompoc.

I swing into the parking lot at the estuary, grab my dog, put him on my clip at my waist, and run clutching my bins and camera, as fast as I can toward the beach, under the RR trestle and out to the concrete platform.

There they are: the four birders who'd arrived before me. Everyone is discouraged. These folks had already put in a fruitless afternoon yesterday looking for this bird. We all gaze half-heartedly at the distant terns, gulls, several groups of long-billed curlews. Brad Hines is nervous. But he'd taken a photo yesterday and it sure looked good for bar-tailed godwit! Yikes, a new county bird for me.

Then, reality strikes. What a colossal waste of time, and why on earth am I, who couldn't identify anything more than a marbled godwit, standing here waiting for something that's gone?

When birders get together waiting for a bird, they do one thing: talk, talk, talk. About birds of course. Remembering the history, recalling the collective body of memories about our patch that we all love. Brad Schram, the king of Santa Barbara County bird totals, was there. He's been birding our county longer than any of us.

So Brad S. starts regaling us with famous birds found in the 1970s, and then Wes Fritz chimes in with birds he saw 15 or 20 years ago when he started birding here. We're all laughing and chatting away. The whole endeavor is pretty silly: no large waders or even a flock of them. The scopes are set up, but there's nothing new to look at.

Finally, at 12:30, I'm hungry, figure I'll pack it in. Everyone agrees it's useless, but they don't leave. I say good-bye.

Since there's no cellphone service anywhere in that windswept estuary, I drive out onto the main road. I pull over at one of the farm road intersections, and text my husband and our local listserve. I tell everyone I am headed for home, that the bird is a no-show thus far... start the car engine... drive toward the outskirts of Lompoc, when my cell rings.

"Turn around and come back!" yells Brad Hines over the phone. I am speechless. I make a quick U-turn in the middle of the road, and then I send out the message to the listserve: "Turned around, bird may be there."

177

That's it.

*I have to hope that the 900 other folks who'll receive it
will understand, because there's no time to do anything more...*

*I nearly kill myself gunning the car as fast as it will go
back to Ocean Beach. I worry that a policeman from the
kiosk at the Vandenberg AFB entrance might see me and
give me a ticket, but so far so good.*

*I hurtle back down the same entrance road, careen
into the parking lot, leave doggie in the car with the
windows down, and rush out to where I'd left the birders.*

*It's there! The bar-tailed godwit is there! I look
through Brad Schram's scope first, an excellent view, as
the bird preens on the far shore.*

*When I examine the familiar cinnamon-colored
shapes of the marbled godwits in that flock, one bird
stands out. It's different: a couple inches shorter in leg
length, with no cinnamon tones at all. The impression
is of a gray bird with a crisply black-and-white speckled
back. A juvenile, a mixed-up youngster.*

*The bar-tailed is putting its long bill underneath a
wing, often hidden behind the taller marbled godwits,
and I notice a pronounced supercilium from the bill
continuing above the eye and beyond. The bar-tailed
is a shorter bird, and the bill appears super-long in
comparison to its "dumpier" structure. I watch it through
the scopes of the two Brads, and then — not more than
five minutes later — all of the godwit flock, 40-50 birds,
flies up and away. We watch as they depart to the south,
over the dunes to our left, out toward the open ocean.
Gone. Never to be seen again.*

*The flock and the bar-tailed with it had been there for
exactly twelve minutes. Somebody looked at their watch,
and it wasn't yet 1 o'clock.*

That's the story of my "godwit luck," but it doesn't stop there.

As soon as I got home, I realized this was the species of shorebird, the bar-tailed godwit, that researchers had just confirmed as the longest non-stop flyer in migration of any other bird. The bar-tailed makes a mind-boggling non-stop migratory flight from Alaska to New Zealand every fall. Over the course of 6-9 days, this species accomplishes a flight of 11,000 kilometers (roughly 6,800 miles) in order to arrive at wintering grounds in the Southern Hemisphere. Picture a flock of godwits high above the Pacific Ocean, buffeted by the winds, pelted by raindrops, and yet onward they fly. How do they manage the fuel load? What's special about bar-tailed godwits?

In one of their first experiments in 2005, ornithologists implanted female bar-tailed godwits with tiny transmitters. They chose females, because they're larger than males, and presumably more able to withstand the slight extra weight.

Subsequently, scientists have figured out several reasons the bar-taileds are capable of this extreme journey. First, the species must eat a significant amount of fat and protein to sustain it. In order to make room for the extra load of fat, some of the digestive organs of the bird have to be re-absorbed during the long flight: the liver, kidneys, and alimentary canal disappear temporarily. When the taxing journey has ended, the organs are restored.

In addition, once the bird is loaded with fuel, it must fly fast and continuously, yet maintain a low metabolic rate, which it does. And, in order not to alter its streamlined shape, the extra fat is mostly stored under the skin in the breast. Finally, these godwits fly in flock formation, which could potentially save on energy.

There's still much we don't understand about the navigation skills of shorebirds, but one aspect stands out. The journey of the bar-tailed godwit is about as far as any bird can migrate without stopping.

14.

Saying Good-Bye and Finding My Own Path

One afternoon in 1999, I was in my childhood room at the family house on Las Canoas Road. The doctor had just visited. Dad and I were quiet. I sat on the bed and he sat in the desk chair. We watched the wild oats as they blew on the hillside. I looked up to the crest of the hill, where the dark green oak still stood, the one that I'd seen grow bigger and bigger since I was in high school.

It was fall, with that lovely soft light. The mountains rose up against the sky and the shadows on them were longer; you could see all the way to La Cumbre Peak if you stood outside in our driveway.

Dad looked out the window from his chair, then turned to me.

"Well, I've had a good life, Joanie."

The doctor had said, "Bob, there's not much more we can do for you."

I thought it was terribly blunt, but I was wrong. It was the right thing to say, the truth. My father was miserable; he had suffered a spontaneous back fracture that was killing him. The pain was so bad he couldn't write anymore. Strong medications played havoc with his frail body. Dad had nothing if he could not be creating words and stories from that brain of his. I understood how important writing was to my life, so I knew how he felt.

Five days later, he was gone. So quick. He'd only been ill for six months. I wasn't prepared at all. Most importantly, I stopped thinking of myself as a daughter. I thought I'd finally grown up, but it turns out it was only a small step in what has become a continuing process, an unfolding. Little by little, I was finding my own way. Mom was still alive, although diminished mentally. Without Dad, life for her was nothing.

Ellen and I were on our own, as we so often found ourselves after Dad died. Our sister Jane lived in Hawaii, and our sister Katherine had passed away. Katherine, plagued by mental infirmities, had had an unhappy life. She'd married, divorced, and had two children. (Thankfully, both of them are well, living here in Santa Barbara.) But while Katherine had some good times and bad, life was hellish for my parents who tried everything in an attempt to give her what she needed. Nothing worked. Her death from emphysema in 1984 was a blessing.

But back to the little red farm house: after we'd settled Mom in a good assisted living facility, Ellen and I spent over a year to get the house cleared of all the manuscripts, papers, letters, and files. Physically, the house had run its course. It was tired. I don't know why the whole place didn't go up in flames from the faulty wiring or why the upstairs toilet didn't sag right down through the kitchen ceiling.

Yet within it were all these valuable thoughts and ideas that my father had composed. It was as if the house was being held upright by the thousands of books in the shelves, the boxes and boxes of manuscripts, the genealogy books stuffed into dresser drawers, magazines old and new propped on top of each other.

This chaos was chuck-a-block with important material. Everything had to be reviewed. Much of it went to the UCSB Library Special Collections, where all of Dad's environmental contributions and writings are catalogued. By the time we finished cleaning out everything, Ellen and I cursed anyone who wrote books, read books, or collected books. We had lifted too many cardboard boxes to the storage unit, agonized over where this piece of writing or that piece should go.

Not surprisingly, it turned out that the most valuable asset my parents had was their collection of thousands of books, some of them rare.

These were our inheritance, these volumes about everything from Chumash daily life to early California expeditions and European art books. Most prized were the calfskin-bound volumes of the classics that Grandfather Faust had ordered from a famous store in London. While in Italy, he had wanted to fill his study with all of Shakespeare, Horace, and Ovid. The bound sets were beautiful, in navy blue, cream, or rich brown. An original Oxford English Dictionary in many heavy volumes was another of the treasures that came to me.

And among this collection of novels, history upon history of ancient and modern wars, biographies of Napoleon, Hitler, and more, I found jewels — books long out of print about natural history, which I could use in my writing. This pleased me, to think that my father had acquired these books for his own research, and now I was reading the same pages and perusing them for ways to write about nature.

But Dad was no longer there. I missed him terribly.

"An Introduction to Birds of the Southern California Coast"

One day in 2002, I got a phone call. It was Rich Stallcup.

As I mentioned, in the late 1960s and 1970s, there were two birders — Guy McCaskie in Southern California and Rich Stallcup in Northern California — who were buddies, and had pushed California birding to new levels. It would take pages to describe Rich's superb career as a teacher, writer, field trip leader, and all-around top California birder.

Rich was only a teen-ager when he started birding, and he had that rare combination of an innate feeling for where birds could be found, an ability to organize records, and a way with words. Furthermore, Rich was a naturalist. Although birds were his specialty, his knowledge of other creatures was widespread. In one of his books "Ocean Birds of the Nearshore Pacific," his descriptions of whales, dolphins, and other denizens of the deep sea are as good as those of the seabirds, which he loved. A renowned natural history educator in Marin County, Rich was also somewhat of a counterculture hero, reflecting his coming of age during the Vietnam War era. He had a quiet, gentle approach to birding, which earned him friends and followers wherever he went. Birds showed up when Rich was there, or at least that's how it felt to many who had been out in the field with him.

Rich had visited Santa Barbara several times, once even done a Christmas Bird Count in Montecito, and I'd met up with him on his own territory in Point Reyes several times in the 1990s.

Imagine my surprise when I heard Rich's quiet voice at the other end of the phone, and my excitement when he started to outline a potential new writing project. Rich was headquartered at Point Reyes National Seashore; he frequently led bird trips and classes there. One year he took Doris Kretschmer and her husband on a memorable bird walk.

Doris was an editor for a series of books from the University of California Press, called the California Natural History Guides. These were small-sized books with concise introductions to many areas of California's natural history. Over the years, I'd collected as many as I could find in used bookstores, and some new ones, too. I was just the kind of customer that U.C. Press sought out. These books were accurately written guides for the interested layperson.

Rich and Doris hit it off, and when he began talking about producing a book on coastal birds of Northern California, she asked him if he knew anyone he could recommend to write one for Southern California as well. She wanted to reinvigorate the California Natural History Series of books.

My name had somehow popped into Rich's mind, and I jumped at the chance. Bingo. I'd hit the jackpot. Yes, to my first university press book! I was over the moon, and so grateful to Rich.

Although I had already started the outline of a regional natural history book that I'd conceived of before Dad passed away, this was too good an opportunity to pass up. I began corresponding with Doris. She was an enthusiastic editor. From time to time I drove up to Berkeley to touch base with the folks at U.C. Press. Everyone was friendly, smart, and encouraging.

I worked hard on each species account, the copious directions to birding sites, and the detailed maps. Don Desjardin, a friend and birder from Ventura County, was the photographer I chose. This was in the early 2000s, just before digital photography took off. Don had a large backlog of bird portraits on slides, which we used. He also haunted the coastal locations where he could get as close as possible to the shorebirds he needed to photograph.

Then one day Peter Gaede knocked on the front door. He and his wife, Lisa, had just moved to Santa Barbara. Fresh from getting his degree in scientific illustration, Peter was eager for work. We were to become good friends and collaborators. I love the fine illustrations Peter created, and I was in awe of his skill as an artist.

But the concept was Rich's idea: focus on birds of the coastal strip, arguably the most visited part of Southern California, and describe them. Then tell readers where to find them, with an emphasis on casual birders with families.

I honestly was not enthusiastic about exploring Southern California south of Santa Barbara. However, I swallowed my fear of horrendous traffic, and my bold ignorance. Where would I go in the region for the best birding experiences? I was fortunate to have birding friends who guided me, pointing me in the right direction for newly restored sites and recently established visitors' centers.

Remarkably, I discovered that coastal Southern California, from Ventura County to San Diego County, has great birding spots. I discovered salt marshes bordering lagoons in northern San Diego County that had been beautifully restored. San Elijo Lagoon was a star example. In Orange County, upper Newport Bay attracted a fantastic array, including a healthy population of Ridgeway's rail, the endangered subspecies of clapper rail found in our region.

Another location, Bolsa Chica Ecological Reserve, is a lagoon famous for nesting terns and gulls. Often, the sites were within shouting distance of a shopping mall or a high-rise apartment complex, but that doesn't bother birds. The mild climate and proximity to the ocean will still lure migrating and wintering birds to Southern California, if habitat restoration continues.

Currently, authorities are talking about bulldozing the concrete from portions of the Los Angeles River. When I visited there, such ideas were only a dream. But you could still see masses of western sandpipers feeding on the algae flats in the riverbed if you watched from near the Willow Street bridge, which is minutes away from Los Angeles' massively traveled 710 Freeway.

The book, "An Introduction to Birds of the Southern California Coast," was published in 2006. We had a big book signing at the Museum of Natural History. I was ecstatic, until I read a hideous review of our book in *Birding* magazine's newsletter, called *Winging It*. Humiliated, tearful, furious, I realized not everybody was on my wavelength. Just because this reviewer panned my book, that didn't mean that everyone else hated it. But it was a bitter pill, and another call to armor my sensitive self against this kind of attack. It's not personal, it's just part of life.

In the end, Rich Stallcup and others completed a guide to birds of the Northern California coast, but it was published posthumously. Rich passed away from leukemia in 2012. He was too young, way too young, but heralded by all who knew him as one of the finest characters and most talented birders in California, if not North America.

Renewing Museum Ties

After Dad died, my life changed unalterably. I was released from the bonds of being the oldest. No longer needing to be the dutiful daughter to my adored father, I felt a new freedom. I continued to reach for the things that I'd always wanted to do. I was a birder and a nature writer.

My brain, which had been idle for too many years, was begging for nourishment. I had always been a fact person, loved the solid stuff that you couldn't argue with, loved the science.

Give me something to hold onto. A body of knowledge that I can go to whenever I take a walk on the local trails. Bricks out of which I might build a house of nature, a place of refuge when life overwhelms me.

Luckily I realized that here in my own area was all that I was searching for: the geology, the botany, the weather, and the extraordinary diversity of life in our region. I was in a hurry to understand the aspects of the natural world beyond birds. Birds would always be my passion, but they fit into a bigger story. Fish in the streams, whales in the ocean — I needed to learn about all these other elements of natural history.

But to begin at the beginning, I must go back to the late 1970s when I first became a docent at the Santa Barbara Museum of Natural History. Remembering my own youthful rambles around those hallowed halls, I was keen to give back. After frequently taking my young family through the museum and its environs, I was eager to sign up to give tours to school children and to learn more about each of the museum exhibits. It was like settling in to a place I belonged. The museum was my second home.

Mary Gosselin, who headed the Docent Program at the museum, was an excellent teacher and an inspiration to me. We later became friends and she came along to help me out with the bird classes toward the end of my teaching career.

Later on, I became acquainted with most of the curators, and I discovered the potential of a research museum like ours. Curators steeped in a variety of disciplines had an obligation to share their expertise with the community. They were approachable scientists, answered my questions, never made me feel like an idiot when my ignorance was as plain as day. The fact that scientists with a wealth of knowledge about Santa Barbara's surroundings were within my reach was crucial. I had no scientific background, but when I began to take the study of natural science seriously, a whole new world unfolded.

Without the Museum of Natural History and the mentors I had there, any further study of birds and nature would have been impossible. Had I not had an institution where helpful people showed me the ropes, I would have foundered.

When I first showed up at the museum library, Terri Sheridan was there, anxious to help. Depending upon what my latest writing project was, I might spend whole afternoons down in the library basement, going through books in the stacks. I can still smell the cool, stale air down there, as I sat on the little stool gazing at row upon row of books about natural history. Then, gathering my heavy treasures with me, I'd lug them up the stairs to the long tables in the main library room. Here, I chose the volumes I needed. Out came the yellow legal tablet. In long-hand, I wrote. No laptops in those days.

I couldn't bring the books home, as the museum is a reference library. The way to get anything accomplished was to work there in that quiet room with the high ceiling, the fireplace, and the portrait of Max Fleischmann staring down at me. Nothing broke my concentration; I was transported to that place the researcher craves, where the perfect sentences about a certain species of bird, or a particular passage describing the habits of a bear, would send my pen dashing across the paper. My brain was full up, but I wanted more. Pages and pages of notes and citations.

I frequently dropped by the Vertebrate Lab. Here, where the mammals and birds are prepared, is the heart of the museum for bird lovers. Behind the scenes, stored in floor-to-ceiling cabinets, are the "skins," the working collection of birds procured for the museum since its founding in 1916. Here too is the museum's sizable collection of nests and eggs.

Jan Hamber was the first curator of ornithology I knew, because she and Dad had been friends due to their work saving condors. Jan was a great example to me; she was a Cornell graduate and she knew her birds in an era when there weren't many women doing field work.

Later on, Paul Collins and Krista Fahy guided my research. Both local UCSB graduates, Paul and Krista approached birding from a different angle. They weren't "birders" as such, they were biologists with scientific backgrounds. Paul possessed especially broad knowledge about a number of different species of regional reptiles, birds, and mammals.

This was where I belonged, contributing my time to a nonprofit with which I had a history. My Easton grandparents had been big supporters of the Museum of Natural History and the Santa Barbara Botanic Garden. They and their friends, including Dr. and Mrs. Henry Pritchett, and Pearl Chase, believed in supporting these unique institutions, which were exceptional for a community of our size. Dr. Pritchett had been head of the Carnegie Foundation for years.

In addition, my dad had been named a Research Associate in the museum's Department of Anthropology during Travis Hudson's tenure there. So the family tradition continued.

By the late 1990s and early 2000s, I was on the museum Board of Trustees, where I served two terms. This increased my commitment because I understood how complicated a museum's operation as a non-profit institution can be. I volunteered to organize various field trips, and thrived on planning these while mingling with the participants as we embarked on many a nature adventure. Eventually, I became a Research Associate in the Vertebrate Zoology Department, a courtesy title that Paul Collins had bestowed, but one that I held dear.

When I wandered beside Mission Creek on the museum grounds and looked up the steep hill toward the Santa Barbara Mission, I remembered long ago when I visited my grandparents in their house nearby on Garden Street. The back lawn of that house had a stone wall with a gate that opened down toward the shaded hillside to Mission Creek. We girls were never allowed to go down there, for fear of poison oak and other unspoken dangers. But I knew the museum was there somewhere, and in my dreams I thought I might be able to sneak down to it.

15.

Looking Through A Wider Lens

"The achievement of a first-rate thing is so rare that it is worth doing second-rate work for a lifetime in order to produce one or two perfect things. Even if the perfect thing is never actually produced, the life of second-rate achievement is justified by the quest for first-rateness which inspired it."

"Testament of Experience," by Vera Brittain, page 413

Increasingly, my thoughts would hark back to an idea I'd harbored for years, and had mentioned to Dad when he was alive. I wanted to write a natural history of the Santa Barbara region.

My busy mind needed the stuff that makes a knowledge junkie like me feel excited, fulfilled, energized. New facts and figures were dangling in front of me, urging me on. I couldn't get the project out of my head. But was I the one to do it? Surely somebody at UCSB or the Museum of Natural History was more qualified.

I chewed this over and over. I went to Karl Hutterer, then the Executive Director of the Museum of Natural History, and showed him my outline for a natural history book of our region, beginning with geology and ending with animals of the backyard. I was brash, just plunged in, even suggesting the museum might want to be involved. Karl thought it was a good idea.

In addition, my friend Paul Collins, the curator, got me started by loaning me a wealth of material. Without these two, I would never have had the courage to tackle this behemoth.

And as I often did, I went to my sister's house to ask her advice. Ellen had published three books through her gallery, and she was wise about big projects.

"Joanie, tell me. If you could just walk away from this, how would you feel if you decided not to pursue writing this natural history book," she asked. "Would that be a relief?"

I stared at her. I could not stop now. I was too far in. So I made the decision and assembled a sample chapter of the proposed book. I presumed it was a fruitless endeavor, but I had to *act*.

As my focus, I picked a habitat that I knew well, the Carpinteria Salt Marsh. Peter Gaede, talented illustrator and birder, agreed to create a couple of illustrations. And Stuart Wilson, a fine entomologist and photographer, came up with some superb photos, on the chance that this project might fly.

I outlined the book proposal, wrote the text for the chapter, included the art and photography samples, and sent off the packet to a handful of small publishers.

One day in January 2008, while routinely scanning my e-mail, I saw a message from Heyday, a well-known publisher in the San Francisco Bay Area. I jumped up from my computer and called as loud as I could for Gib to come. And the yelp I made was one of pure, unexpected joy. Heyday editor Gayle Wattawa had read my sample and liked my writing.

I drove to Berkeley to meet Heyday's founder Malcolm Margolin, one of those legendary characters that you can't believe exist in the real world. Malcolm had arrived in Berkeley in a VW bus in the 1970s, and he was the real thing — a hippie who'd made a success of himself by writing and publishing books.

But Malcolm was also a businessman. Like many who have made it in the publishing world, he was big on partnerships. And it was he who suggested the Santa Barbara Museum of Natural History might be a help in fundraising for the expenses of publishing the kind of book I'd envisioned. (Malcolm knew Karl Hutterer.)

He said, if you want a regional book like this to see the light of day, you are going to have to spend some time fundraising.

My heart sank. I hated fundraising.

However, I was underestimating our extraordinary museum. Caroline Grange of their Development Department gave me hope and encouragement. Over a period of four years, while I wrote the bulk of the book, the fundraising went right along.

With the museum as co-publisher, people who wished to could give a tax-deductible gift to that institution in support of the proposed book. On behalf of the museum, I wrote to everyone I knew asking for money. I swallowed my embarrassment, deeply convinced that the world needed this book, and not ashamed to ask my friends or museum supporters to step up to the plate.

If you want something badly, you feel it in the pit of your stomach, and the only way to get rid of this is to act. Being passive doesn't work when you're old enough to be a grandmother. I was on fire.

The Role of Geology

As I look back on my outdoor adventures, I see that I was preparing for this book research long before I began writing it all down.

Early on in my life, the mountains, their shapes, the hidden forests and the montane birds had drawn me in. I wanted to know why they were arranged in this or that direction, what valleys I had to cross to get to them.

I was in love with the land, but I didn't know the science behind ridges and rivers. I didn't know how they were formed or why they were here. I knew little about geologic time.

In 1994, I had been frequently flying between Santa Barbara and Sacramento, because Gib's mother, to whom I was close, was ill with cancer, and I visited her there. As the little commuter plane hummed its way from north to south on the return trip to Santa Barbara, I would sit with my binoculars looking down at the land beneath me.

There I was, obsessed by a bunch of mountain ranges from the window of a plane.

NATURE JOURNAL: MAY 29, 1994
Flying Over Santa Barbara Backcountry

On a clear spring day, I see below me the dry, humped foothills of the Temblor Range as the plane banks to start its approach toward my backcountry. I look east at the flat Carrizo Plain and the white sandy playa of Soda Lake in the distance. Mt. Pinos emerges on the horizon — big and round with purple haze gathered at its feet. This, the highest mountain in our region, is surrounded by other peaks that lean up against it. And the whole Mt. Pinos group is nicknamed the Big Knot, I later learn. It's obvious why from up here: the Temblor, the Caliente, the Sierra Madre and the San Rafael ranges strike out in a northwest direction, like ribbons from a knot. Between the ranges lie the valleys, some with dry riverbeds as they make their way to the Pacific.

Soon enough, we fly directly over the Sierra Madre range. Roads and firebreaks scar the tops of the mountains here. I can't see the potreros, because we're too far west, but I can follow the way the Sierra Madre range curves east and hooks into the San Rafaels, forming a horseshoe. Then there's far-angled Madulce Peak — a stony monster of a mountain — and at last closer, closer and we're over the north side of Big Pine Mountain. My Big Pine. In surprising detail, I see the green coniferous forest and even the chokecherry patch with the jeep road running through it.

In the forest, where the thick-trunked incense cedars and slender white firs grow, that's where my heart lies. I can imagine the steep north slope, the smell of the

*pines, the Western tanagers singing from the treetops, the
chickadees popping in and out of nest cavities. Soon, I'll
be studying the birds for another season.*

*Perhaps my precious Big Pine Mountain exists more
in my imagination than as a real place. But I know this
spot is a fantasy that my mind revisits, a refuge of peace
and renewal.*

*Closer still, I see Lake Cachuma slide by beneath
the wing of the plane. And then — quick as a minute
— the sea! The bright, aquamarine ocean and yellow
Guadalupe Dunes are below us.*

*The plane circles back along the coast, getting ready
to land in the tiny Santa Barbara airport that I've known
for years.*

I'm home.

So scant was my knowledge about the geology of our region, I sensed it would be the most difficult chapter to write. So I attacked it first.

Professor Bruce Tiffney was on the museum's Board of Trustees with me, and we discussed paleontology one day in his office at UCSB. Being a paleobotanist, Bruce had access to all the online research papers, which, at the time, weren't available to the average person who wasn't linked into the university's educational network. And then he hinted at which animals and plants inhabited our area millions of years ago: three-toed camels in the Cuyama Valley, a clam on top of Tranquillon Mountain, a miniaturized horse in the Sespe region. My imagination went wild.

My first interview was with Dr. Bob Norris, who welcomed me, a total stranger, into the living room of his home. A renowned UCSB professor of geology, Bob was about to finish his own book on the geology of Santa Barbara County. He possessed that rare gift of making complex ideas seem simple. Yet when he started talking about the radiolarian chert fossils on Figueroa Mountain and casually mentioned that they were derived from an ancient sea, I glimpsed the scope of the material I didn't know. It was huge.

Another concept that had to be explained was the theory of plate tectonics, that is, the movements of surface chunks of our planet's crust, and how they've influenced the way our land looks now. Professor Tanya Atwater, arguably the most famous person in my high school class, had superb educational outreach skills. After talking with her, I could explain the complexities of geologic history to my readers. The online diagrams showing how our Santa Ynez Mountains ended up traveling from the San Diego area, to their present east-west orientation along the south central coast, started to make sense. Tanya had a flare for translating scientific papers into accessible knowledge for teachers.

However, I had to wade through other challenging references on my own. To be honest, the biggest hurdle in writing what had by now been given the title "A Naturalist's Guide to the Santa Barbara Region" was learning how to read a scientific paper. I confess that when I first started to peruse the research, I felt intimidated. But with time, I learned to cut to the heart of the abstract (the summary) of the scientific experiment that was being presented. Scientists like jargon, but you have to learn how to get to the meat of what they're saying. If you can read, you can do it. Often, the results of a good research paper can be stated in one sentence.

When I walked away from my desk knowing that I'd understood a complicated idea and had teased it apart to explain to my readers, I was infused with power. I was totally happy.

Thomas W. Dibblee, Jr., known as "the geologists' geologist," was a man who had literally walked every mile of our region's terrain while mapping it. During the course of organizing special field trips for the museum, I was able to meet and talk with Tom. He had grown up on the lovely San Julian Ranch, and our committee planned a day I'll never forget: a hike with Tom up to a nearby ridge overlooking the Jalama Valley, and a catered lunch under the arbor of the historic ranch house.

It was news to me that geology could be mapped. Good field geologists can tell by looking at the earth's surface what went on beneath that surface and what kinds of rocks you could expect to find deep down. Tom had an unparalleled knack for this. He tramped all over remote regions, often sleeping in his car when night came. When in 1947, he suggested to his boss at the time, Richfield Oil Co., that they might dig in certain areas of the Cuyama Valley, they followed his advice, which resulted in a big oil strike (the Russell Ranch Oil Field), together with the discovery of the South Cuyama oil field.

Tom Dibblee retired in 1977 and sometimes volunteered for the Los Padres National Forest. One of my treasured references was a little booklet put out by the Los Padres Interpretive group, which I had found among my father's papers. In it was a map of the San Rafael Mountains with indications of rock types and where they were found. It was so perfect. So easy to understand. Dibblee drew it, of course, but the fact that Dad had saved and underlined parts of it in red made me realize how curious my father always was about everything. I missed him so.

My way of sorting out all that I'd learned about geologic history in our region was to create a big, messy chart in pencil on an enormous piece of butcher block paper. Physically spreading out facts and figures in sequence with columns and dates allowed me to write coherently.

I spent over two years, including interruptions, composing the geology chapter. You see, I'd picked a region with a turbulent geologic history, not some boring place without volcanoes, earthquakes, or subduction events. On the edge of this relatively young continent, the coast of California was right in the thick of it. No wonder I was on fire.

Botany the Easy Way

Compared to geology, other fields of science were easy.

The world of botany in all its intricate beauty lay before me every spring in coastal Santa Barbara, and in summer in the mountains — both locally and in the Eastern Sierra Nevada. And since I was a hiker, I went slowly and examined the plants.

When I first came to the joy of wildflowers, Philip Munz was the authority. I carried his portable Munz flower guides everywhere, including "California Shore Wildflowers," "California Desert Wildflowers," and "California Mountain Wildflowers."

Dad had bought me Munz's "A Flora of Southern California," and I began to try to key plants. I loved the Latin names, the intricacy of the blooms, the way the flowers stayed put so you could try to figure them out. I carried a perfect small plant press on field trips. That way I collected a plant I wasn't sure of, and pressed it flat between two pieces of newspaper, padded on either side with two sheets of green blotter paper and stiff cardboard. The press frame was of balsa wood tightened with a strap. When I got home, I opened the press and there was the now-flattened but still remarkably lifelike blossom or leaf.

In 1985 I went on my first botany field trip, to Jualachichi Summit on Jalama Road. The trip was part of a wildflower class that Ellen was taking at the Santa Barbara Botanic Garden, taught by Steve Junak, and I asked if I could tag along.

And here it came, a bevy of new facts about plants.

Steve showed us a special area of shade-loving, moisture-dependent plants that grew on the north-facing slope of the ridge. Cooled by sea breezes, and sheltered from direct sun, several species were relicts from a cooler age. I saw tanbark oak, wood strawberry and my first closed cone pine, the bishop pine.

Steve explained that Point Conception created a rough division between plants with northern and southern affinities in our state. That was a thunderbolt, a theme that made understanding botany in our county so much easier. Here in Santa Barbara we are in a transition area between Northern and Southern California. No wonder it's so diverse in plant species.

I learned the importance of scientific classification based on similarities among plant families, but I was never diligent enough to recognize the tiny parts of a plant that require examination with a hand lens, sometimes even a microscope. I decided right then to have fun with botany, and realized I'd never get to the level I'd achieved in birding.

Birding is forgiving. The English names are standardized, so there isn't the pressure to learn the scientific names. In botany, plants can be called an array of colloquial names, and nobody really cares, because the Latin scientific name is what identifies the plant. Obviously, I wanted to know the names of the common plants. And that I did, as well as becoming familiar with the plant communities in our region.

The problem with plants is that there are so many of them, compared to birds. For example, roughly 2,000 plant species inhabit Santa Barbara County alone compared to just over 500 bird species.

Again, a keystone book led me forward. Clif Smith, a friend of Dad's and an eminent local botanist, had written "A Flora of the Santa Barbara Region, California," first in 1976, then reprinted in 1998. The importance of this book, which describes all our plants, is its local point of view. Clif himself had explored almost every location he mentioned when it came to where to find certain plants. So if you happened to be along a popular trail or up a particular canyon, you were able to pinpoint the plant you didn't know by seeing where it was commonly found in Clif's book. This was invaluable.

Fortunately, I happened upon a mentor, Cathy Rose. Cathy was tops at making botany user-friendly. She had been an award-winning English teacher, and spent every summer tramping through Yosemite with famous botanists, or scrambling around the canyons of Borrego Springs in spring wildflower season.

Since I spent many summers in the Eastern Sierra, and Cathy had a house there, we'd often meet for spectacular hikes. These were little-known, cross-country hikes that Cathy was familiar with. Dana Plateau, Granite Divide, Shepherd's Crest — lots of tough, steep, exhilarating treks to find hidden plants that only a few die-hards were aware of. Here was Cathy, older than I, and off she went, like a mountain goat up those shale hillsides, way, way up. I was out of breath, but onward she pushed.

I cannot describe how exciting this all was to me. Botany, like so many other disciplines in the natural sciences, is like looking at a catalogue of myriad species. Whether you go up or down on the altitudinal scale, you find similarities within a genus. And once you learn the families, and the most common genera within those families, you can apply those similarities to wherever you are, if you have a good field guide to the plants of a region.

Now, we have the various websites on our phones, which makes it easier. You can look up a photo of any plant in California. But at that time, you would get home after a hard day of hiking and botanizing, and you could examine your plants, keying them out using a local flora. Even a simple guide with photos of flowers is a way to start. I felt I had to put a name to each piece of the botany puzzle I saw before me — whether it was in the mountains, the desert, or right here at home.

Another highlight was field trips with Bob Haller out of the Santa Barbara Botanic Garden. Haller, a former UCSB professor, was tireless. We would get back to Santa Barbara from a field trip to local spots and it was 10 p.m. But we had learned our conifers, or our oaks or whatever was the emphasis of the outing. And there I was, riding along with people who knew what they were doing. I kept my mouth shut. This is how the self-taught student survives: carry a pencil, a notebook, and keep your mouth shut.

Eventually, the Jepson Manual came out, and there was much I had to do to become up-to-date. Interestingly, the introductory material in both editions of that important volume was to be a huge plus in my understanding of our region's climate and plant life for my own book.

Amphibians

I backed away from my focus on birding. The power of widening my research into other fields, and learning fresh facts, filled me with strength. At the same time, I felt I had to learn more than I would ever write. I'd found that out in teaching. In order to explain a concept, you have to dig beyond what you'll tell your students or readers.

Some of the most memorable lessons were those I stumbled upon while wandering around on my own. For example, I was fascinated by the amphibians. Yes, it must've been the chorus frog tadpoles I caught as a child, because I fell in love all over again with frogs and toads. The amphibious lifestyle, the magnificent change — known as metamorphosis — from a water-dwelling creature to a land-lubber, is how frogs and toads survive.

In the book, I wrote about my night in Santa Maria searching for tiger salamanders, but I'd had other nocturnal escapades. The journal entry below describes a night out observing Western toads.

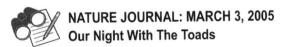

NATURE JOURNAL: MARCH 3, 2005
Our Night With The Toads

Rain, rain, rain. Week after week the winter nights are wet ones. Water, that rare component of Southern California's landscape, lies everywhere: puddles overflowing, creeks running high, wetlands flooding. This is the year to be out watching for frogs, toads, and salamanders. But I don't know that. I am out birding.

Marilyn Harding and I slip on our rubber boots to go walk in the mud around our favorite farm pond, one that lies in a low place among the planted agricultural fields of Carpinteria. Over the years, we've watched this pond. She grew up near here, and she notices the water levels, and the birds that pass through.

This morning we arrive at the pond to look for birds. The pond is full to the brim and it's harboring mallards, ruddy ducks, and coots. Our feet slip and slide as we clomp through chunks of muddy earth. You can't walk without your boots getting clogged and gunked with goo. We love it.

From the neighboring hillside, I hear a strange, high peeping noise. At first I think its a bird, a pygmy-owl — a short "toot" or "peep" given persistently from the gopher hole-pocked hillside. With our binoculars, we carefully scour that slope that rises up several feet away from the pond itself.

At last Marilyn spots him. Almost hidden at the round entrance to a gopher hole sits a frog or toad. That's where the noise is coming from, we guess. It must be an advertising male. We don't know what species it is, but I'm determined to go home and read up on this.

We both decide to come back tonight to see if we can solve the mystery. Surely this animal will be active tonight and we can check him out.

8 p.m. The moon is up and hides behind the clouds. Shadows play over the ag fields. Very still and quiet.

The sound of a coyote barking from a distant field startles us. Across the valley, another coyote answers.

We grab our flashlights.

We begin to walk slowly through the puddles, then crawl under the fence.

Now we notice there's a row of birds spaced at intervals along the edge of the pond: black-crowned night-herons, medium-sized herons with black backs and white forefronts. Their favorite food is frogs. Their bills are sharp.

The birds stare fixedly at the edge of the pond and the muddy slope surrounding it. When we get there, we see why.

It's mating night at the pond for western toads!

And I'm hearing over and over again that soft chirping sound, the sound of the males calling for the females. The females, of course, are in control. They're the ones that, like most amphibians, journey cross-country to the nearest pond to find a male. And the males are waiting, oh yes, they are waiting. And as soon as the female comes near the pond, she's jumped on by not one, not two, but three of the eager males. This frog sex is called

amplexus, and it appears to go on all night. For hours,
these males hope that their genes will be the ones to
fertilize the female before she lays her eggs.

Western toads inhabit gopher or ground squirrel
burrows during most of the year, only coming to the
ponds to mate. And what I'd heard that morning was
the call of the male toads, the soft "peeping" call, just
practicing for the evening's activities.

So here we are, in the moonlit night, the deadly row
of night-herons waiting for an unwary toad, and the sight
of hundreds of toads hanging onto each other at the edge
of the pond.

Western toads don't have the typical larynx of most
frogs, so they can't give the full-throated croaking sounds
most frogs make. But whatever their noise, it seems to
be working with the females. Marilyn and I feel like
we've been to an X-rated movie — not much foreplay
but lots of sex . . . .

A Community Effort

I could fill pages with the names of individuals who helped me with this book-writing endeavor, this compilation of knowledge from a multitude of sources. I learned that certain scientists at the top of their field are extremely generous with their time. They welcomed my intrusion, or so they said. They shared online versions of scientific papers they'd written (this was before some papers were not as widely available as they are now), and allowed me to accompany them on field trips.

Picture this, a housewife affiliated with the museum contacts a university professor or a curator and says she's writing this or that type of book. Well, you'd never heard of her, and you said sure, come and talk to me . . . probably secretly thinking oh no, what a waste of time.

But for the most part, these authorities never, ever made me feel frivolous or stupid.

There's one person in particular without whose extensive library of science books I could not have proceeded, and that's Larry Ballard. Larry is one of a kind in that he's a botanist first, but he's also a birder and a talented naturalist. We are of the same generation; we still use books as references. Granted, there's more online now than when I first started writing my book, but I craved the written word without a screen behind it. Whenever I needed a book or some background in a subject, I contacted Larry first. Indeed, his willingness to share reference materials with me and to guide me through a maze of questions, whatever the subject, were crucial to the completion of the book.

When you write your heart and soul into a book, people come forth to help. Peter Gaede and Stuart Wilson, my patient partners, were in from the beginning, and my gratitude to them is boundless. But as I wipe tears from my eyes in writing these words, there were so many unsung heroes who may never know how much their support and help meant to me when I finally launched "A Naturalist's Guide to the Santa Barbara Region."

Northern Pygmy-Owl
(C. Marantz)

Great Gray Owl (C. Marantz)

Hepatic Tanager
(H. Ranson)

Grace's Warbler
(C. Marantz)

TOP: *Zone-tailed Hawk* (H.Ranson)

MIDDLE: *Black-headed Grosbeak* (R. Goodell)

Western Tanager (author)

Osprey (G. Kincaid)

Hooded Oriole (R. Goodell)

Bonaparte's Gull (G. Kincaid)

Pacific Loon (G. Kincaid)

Parasitic Jaeger - juvenile (C. Marantz)

Phalaropes in migration (D. Pereksta)

Western Sandpiper - adult (G. Kincaid)

Red-necked Phalarope (D. Pereksta)

Semipalmated Sandpiper - juvenile (G. Kincaid)

Western Sandpiper - juvenile (G. Kincaid)

Curlew Sandpiper (J. Hardie)

Bar tailed Godwit (W. Fritz)

Nazca Booby (C. Scotland)

Broad-winged Hawk (B. Hacker)

Tristram's Storm-Petrel (D. Pereksta)

Blue-winged Warbler
(C. Scotland)

16.

2018: A Year To Remember

After "A Naturalist's Guide to the Santa Barbara Region" was published in 2013, I entered a golden period. The reaction from the Santa Barbara community of nature lovers and natural history buffs was overwhelmingly positive. With the help of the Museum of Natural History and others, I had made a contribution to the literature of the Santa Barbara region. My cup runneth over.

Since 2000, our daughter, Jenny, and her husband, Kevin, had settled in Los Angeles, where they had careers on the staff of the UCLA Law School Library. I was excited to have them nearby, but nothing prepared me for the arrival of grandchildren. I was bowled over by the love I felt for those two adorable kids — Alex and Annabel. From the time they were toddlers, they visited Gib and me, often for a week or two at a time. Every chance I could, I took them out in nature.

I was able to share many of my discoveries from the book. Ellen and I would load up our grandchildren on a day when the tide was super low, and we'd have adventures among the tidepools at Coal Oil Point.

Alex and Annabel and their cousins found out how much fun it was to collect the creatures we found, and put them in a bucket full of saltwater, all to be gently released at the end of our visit.

One summer when Alex was staying with us, we sat down to dinner with a coast range newt floating in a glass bowl full of creek water as a centerpiece. We'd hiked up Cold Spring Trail, and carefully netted a lovely orange newt, one of many that Alex's sharp eyes spotted. I knew it was wrong to bring it home, but the newt was simply on loan and went right back into the creek after dinner. When you're ten years old, this sort of stuff is cool. I knew I had to get my licks in while I could, because once the teen-age years hit, all bets were off.

Meanwhile, Gib and I were able to take some great cultural trips to Western Europe. And when I returned, I'd write up a blog for my website, http://joaneastonlentz.com/, which I'd launched to publicize my book. Whenever we traveled, I fit in a day or two for birding, usually with a knowledgeable guide, and I found satisfaction in summarizing these adventures with a blog on my website. But it was so impermanent. I longed for another writing project.

Since 1999, Ellen and I had parked all those cardboard file boxes from our parents' house in a waterproof storage shed on my property. Stacked to the ceiling, the boxes contained letters, photos, diaries, scrapbooks, and family memorabilia going way back.

At first, I was filled with anticipation. I would get this chaos organized. Box by box I labelled and categorized the contents. There might be a book in here. Would I want to compile a family history by putting together the genealogical materials that my father had acquired? When I mentioned that I was contemplating writing a family history, people who had known my parents exclaimed in delight. My parents and grandparents were held in high esteem here in Santa Barbara. I was proud of their achievements.

Original material sat right there in front of me, loads of it. I pored over letters, sorted through manuscripts, tossed out duplicates. Torn between the duty of preserving the Eastons and the Fausts in their glory, and a desire to write a book about my own life, I grew increasingly uncomfortable.

Several of my friends were happily delving into their family histories and writing them up for the next generation. I forced myself to give it a try. I was the oldest daughter. It was my responsibility to research Great Grandfather Olney's Civil War service, or Grandmother Easton's involvement in the Garden Club of Santa Barbara. And here was Grandfather Faust, otherwise known as Max Brand, the famous Western writer, like Zane Grey or Louis L' Amour; indeed, he already had his own collection of material at the Bancroft Library at U.C. Berkeley.

After months of work on three different versions of a family history, it all ended up in the trash. The stuff belonged to other lives. I was suffocated by personal letters and oral histories. Founding colonists, Episcopal ministers, outstanding lawyers — their stories were intriguing, but they didn't belong to me. Smothering me, in layer after layer, the achievements of my ancestors, including my own adored parents, were burying me.

As a naturalist with a passion for birds, I wanted to share my own experiences.

Slowly, it dawned. There's a book here, but it lies outside of these boxes. My parents had already written books about their lives; much of the family material of historical interest should go to the UCSB library, where there's a Robert E. (Grandfather) and a Robert O. (Dad) Easton collection. But there won't be a book outlining who did what from me. Writers want their own story told, and they are formidable when their minds are made up.

I wanted to write about my own life, the one about me and the birds.

Meanwhile, in recent years I'd harbored an uneasy feeling. When it came to birding and writing, a frightening sense of urgency swept over me at intervals. When I asked my close friends, they didn't share the feeling that time was running out, or that our bodies might be running down. They weren't worried. Everyone was meeting the challenges of getting older, discovering that hearing aids were great for birders, making an extra visit or two to a doctor. No big deal.

Not me. I could not forget that time was ticking away. The older I got, the more anxious I became to reach my goals. I had pieces I wanted to write, places to go, birds to see.

I felt the gun in my back, the precipice looming into which I might tumble. I had to hurry, hurry to get the living in, get the experiences churning over. I often mentioned this to my family and others who knew me. They laughed. My daughter said, "Mom, you're so young and full of energy, relax, enjoy life!" And my friends said, "I don't feel that at all; I just want to kick back and relax now . . ." Did I have a premonition of what was in my future?

Winter 2018:
Mud and Disaster in Montecito

We got the automatic alert on our phones: a big storm, the first of the season, was headed our way. Weather charts were ominous; I worried because I'd never seen such devastation as the recent Thomas Fire had caused in the mountains above Montecito. The fire had started in early December 2017, and burned until early January. It was the first indication that nature as we knew it may be changing forever. But I didn't have an inkling, nor did anyone else, of just what a hideously "perfect" storm lay ahead.

We were told to evacuate, but were in the voluntary area so we stayed. We had heard of evacuation fatigue and we figured lots of people had it. Living in an area south of East Valley Road (Highway 192), many of us had been told not to worry, that those who lived closer to the burn in more upslope properties had more to fear.

How little we knew.

I slept restlessly, my phone ringing its alarm tone from time to time. About 3:30 a.m. on Jan. 9, I heard the raindrops. It started raining harder, but nothing to worry about. After all, we'd been through heavy rain before. And we sure needed it at this point.

I got up to check the towels, with which I'd lined the thresholds of the deck doors to prevent flooding. I looked to the north, up toward the mountains where an orange glow lit up the sky. Was it fire in the Upper Village? But rain was pouring down, so whatever fire had started was probably okay. Later, I found out it had been a utility pole uprooted by the mud flow that had fallen on a gas pipe, igniting a set of flames. Two houses had been destroyed and several people were badly injured. The rain continued to pound on the roof, then the power went out. We went back to sleep.

Still sprinkling on and off, the skies were gray and cloudy. I went to my car and backed it out, charging my cellphone's battery (we were so hopelessly unprepared for emergencies then). Marilyn, who lives nearby, was walking into the driveway clutching her umbrella. We thought we would walk over to Montecito Union School to see what was happening. We couldn't understand all those helicopters that whined overhead — flying so low, never a good sign.

As we approached the school parking lot, we saw two yellow-suited, emergency responders resting in the back of their truck. The young men were covered with mud, totally exhausted. They told us they had been up for hours rescuing people. We were aghast. You mean you actually pulled people out of creeks? Yes, and from rooftops where they had been stranded. Marilyn and I stared at each other. Living where we did, we were blind to the fact that people near the creeks, which had choked and overflowed with mud and debris, were in critical danger. We had never experienced a debris flow, never heard of a mudslide.

We looked up to the mountains again and saw wisps of smoke. The smell everywhere was acrid, toxic, as if odd substances were being unleashed: plastics, metals, sewage. It reminded me of days during the Thomas Fire, before we had to evacuate for nine days. Then, it wasn't only vegetation burning, but the contents of homes and people's belongings.

Gradually, as Gib walked one way and I walked another, we saw the utter devastation that had taken place only a few blocks from us, of which we had been unaware during the night. I walked along Schoolhouse Road to Hot Springs Road. Looking south, the bridge that for years had sufficed to cross Montecito Creek — gone. The guardrail was ripped aside, and monstrous eucalyptus trees with 15 foot-high root balls lay in the mud. The whole of Hot Springs Road was a river of mud, especially at the "triangle" in front of Casa Dorinda.

But I dared not walk that far down. Policemen were keeping people away. Onlookers were told to stay back. And then I heard the word "bodies." Yes, dead bodies were being found. This was serious and I began to quietly cry, to mourn those poor, unsuspecting souls who had been terribly unlucky. Seeing the power and violence of the destruction was like viewing a war zone. Mud levels had risen above windows in the houses that still stood, silent, ravaged, empty.

Power lines looped down to within inches of the ground along Hot Springs Road. Utility poles lay turned over like matchsticks — tall, metal utility poles that reached to the sky, now downed in a mud bath several feet thick. Who knew *when* we'd ever get electricity, wifi, cable again?

The sky was beginning to clear and the showers stopped. A beautiful rainbow spread above Montecito. I hoped it was over and everything would turn out fine, but that was dreaming. It had just begun.

As the hours dragged on and the following night turned to morning, we decided to leave. All of Montecito needed to evacuate. The job of cleaning up and putting together a temporary infrastructure so that people could live in their homes again would take weeks. Gib and I were out of our house for 26 days in total.

I packed in a second, threw things helter-skelter in suitcases, left the refrigerator full of food and departed. A few folks on our street were staying in place, but most were leaving, especially those of us without power. From then on, we were gypsies, eventually landing in a condo loaned to us by an acquaintance who appeared out of nowhere and offered it to us.

If we needed to get back to our house for any reason during this permanent evacuation period, we had to park our car and ride with a sheriff or police officer to gain access. We had medicines to collect and a few other essentials, so one day we rode back through Montecito in the back of a cop car.

As we were driven along the streets of our devastated Montecito, tears came to my eyes again as I saw what had happened. We learned that 21 people lost their lives and two others were never found. Unsuspecting people who just happened to be in the wrong place during the debris flow had been carried away, killed or injured, with all they owned destroyed. I grieved for them and I felt guilty that we had made it through unscathed.

One of the officers told us we had five minutes to collect our items. But when we opened the back door and smelled the kitchen, I begged them to let me fill some plastic bags with the rotting food in my refrigerator.

The officers were nice — always. It took an extra ten minutes, but I got that food into the garbage can and I was able to calm down. Our house looked forlorn, but there it was, waiting for us. Think of those who had an empty lot and a pile of wood and concrete to call home now. One of my buddies, Alice Van de Water, a birder, had been trapped in her dining room by a wall of mud, been rescued by the Fire Department, and now faced a ruined home.

Meanwhile, because we only had one car, my birding friends were kind enough to pick me up and take me out. It was delightful to be birding again, to get my mind off my transient lifestyle, to get back to my touchstone.

At last, on Jan. 26, we were allowed home. The first thing I did was drive over to Carol Goodell's house to see the damage there. I knew it had been extensive, but nothing prepared me for the sights I saw on East Valley Lane, adjacent to San Ysidro Creek. Mud was everywhere, having destroyed the driveways of our good friends — Brian and Joanne Rapp, and Bob and Carol Goodell. I saw metal dumpsters crumpled like Tinker Toys. Mansion after well-built mansion lay in ruins, wrecked by mud flowing through and around them. A field of giant boulders, logs, and mud, that's what the former shady creekside area had become.

The same situation had occurred at my favorite place: Cold Spring Creek where the trailhead meets East Mountain Drive. Here, where the mudflow could be measured by looking up at a sycamore tree that had a mudline twenty feet high, I saw what they meant by debris flow. Ripping gas lines and water lines before it, a wall of mud and burned detritus had hurtled through that canyon. Cresting the debris basin dam, the flow gathered even more power as it overflowed the creekbed. For years,

I had hiked up East Mountain Drive to the Cold Springs trailhead and then onto the trail itself. But now the trailhead was gouged, the old creek crossing was a steep crevasse lined with boulders, the lovely riparian vegetation that used to grow on either side of the creek had vanished. What remained was a sunny, wide field of rocks.

Sadness overcame me. Watching the accelerated pace of environmental change left me unmoored, as though stranded in an earlier era. Fires and debris flows this big are environmental cascades affecting us into the next hundred years. The landscape is altered forever.

When the rainwater hit those burned slopes, nothing held. The rain was like pouring water on a waxed surface, and if there were boulders sitting on that surface, they just rolled right down along with everything else. By the time the water collected in the creeks, it was a swirling torrent moving at 30 miles per hour. And because boulders are round and slide easily, down they came off the hillsides. After all, they are round because they've been pounded that way by *centuries* of rolling downward.

We know this from studying geologic time, but we're seeing the immediate results in this mudslide. Every so often the cog slips, the wheel of evolution moves, the mutation sprouts, and change happens. For centuries, change may move slowly, but certain catastrophic events, whether due to climate modification or random chance, advance the clock.

Interestingly, most people have a glorified view of the natural world as a benign adjunct to the Anthropocene (the human) Era. Nothing could be further from the truth. The basic principles of all the natural sciences illustrate that humans have only a certain amount of control over what occurs on our planet. Survival is key, whatever the organism. We each are part of a much bigger story than our own. That's why I like studying biology; not everything is warm and fuzzy, comprehensible, and computed. Oh no . . . .

Summer–Fall 2018:
Birding At Its Best

In hindsight, an event like the debris flow in Montecito isn't unexpected when viewed as part of California's volatile weather pattern.

Already prone to drought and flood, our weather situation is exacerbated by climate warming. In the last decade, drought, intense wildfires, and occasional floods were the norm. Scientists predict these extreme events will happen more frequently in the future.

The same is true for our offshore waters which comprise a sort of litmus test for what's happening in the vast Pacific Ocean. The waters of the Santa Barbara Basin in our Santa Barbara Channel, just offshore, reflect the "flickers" in climate — the warming and the cooling that might be initiated by weather phenomena great distances away. For example, when sea surface temperatures change and we have an "El Nino" event, warm waters flood through the ecosystem affecting kelp beds, tidepool organisms, and birds in the channel.

Fast-forward to current conditions in our offshore waters: researchers taking core samples from the bottom of the channel found an acidification rate twice as fast as the global average, making it difficult for crabs, clams, and oysters to build their shells. This may be a result of increased carbon dioxide caused by man-made emissions, or it could be a normal weather fluctuation caused by one of those climate "flickers" that originate way out in the Pacific, otherwise known as the Pacific Decadal Oscillation. Disagreements abound.

Since 2013, local birders had known of the change occurring in water temperatures, because it was reflected in bird life. Boobies are a group of birds related to pelicans that frequent subtropical waters off the Pacific coast of Mexico all the way to the Galapagos. Normally considered rare around here, the brown booby, a silly-looking bird with a big bill that dives for fish, had been seen regularly. By 2019, the boobies were to record successful nesting for the first time on Sutil Island, a deserted rock offshore of Santa Barbara Island out in the channel.

As time went on, this warm water event — not a classic El Nino but a definite plume of warm water offshore — drew several species of boobies to the Channel.

In sum, I was excited to hop on a boat with lots of other birders and explore what was out there.

NATURE JOURNAL: JULY 25, 2018
Pelagic Trip Toward San Nicholas Island

We're off in the gray dawn, chugging slowly out of Ventura Harbor with a boat full of birders. These well-organized pelagic trips, run by Ventura leader Dave Pereksta, quickly fill with birders from all over.

What I notice, now that I own a little entry-level zoom camera, is the fancy camera gear. All the serious birders carry top cameras. The few that aren't serious birders are serious photographers. I slink to the side as these people rattle off the shots when a bird skims across the water. "Tat-tat-tat-tat-tat-tat-tat-tat" they clicked away in burst after burst. Afterward, each photographer is glued to the camera playback screen trying to see what the camera saw. The camera's eyes are faster than ours — a point that was to be made over and over on this adventure.

The difference between this and other pelagic trips I've been on is that there are scads of birds to see. Seabirds (called pelagic birds), which come to land once a year to nest, ply the ocean waters of the world searching for food.

For example the sooty shearwaters, looking like plump, dark brown gulls, are gorging themselves on the squid and anchovies. Many are so stuffed they barely clear the water after pattering along the surface with both feet to become airborne. Sooties have a graceful flight pattern, first one wing-tip skimming the waves, then the other.

But these sooties are far from home, feeding in California waters. They nest way down in the Southern Hemisphere on small islands off New Zealand and Australia.

All of a sudden a shout goes out from the top deck: "Cook's petrel!"

The "gadfly" petrels, known as Pterodromas, are the holy grail of pelagic birders, and I've never seen one before. Named for their erratic flight (evading gadflies or horseflies), Pterodroma petrels are also true wanderers. This species, Cook's petrel, nests only on islets adjacent to the North Island of New Zealand.

This graceful Cook's petrel is snowy white below, with slender wings coming to a point; it's got a marvelous way of arcing up high in flight, then zooming down skimming across the water. We even see some Cook's sitting on the water, feasting on small bait-fish.

Following along this edge of the undersea Santa Cruz Basin, in the waters deep beneath our boat, we hit more pay dirt — storm-petrels. If you want to know what a storm-petrel looks like, think of a large swallow darting in front of the boat, that's your storm-petrel. Swallows are difficult enough to get your binoculars on, but try this with the boat bobbing up and down and these tiny birds flying fast away from you.

I stand at the bow, refusing to be elbowed out by any of the top birders, including a couple of the leaders on the boat. I'm hanging onto the railing obnoxiously, reluctant to go get a snack or sit down. If you lose your place, you might miss whatever bird flies across the bow, plus you have a good view of the horizon.

Finally, we arrive in what are technically Santa Barbara County waters, the area surrounding Santa Barbara Island.

I decide to walk back to the stern, see what's happening back there. This is the realm of Wes Fritz, the guy who's a master chummer. He dispenses treats that attract seabirds. First it's popcorn, kept in a huge plastic bag hanging from the railing. He reaches in and flings a handful toward the boat's wake. But when he wants to go full bore, he picks up his secret "juice" jug, which is filled with an essence of fish oil that will "lay down a slick" if he pours it into the ocean. This juice, which seabirds can smell from miles away, is irresistible. Hunger lures them in.

So here I sit, comfortably chatting with Wes and friends, when a cry goes up "Booby, booby, stop the boat!"

Since we're approaching Santa Barbara Island, everyone is expecting it to be a Brown Booby, the common species. But no.

"It's a white booby!" And the message gets up to the wheelhouse, the boat slows down. Turns out it's an entirely different Nazca booby from the one we had seen earlier today (in Ventura County) and, because we're in Santa Barbara County waters, I get to count it as my 450th Santa Barbara County bird. I'm bursting with happiness. Everyone goes nuts, and the Nazca booby just keeps on flying off into the distance while we all hug each other in shock.

On Sutil Rock off Santa Barbara Island, we count nearly forty brown boobies, no longer a rare sight. We gaze far up to the top of the rock, then spy the adult boobies courting. Sitting atop rudimentary nesting

*mounds, they proffer each other sticks and rub bills.
Are we on a desert island off Baja or really in the Santa
Barbara Channel? Difficult to believe.*

*But it was after the trip was over that the unbelievable
part came to light.*

*You know how the camera can be faster than the
human eye? Well, after these bird experts who were
photographers got home and looked through their
images, they found out they'd seen really rare birds
that were only caught on camera!*

*This was slightly annoying to many participants, but
I say, so what?*

*So what if we missed a gorgeous Tristram's storm-
petrel, an extremely rare vagrant from Japan. Same
situation with a wedge-rumped storm-petrel: at the time,
nobody, not the leaders or the participants, actually
called out this bird. But the camera lenses had captured
the wedge-rumped, and that was the proof that we'd
actually had these two birds on the voyage. But did we?
Does it count if you don't know you saw a bird at the
time but the camera proves you did?*

*I've seen the textbook-gorgeous photo Dave Pereksta
has of the Tristram's. Did he know he had it, and would
he count it? I have no idea, but the more important
point is that these are records of bird species that can
be sent to the California Bird Records Committee. These
extraordinary seabirds will be included in the literature,
regardless of who saw what.*

*Watching all of this life in the sea is intoxicating.
An ecstasy of appreciation for the vastness of the
ocean, these exceptional seabirds, and the fun of going
birding on the ocean — it all adds up to my best pelagic
adventure!*

The fall of 2018 brought more new discoveries and appreciation, as these two September and October journal entries show.

 NATURE JOURNAL: SEPTEMBER 27, 2018
Hawk Watch in Montecito

I seize every opportunity I can to be outside, to see it all this fall: the creek bottom at Carpinteria Creek, the Tijuana tipu trees full of warblers, the eucalyptus trees full of 'lerps' on which the warblers feed in Goleta, and every afternoon: up to Bella Vista to hawk watch.

I've never done this, never let myself go as much as I wanted to. My body protests. I push on.

I can't live without being an observer at this fall movement of hawks, flycatchers, warblers, sandpipers. These birds of all kinds traveling through our space, this narrow coastal plain where the mountains meet the sea. All these species migrating south. In order not to miss out, you have to go birding every day.

One of my favorites is the hawk watch on Bella Vista Drive, a winding road that leads across Romero Creek in Montecito, and ascends to where you can see the range of the Santa Ynez Mountains to the north.

Here, you park your car, and have a view of the ridge-top straight above.

After the severe Thomas Fire burn last winter and the ensuing mudslide debacle, these mountains look like a desert. Their sandstone bedrock exposed, boulders and rocks of all sizes lie scattered on the steep slopes. Small patches of green shrubs at the base indicate regeneration, but it's largely a landscape of scorched branches against a mountain wall.

A water tank, an enormous rusted cylinder, lies toppled on one of the distant promontories. I wonder what it was like the night that tank burned, what an inferno it must've been.

Looming above me in the warm fall afternoon, the mountain stretches up to the blue sky above. That's where I'm focusing my binoculars, where the black specks appear. The migrating hawks fly from west to east along the top of the ridge, occasionally crossing the face.

The hawks don't mind about the fire scars, the devastation. They are in it for the topography, for the slant and the wind lift, the boost of hot air to pump them up, then send them on their way. Although stripped of vegetation, the slopes still promote the warm updrafts, and that's what the raptors need.

We aren't skilled at hawk watching here in Santa Barbara. Eric Culbertson, a Carpinteria resident, is the one who single-handedly figured out this spot on Bella Vista where you can watch the hawks come over the Santa Ynez Mountains.

Yesterday a hefty golden eagle came soaring low, passing from west to east and then back again, with good views as it flew close. We could see the buffy head and undertail, the large brown-fingered wing-tips, and the sheer size of the bird compared to a red-tailed hawk.

By far the most common raptor is the red-tailed hawk, and some of these aren't migrating at all, they're locals — hanging out and riding the thermals for the heck of it. Today is the chosen day, Sept. 27, within the window of time when the scarce broad-winged hawks come through. We've looked at the Golden Gate Raptor Observatory numbers online, and yesterday they had many broad-winged hawks pass by up in the Bay Area.

*The day is warm with fog hanging just offshore.
I arrive around 3 pm, to be joined shortly by other
birders. Our binoculars are glued to the ridgetop.
Suddenly high or low, a speck in the sky turns into a
sharp-shinned hawk or a Cooper's, they circle briefly,
then zoom, off they go to the east. Riding over the
ridgetops, then flying fast, fast, fast away from us along
the sloping south sides of the mountains.*

*As we stand there chatting, we nearly miss the four
broad-winged hawks!*

*John Callender walks over to look to the west. He
sees a small hawk flying toward him. Then we spot
more hawks as they circle up and up. Small hawks,
very pale underneath, just tilting and rising upward
with the thermals. The immatures are whitish with a
dark trim round the outside edges of the wing tips and
hindwing. Picture a miniature red-shouldered hawk,
with fat wings, and white underparts, that's a broad-
winged hawk.*

*And so the four broad-wings lazily soar into the
distance, heading east and low, out over the coastal
plain, eventually drifting closer to the mountains to hold
onto that rising warm air.*

*These broad-winged hawks, seldom seen in Santa
Barbara, are on their way to South America. If they're
immatures, perhaps the birds are discovering a new
route south. We don't know. We don't know if they
fly down the interior valleys and hop over the ridge
here at Romero Canyon.*

*All we can do is gasp in astonishment, as these
lovely hawks glide south. Watching hawk migration
is a new window into the world of birds for me.*

NATURE JOURNAL: OCTOBER 13, 2018
Blue-winged Warbler

Just when I thought it was all over, the best fall I ever had kept on giving . . . today.

I was thinking it was done. The excitement passed. But there was a southern storm in the L.A. area with rain & lightning. And Nick Lethaby had posted a message to the listserve that this could be good for migrants from the north, because they'd be stopped in their tracks right here in Santa Barbara, if we got lucky. Not sure if that's why Nick himself was out birding Carp Creek this morning, but when my cell phone rang, it was Nick with news. He'd found a blue-winged warbler at Carp Creek north of the 8th Street bridge, but he'd looked for it for an hour and couldn't refind the bird.

Oh no, it's gotta be there! Marilyn is up for a chase, so off we go together. We park on the east side of the 8th Street bridge, and walk across it. Then, slipping and sliding, we grab onto willow branches to break our downward scoot, and land in the creek.

The creek bed is an easy, dry walk right down the middle. Nick is there, and pretty soon, one by one local birders arrive. Nick says he's sure the blue-winged was with a flock that had headed up the creek, so off he goes to search.

But we stay put, our necks craning backward to look up through the brownish-yellow leaves of the cottonwoods. The day is overcast, warm, cloudy and calm — perfect conditions. Where the heck is this bird?

Larry Ballard, standing right beside me, quietly says, "I've got it!" And there it is, in the low-hanging branches of a coast live oak first, then it pops into the cottonwood, a big thick-trunked tree, with masses of yellow leaves to look through.

But I can't see it. I panic. Am I the stupidest one in the group, are others seeing it?

Other folks have spotted the bird, and I'm afraid it'll leave before I get to see it.

Where, where, where? The peeping, supplicant call of the birder with bad eyes, like me.

At last I see a bright yellow warbler from underneath, with a black line through its eye, and I know I've got it. Let it please show me more, please? It does. The soft blue-hued wings display two thin wing bars. The head and breast are of that brilliant yellow, reminiscent of a prothonotary warbler, that orange-yellow breast and crown.

I think it's a first-year male, but it surely is an outstanding warbler, and a first county record. Number 453 in Santa Barbara County for me. Reminding me of a day in fall many, many years ago when a bunch of us stormed through the Santa Barbara Botanic Garden and saw the golden-winged warbler, which, if you come right down to it, is perhaps a more spectacular bird even than this blue-winged. But not by much.

After the excitement of seeing the blue-winged warbler, Marilyn and I make our way down-creek. We are delighted by the common warbler species as they bathe in the remaining puddles. Such beauty, such peaceful moments.

I remember all the times I've walked through that creek with my rubber boots, stepping over the rocks, and there would've been Karen Bridgers, right beside me: "Joanie, we've got to find something good for Paul!"

To find a great fall bird on Carp Creek is to unreel the spool of time back to an era when this place dwarfed all others in its ability to attract migrants in fall. There were no Tipuana tipu trees, no lerp psyllids in the eucalyptus. Now these non-native trees full of bugs are rivaling the traditional places we birded in the fall, but I miss going along the creeks. The old-fashioned way . . .

Since June of that year, when I saw the Mississippi kite, I'd added six new birds to my county list, more than I've added over the last five years. Excitement, changes — climate and otherwise. Warming waters, boobies, Santa Barbara County is on the map for rarities now. Everyone is energized!

17.

Breathless

The year 2018 held another surprise for me and it had nothing to do with birds.

Day to day, I was busier than ever. On October 31, I hiked from the bottom of the road to Pino Alto Picnic Ground on Figueroa Mountain, up to the lookout tower and back, with Florence Sanchez.

On November 4, I wheedled Carol Goodell into accompanying me on yet another chase. The day before, Wes Fritz had photographed a varied bunting (another first county record) at Gaviota State Park, but nobody else got to see it. Flushed in a second, that bunting.

Birders being birders, we couldn't stop returning to the spot . . . just on the off chance . . .

After a rare bird is found, there's a phenomenon that used to be called the Patagonia Picnic Table Effect. It originated in a famous place in Southeastern Arizona, a small town called Patagonia, near where there was a picnic table at a rest stop. Birders would stop there looking for a target bird, like the rose-throated becard. And they'd either see the becard or not, but they'd be on the lookout for other birds, and that's how even *more* interesting birds had been located; birders were now taking the time to seek out what else might be at that location.

Consequently, that day when Carol and I arrived at Gaviota, we saw some neat birds that others had discovered while trying to find the famous bunting. Gray catbird, white-throated sparrow, and palm warbler, to name a few. Other birders had located even more unusual birds earlier in the morning. I chatted with Curtis Marantz and Tom Edell, while feeling perfectly fine.

It was my last day of breathing normally.

The next morning, I woke up slightly out of breath. I didn't worry about it, but it was weird. Nothing to get upset about, a slight panting. I let some days go by. My birthday arrived. I was overbooked.

The breathlessness worsened.

At last I called my doctor, and had a scan of my lungs. Bad stuff going on in there. More days of waiting to see a pulmonologist, who gave me an oxygen tank as a good-bye present. That was when I understood that I wouldn't be able to breathe without oxygen for . . . who knew, surely only temporarily? But what about forever? I had never relied on oxygen before in my life. Terrifying — and anxiety only made it worse. I was panting, panting, always breathless.

That Friday night, my oxygen tank ran out and the new supply was late. Gib was going crazy, and I was sure I'd die gasping for breath on the kitchen floor. We called 9-1-1.

Safely delivered to Cottage Hospital in the ambulance, I would not return home for over a month.

Eventually, they took me upstairs to the Intensive Care Unit. This is where patients with serious pulmonary diseases stay. Doctors make rounds, medical students are doing residencies, and you can watch it all through a window from your private room. Within my room, gathered around me were the most advanced systems of I.V. delivery tubes, respirators, valves, and suction monitors anywhere in the world. Cardiac, pulmonary, gastro, they've got you covered, any kind of critical care.

The doctors flooded my system with Prednisone, an anti-inflammatory steroid. The worst side effect, insomnia, was the special hell I had to go through for the first five nights as I lay unable to sleep.

Don't get me wrong. If you're as sick as I was, you want to be at Cottage Hospital. The night nurses were my favorite: young, top-notch, dedicated, loved their job. They said they looked forward to coming to work every day to watch patients get better. They kept talking about people being cured and walking out. Are you kidding? I was being bombarded by 40 liters of oxygen whooshing out of a giant tube night and day. It was hard for me to believe that I'd ever live a normal life again. Was this thing I had — acute interstitial pneumonitis — going to let me live or die, go forward with restraints, or never go birding again?

Every one of my friends, including my birding buddies, and all my family near and far flooded me with cards and messages of good will. I was afraid to open them. I wanted to see if I was going to be okay. I couldn't bear it. I cried every time Gib visited with his briefcase full of cards and letters. If I didn't survive, I'd be letting every one of them down. So I saved the messages as good luck charms to read when I felt better.

Ushered into another universe, I was blindfolded, rudderless. Where was I supposed to go and what was I to do now? With my mind, that is. You would be surprised how much you count on the future to be "normal." But all semblance of normality was out the window now. No roadmaps here, no guideposts. Just the night aide that empties the bedpan, the stoic nurse giving me meds, and a parade of doctors listening to my chest.

Through stethoscopes, the doctors heard the sound of my lungs —like paper crinkling. They shook their heads. None of the pulmonologists could explain why this had occurred, what caused it, or what the prognosis was. Question after question was hurled into the ether with no answers.

Random events. Stuff happens.

It was inconceivable that this might be out of my control. I knew I was subject to the vagaries of the future, but when it happened — I was hit with a bombshell. I knew I had to adapt to aging, but wasn't that *slowly*? I was felled, cut down with no warning. Here I was on my own, battling, fighting my way back one minute at a time. I thought of myself as so young, so active, in good shape, faithfully attending exercise class, etc. The swift onset: that's the soul-destroying angle. Was I not grateful enough for my fabulous life? I was still thinking in that 1950s mindset.

If you're a good girl and play fair, you can avoid bad things happening. The unfairness of the 1950s mantra, both in its prediction and in its outcome, knocked me flat.

* * *

The first thing I noticed in I.C.U. were the sounds. Like most birders, I'm sensitive to noise.

Above my bed, a computer screen showed a series of horizontal fluorescent yellow, green, white, and blue fluctuating lines moving across a graph: high loops and low ones. For example, when I talked, my white line graph went up and down twice as fast, measured by those sticky things on my body that record heart rate.

However, the most important line was the blue line. It measured the oxygen level in my blood. I needed to stay above 92. After the slightest movement to reach something on the nightstand or to open my mouth to talk, the oxygen sound turned into a full-blown alarm bell if the number fell below 92.

"Joan, you're dropping too fast!" The nurse came hurrying in. "Stop, and breathe in through your nose and out through your mouth!"

I gasped. I reached for air and there was none to be had, none that would penetrate the fistulas of disease that were winding in and around the openings in my lungs. Somebody had put plastic wrap around my lungs and sealed it tightly. Disease had filled the spaces and tissues, some virus we didn't know of. Nobody had answers.

As I lay tossing and turning in the I.C.U., the beeps and pings and whistles drove me mad. I imagined I was in an altered state of nature.

It was man-made, but contained reminders of a world outside these walls where I used to wander and explore. Where I was happiest — birding outside. But since this world was no longer available to me, I created my own in that hospital room.

On the overhead monitor each line emits its signal that registers to the nurse what the body is doing. "Ping-ping-ping" is a friendly reassuring note, reminiscent of the staccato hoot of a Northern Saw-whet Owl.

My favorite was the comforting chirp, the lilting upward swing of the note that said "All's well!" with the oxygen in my blood — the blue line.

I was delighted to find this sound reminded me of the call of the Flammulated Owl.

I lay there in the midst of this high-tech environment, and yet I found the sounds were similar to those I'd heard from the forests, from the field trips to our local mountains, from the owl-watching nights waiting to catch those delicate calls of the Flammulated Owl signaling to its mate.

"Zeeee-oop?, zee-oop?, zee-oop?" Just the hint of an upward note at the end of each "oop," that's how the Flammulated Owl lets itself be known to others of its kind. Impossibly difficult to see these tiny owls, but still, you have the sound, like a miniature waltz, if you are only there to hear it.

And as I lay listening in the hospital, I heard the Flammulated Owl calling from the monitor above my bed. I didn't know if I would ever walk out of there as a person who could still go birding. I didn't know if the computer sound above my bed would ever again be a real owl singing to me in the whispering pines above my tent.

But I knew right then that if I couldn't have that experience, it was a good bet I would still figure out a way to keep birding in my life no matter what.

Old Overnight

From the very beginning, a phrase popped into my brain: old overnight.

Old overnight. That's the way I thought of myself.

When I got out of the hospital, I didn't realize how weak I was. Gib had borrowed medical equipment from the Visiting Nurses Association — a generous non-profit in town. I looked around when I got home. My husband had installed a commode for the bathroom, a stool for the shower, and a walker was parked outside the back door.

It looked like a place for the old and the sick. I shuddered.

This is the beginning, and call it what you will, life *before* death is going to be the challenging part. Death will approach in slow downward plateaus, as Atul Gawande tells us in his marvelous book, "Being Mortal." So either you take a step down to the next level, stop whining, and get on with it, or you pack it in. Your choice.

When the self help books tell me to call upon resilience and to adapt to new restrictions, this is what they mean. Like the birds around me, either I modify my habits to fit the new conditions, or I will not make it.

Moreover, I struggled with other feelings, some I'd admit only to myself.

How many times had I seen a person with a handicap and turned away. Those oxygen tubes coming out of a person's nose are repulsive. I recoiled from disabilities, because I was terrified. I couldn't empathize because I was thinking of myself and how it would affect me, make me infirm, out of the mainstream — old.

Thinking back on it, was I as kind, thoughtful, caring, or considerate *enough* to those who were older or had special handicaps? I recalled some of the struggles Gib's parents and mine fought as they aged. But no, I was too busy being youthful, priding myself on all that I could still do, contemplating with fear and avoidance any change in my active lifestyle or my youthful appearance.

During the last week of my hospital stay, I was placed in the Rehabilitation Center. The days were packed with organized physical therapy. I was given a wheelchair, which I learned to maneuver, and a green oxygen tank was attached to the back of it with life-giving air. I could only walk on my own pushing the tank for short distances, while accompanied by a therapist. When I stood up, my legs felt funny and my feet were like sponges. Having been in bed for three weeks, my limbs had forgotten how to move. And whenever I did anything more than just sit, my blood oxygen level dropped precipitously; I was gasping for air time after time.

All around me in those rooms at Cottage Rehab were examples of courage and determination on the part of the patients, people from all walks of life. I studied their faces, overheard their life stories, realized that accidents, strokes, and unexpected consequences occur. Nobody was warned ahead of time, and yet they'd soldiered on. Now it was my turn. I learned precious lessons there.

When I returned home, Christmas was upon us in a few days. No Christmas tree, no decorations. Lots of family, lots of friends, but oh so tired. I was so, so tired all the time. The extra oxygen was essential, and I was afraid to be without it for even a minute.

Little did I realize that I was beginning a long road — the one that leads to a life coping with chronic disease.

Teaching My Body to Work Again

I have a lung disease for which there's no cure; my lung capacity will continue to deteriorate over time. It's not cancer; I don't have to go through chemo. I am not in pain, at least not now. And, I know what I will die from. When it comes to lung issues, I suspect that my DNA has a faulty chromosome. As a child I suffered from asthma. Lung disease runs in our family; one of my sisters has COPD and the other had emphysema.

The problem is that, typically, a human being requires close to 24,000 breaths of oxygen-loaded air in a day. It's what makes the miraculous body we occupy operate smoothly. A healthy person is hardly aware that they're breathing, so automatic is this hum-drum yet crucial function. But me? My lungs are ravaged by the virus that attacked them, and I retain about half my normal breathing capacity. The scar tissue created by the virus is called fibrosis. It is progressive.

From the beginning, I sensed exercise was the crucial ingredient for my improvement. I had to get stronger, and I set up my own regimen at home.

Brilliant advances in oxygen delivery to patients gave me the freedom to experiment, once I was able to walk around. I have a little oxygen concentrator, which weighs about five pounds. By grabbing oxygen out of the air, this device sends it up my nose via a cannula (nose tube) and I can use it to breathe during exercise and movement of any kind. The machine runs on batteries that need to be replaced every couple of hours.

My earliest exercise routine consisted of me wheeling my walker with the oxygen concentrator in it (attached to my nose by the tube) around and around our paved driveway. The driveway has a small slope. I could feel it every time I went uphill. That was a struggle that never left me, because walking uphill is hard for patients with my disease. The damaged tissues can't supply the blood vessels with enough oxygen when you need it fast, like in climbing stairs or going up a hill.

After two or three circuits, I stopped, sat down on the walker, and measured my blood oxygen level. It was always low, and yet . . . after a minute or two of rest, the numbers started to climb up. I had to practice breathing techniques and make my diaphragm work. The lungs aren't a muscle and they won't recover, but you *can* increase the amount of blood oxygen you process by exercising with oxygen.

Round and round the driveway I walked that winter of 2019, a rainy, cold, and beautiful one. For the first time in years, the drought had lifted. It wasn't gone, but the rains were coming regularly and lightly. The fear of a recurring mudslide in Montecito proved groundless. All of us were celebrating nature's regeneration.

On the Internet I found a collapsible trolley, and I seized the chance to be able to wheel something around that would hold my concentrator. I could use it inside or out. Mobility was key.

Therefore, the original walker sat unused in our back mud room, which was open to the outside, although covered by a roof.

One day I walked out the back door and noticed a pair of Bewick's wrens fussing around that outdoor room. Gib reported that he'd seen one of them going in and out of my walker, which had a small pouch underneath the seat. From then on, the wrens commenced building a nest in my walker.

The wrens provided us with great happiness and eventual heartache. The amount of pliable grasses, leaves, and sticks those two birds brought in was huge. Finally, they made a cup of fluffy down feathers in the top of the jumble, and there they laid six spotted blue eggs. A pair of cats that roamed the neighborhood had the uncanny sense to find that nest, vandalize it, and kill the young brood.

(Note: In 2020, the same pair of Bewick's Wrens had a nest inside the rim of the fluorescent light affixed to the ceiling of the back porch room. Safe, warm, and out of reach, the nestlings successfully fledged.)

Continuing Birding

Let me go back a bit and recall what I had done for the 2018 Christmas Bird Count, held on January 5, 2019. I had been participating in the CBC since 1974, and I wasn't about to stop now after forty-six years.

The day was cold and cloudy with rain threatening. I sat snuggled in my bathrobe in a rocking chair, looking out the window, and counting the birds at my feeders in the backyard. For the first time since becoming a birder, I was housebound for the CBC. My friends did what surveying they could in Montecito, but it was a nasty weather day.

Looking out the window, I carefully tallied the number and species of birds at my feeder. I even saw for the first time a rare subspecies known as the "Cassiar's" junco. This little sparrow, which I didn't recognize at the time, was one of the Rocky Mountain forms of the dark-eyed junco, and we seldom get it here. Subsequently, I was able to get a photo. But I never forgot it was present on the CBC. I was birding the moment I could get out of bed.

Months ticked by. I was referred to a guru pulmonary doctor, who had an office at the UCLA Medical Center, and Gib and I made trips to Los Angeles frequently.

During our first visit, I hung on every word this famous doctor said. Even he was surprised at the suddenness of my "acute event" as they called it. The big unanswered question: was I ever going to get better? Only time and the CT scans of my lungs would tell. Doctors at that high level are like gods, but there's much they don't know. I worshipped this guy. I would've done anything he suggested. He said wait and see.

* * *

Back home, my life slowly became more normal for two reasons.

First, I had the best caregiver in the world, a loving husband. Gib handled everything those first months and still does: laundry, cooking, going to the grocery store, you name it. Perhaps I knew what I was doing all those years ago when I was only 22 and got married. However, I couldn't possibly have anticipated the way I need him now and what a rock he's been.

Second, I grew stronger. If you use supplemental oxygen during exercise, you can train your body to do things it couldn't normally do without oxygen. I was blessed with wonderful rehab therapists.

Gratitude washed over me at the oddest moments. When I slowed down and stopped rushing from one event to another, I noticed these fleeting seconds. I teared up at the most ordinary of times. Particularly when joyful, the tears came rolling down over my plump, Prednisone-swollen cheeks.

I couldn't get over how beautiful ordinary life could be. Every day was the best. Normal was terrific. Sudden feelings of kindness, generosity, and love washed over me as though I were having a religious epiphany almost daily.

Being with my grandchildren was especially moving that first year. To be close to youth, to share their lives for a moment, to see the laughter in their eyes, to help Alex with his driving license ("Let's go driving, Nana!") and to have Annabel up here for her summer vacation ("Let's go shopping, Nana!") caused me to weep quietly in private at my immense good fortune. I'd been given another year.

Through it all, exercise and birding restored my body and soul.

Exercise made me strong so I could be more active, and birding saved my life. I repeat that: birding saved my life.

In the early days, I could always relax on the deck in the sun and watch the birds at my feeder or at the small pond in my garden. I made a cup of tea, and sat outside as much as I could. The beauty of eBird is that I made a list of the species I saw. Making a list set parameters for me, and I felt I was providing data, even though it was only from my backyard. I made lots of Pimiento Lane lists that first year.

Meanwhile, my birding friends didn't desert me, far from it. They were game to take me out birding, my oxygen concentrator in the trolley, extra batteries in someone's backpack. When I was in the car, I had a cord that went to my concentrator which charged my battery, giving me more time. The most difficult part was organizing everything, making sure I was self-sufficient with my oxygen, not to speak of binoculars, camera, my dog Bud on a leash, and so forth.

One day I started laughing and I couldn't stop. My friend, Libby Patten, had the idea and coined the phrase: I was the "Velcro birder," held together by various contraptions. Straps around my neck, my waist, my shoulders. So strong was my desire to go birding, I put up with all of the inconveniences, the frustrations, and the *time* it took to get oneself out the door.

Here I was, draped with gadgets, but I could still go birding!

List of accoutrements for a birding outing:

Ugly black Velcro brace to support my back

Scarf, vest, jacket

Hearing aids to hear the birds sing

Worn-out floppy birding hat

Fanny pack with Bud's treats, my water bottle, Kleenex

Binoculars around neck

Camera hanging off shoulder

Oxygen concentrator on trolley, with extra battery underneath

Sun gloves to protect hands

Phone for keeping the bird list

Bud's leash and hook to attach him to my waistband

As I lay in that hospital bed months before, I never imagined that I would experience the thrill of being able to go birding again. I thought it was lost forever.

I was determined. Bring on the cords that kept getting caught on things, the injured ribs I got from lifting that oxygen concentrator around, the constant breathlessness when I leaned over to change the battery. Birding was there for me. I couldn't go on rough trails or negotiate hills, but I was outside.

I was out in nature, absorbing the fresh air replete with oxygen. And the birds with their sounds. I sensed that old happiness rising within me when I was able to hear the ruby-crowned kinglet's song as it practiced up for spring. I kept track of the pair of red-tailed hawks that perched on a redwood tree near our house.

Figuring out where the pair of red-tails might nest, hearing all the bird sounds with my hearing aids, finding an unusual or rare bird, or even chasing one upon occasion — it was all still accessible. My go-to remedy still worked, and performed wonderfully. Being outside took me away, focused my mind on something other than my bodily state, and kept me engaged with the latest happenings in the bird world. Besides, there's more oxygen outside than in.

I'll admit there are good days and bad days. Walking uphill lugging that oxygen machine is a Sisyphean task. It never gets easier. I learned, though, that no matter how crummy I felt, I was better after a walk outside. Although I ingested a cocktail of drugs every morning, I am convinced it was the natural world that made my body yearn for wellness.

The mental battle is the toughest one. The mind is a demon grasping at horrors and holding onto fear. Panic and anxiety are the worst emotions for an oxygen-deprived body. And what sensitive person with a lung disease wouldn't have them? The runaway mind, the disease like a vine strangling my lungs, pulling me down, inexorably down, down, down. How fast and how much time left, nobody knew.

But I'd made a vow while in my hospital bed. I will finish a memoir describing my life with birds, my growing up in Santa Barbara, my passion for nature in this place I live, if I ever leave this bed.

Writing this book has given me a purpose and helped me heal. I found that while writing in my study, sitting at my desk, I needed no supplemental oxygen. I was quiet, not taking any extra breaths and not talking. I loved the time when I was simply breathing normal air, without the oxygen machine and those two prongs up my nose.

I looked forward to those afternoons of writing, and the more I wrote the more committed I was to sharing my life with others.

To come to this decision, I thought long and hard about what I was saying and why my story might be worth reading.

Epilogue

Can Nature Make You Well?

I grew up in glorious Santa Barbara where I was exposed to nature frequently. Born with a fascination for birds, I embraced being outside as part of my daily routine.

Over recent months, as I have struggled to live as normally as possible despite my lung disease and my need for supplemental oxygen, I examined more closely how I spent time. Would being outside have the same benefits as it did before I got sick? I suspected it would, but I was interested in scientific evidence about the restorative powers of birding and nature.

Can *nature* make you well? I feel better with the sun on my skin and the breeze blowing in my face. My spirits lift when I observe the birds on my property or while walking up and down my street. When I'm calm, outside, being quiet, I can turn off my oxygen machine and listen to the birds. I breathe more deeply outside, feel my fears quiet and my body relax.

And then the novel COVID-19 virus enveloped us, stranded us, turned our worst fears into a human crisis. Of all the people who could be considered high risk to perish from COVID-19, I was the ideal candidate.

Moreover, hadn't I just survived one cataclysmic event, the Montecito mudslide, only to turn around and face another? Humans and nature. This time it's us against the microbes, the novel COVID-19, the invisible virus with the deadly mutation. The virus is harmless until it settles in the mucus of your nose, mouth, or eyes. After that, it mutates and takes the form of a disease, one that's particularly damaging to lungs.

As I write, I am in a state of self-isolation and have been for weeks. I see no one, other than my husband, my sole caregiver. But there's one activity I've not had to give up: going outside for a walk in nature. I can still pick an uncrowded location — although that's becoming more of a challenge — and there I am, oxygen concentrator in tow, binoculars at the ready, bird list queued up on the phone. And soon, my mind is out there, up and away from me, gone from the portents of disease and death. My soul is poured into the soft chips, the loud songs, and the beautiful plumages of spring birds arriving in migration.

And good fortune has accompanied my outdoor pursuits. Rarely, extremely rarely, weather conditions align to bring colorful warblers, tanagers, and grosbeaks, that winter in Mexico, right through Santa Barbara (see Chapter 11). This spring, my garden has been flooded like never before with numbers of these black, gold, yellow, and red birds.

Watching the progress of these migrants as they arrive in my garden, then depart up local canyons, and following the pace of spring migration through reports of others around Southern California, has completely absorbed me. My mind is wiped of coronavirus fears. The only reason I'm breathless is to expound my joy, my ecstasy at this unexpected outfall of birds every time I go outside.

At this time of desperate sadness at many lives lost, of worry about our own vulnerabilities, those of us who notice nature are thoroughly engrossed in another spectacle. That's the connection we birders and naturalists have with nature. When you need it most, it's there for you.

* * *

Was it just me? Had others felt this?

First, I reached for a book on my shelf, "The Moth Snowstorm" by Michael McCarthy (2015), a well-known environmental journalist. I found his premise profoundly moving.

"There can be occasions when we suddenly and involuntarily find ourselves loving the natural world with a startling intensity, in a burst of emotion which we may not fully understand, and the only word that seems to me to be appropriate for this feeling is joy, and when I talk of the joy we can find in nature, this is what I mean.

"Joy hints at an unrestrained enthusiasm which may be thought uncool; perhaps a bit lame, a bit old-fashioned. Joy refers to an intense happiness, but one that is set apart. There's an overtone of something more, which we might term a spiritual quality. It looks outward, to another object, another purpose, another power. It signifies a happiness which is a serious business." (McCarthy, page 31, 32)

Joy and a sense of wonder are the two ingredients that McCarthy cites for the powerful hold that the natural world has on us. I feel them strongly.

The next book I looked at was one that Gib had given me a couple years ago: "The Nature Fix" by Florence Williams (2017). I remembered reading it, but I wasn't tuned into the message . . . yet.

"This book explores the science behind what poets and philosophers have known for eons: place matters . . . Thanks to a confluence of demographics and technology, we've pivoted further away from nature than any generation before us. At the same time, we're increasingly burdened by chronic ailments made worse by time spent indoors, from myopia and vitamin D deficiency to obesity, depression, loneliness and anxiety, among others." (Williams, page 4-6)

This was just what I was looking for: could scientific experiments measure the health benefits of being in nature?

So I began reading up, and the other books I sought were written by E. O. Wilson, the famous Harvard entomologist who took the word "biophilia" and used it as a cornerstone of his theory.

He defines biophilia as the innate tendency to focus upon life and life-like forms and in some instances to affiliate with them emotionally. Wilson identifies the innately emotional affiliation of human beings to other living organisms as an evolutionary adaptation aiding in survival. Although no genes have been found for biophilia, it's recognized that our brains respond innately to natural stimuli. Bio*phobia* or fear of nature, for example, is evident in the word snake. Our visual cortex picks up snake patterns more quickly than other kinds of patterns. And what about other phobias — fear of spiders, heights, enclosed places, blood — all are powerful cues inherited from our Pleistocene days.

While visiting Japan, Florence Williams recounted in her book how biophilia combines with "forest bathing" to expand on the theory that because humans evolved in nature, it's where we feel most comfortable. Yoshifumi Miyazaki, physical anthropologist and vice director of the Center for Environment, Health and Field Sciences at Chiba University outside Tokyo, has conducted experiments with hundreds of subjects to prove that "leisurely forest walks, compared to urban walks, deliver a 12 percent decrease in cortisol levels, a 7 percent decrease in sympathetic nerve activity, a 1.4 percent decrease in blood pressure, and a 6 percent decrease in heart rate." (Williams, page 23)

Hundreds of thousands of visitors walk the forest therapy trails in Japan each year, and more parks are planned.

On the other side of the argument are the U.S. scientists that Williams interviewed. They're more interested in the effects of nature on the brain — specifically cognition and creativity.

According to this line of thinking, nature experiences are like a drug that engages what's good, within that default network in the brain where our creative, unstructured, free-ranging thoughts lie. From the office environment — with its computers, cell phones, and constant media bombardment, people need a break. We need the "restorative reprieves," as Williams puts it, that being in nature gives us to put our thinking brains back in balance again. In other words, a sort of "default network" that opens up that side of the brain where stress reduction and the resultant creativity occur.

And then there's my favorite, Roger Ulrich, a psychologist, who, in the 1980s was the first to study the health consequences of having a room with a view. He examined the records of gallbladder-surgery patients over a half dozen years, some of whom had been assigned to rooms with a window view of trees, and some who looked out onto a brick wall. In short, the patients with the green views needed fewer postoperative days in the hospital, requested less pain medication, and were described by nurses as having better attitudes. Ulrich's paper was published in *Science* and has been widely cited. Since then, window experiments have shown that nature views increase worker productivity, reduce stress, and result in higher academic grades and test scores.

The importance of parks, as first expressed and designed by famous landscape architect Frederick Law Olmsted (Central Park and Prospect Park in New York, among many others), is becoming obvious. The health of millions of nature-deprived folks who live in big cities can be improved by simply taking a walk in the park.

Local columnist and nature enthusiast Dan McCaslin writes about the rejuvenation found in our backcountry after hiking and walking. His column in the online journal Noozhawk mentions these same ideas, and, as John Muir said: "Thousands of tired, nerve-shaken, over-civilized people are beginning to find out that going to the mountains is going home; that wildness is a necessity."

Certainly, for my ongoing struggle against this disease, for my search to lead a meaningful life until my time runs out, I must surround myself with the natural world at regular intervals.

In the Anthropocene — the geological age that is influenced by man — we search for a way to cope with the enormous complexity of modern life. Suicide, depression, drug and alcohol dependency appear to be symptoms of people crying for help. Despite the array of modern medical advances, young people are finding themselves unable to survive in the way that our modern era requires.

Those of us a little farther down the road (read "older") have perhaps each found our own path. Many of us crave a way to recalibrate our brain, a need to immerse ourselves as a player in a bigger picture.

Let's say you're going out for a bird walk. It need not be early, but it's in the morning. One of the first sounds you hear is birdsong, which our ears have evolved to associate with safety and a normal day. If you don't hear the birds singing, something is wrong.

In both birds and humans, the ability to respond emotionally to linguistic and musical sounds became critical for mating, communication, and survival. Is this why I like hearing the trills, tweets, and whistles — and figuring out which species they belong to — and even what they might mean?

It turns out that other folks, "non-birders," like birdsong as a sort of background soundtrack. They find it soothing, like listening to running water. I, on the other hand, find birdsong not only soothing, but an integral part of the whole nature experience.

In short, birdsong is another one of the ingredients in a nature outing, along with whatever else you want to throw into the mix: hiking, walking, wildflowers, tall trees, birds, butterflies, dragonflies, mammals (national parks are full of them), and fresh air.

And then I went online and found this article: "Nature and mental health: An ecosystem service perspective."

Here, a group of researchers had written a paper in *Science Advances* (24 Jul 2019). The first sentence of the abstract reads: "A growing body of empirical evidence is revealing the value of nature experience for mental health. With rapid urbanization and declines in human contact with nature globally, crucial decisions must be made about how to preserve and enhance opportunities for nature experience."

If you're feeling overly reactive and stressed, try taking a walk outside. Notice if you are more relaxed and focused afterward. Researchers can prove there are bodily changes; it depends upon the person.

Can nature make you well? Maybe.

Can nature make you better? Absolutely!

Glossary
of Birding Terms

Christmas Bird Count (CBC) - An annual census held on a pre-arranged day when birders go out for 24 hours and count all the birds they see within a predetermined "count circle." The circle is defined by a 15-mile diameter from a central point. Count Day must be chosen from the 3-week period from mid-December to early January. Formerly, the CBC often centered around or near a settled community, but increasingly it takes place in a variety of habitats.

County Coordinator - Someone who keeps track of all the bird records within a county and sends in a report to the national magazine, *North American Birds*. The records are published quarterly, along with those from other regions of North America.

County list - All the birds a birder has seen within a specific county; a "county bird" is one of these.

Diatom - A microscopic unicellular organism which is found on mudflats and ocean bottoms throughout the world.

eBird - A worldwide database organized by the Cornell Laboratory of Ornithology. When birding, birders carry smartphones with them, and check off the birds they see or hear at that location from a list provided by the app. Birders' photos and bird recordings may accompany the list.

Landbirds - An informal way of referring to species of birds that live on or over land. Often referred to as Passerines, or perching birds, these are the smaller birds, such as flycatchers, warblers and sparrows, to name a few.

Life list - All the birds a birder has seen in a lifetime; a "life bird" is one of these.

Migrant - A migrating bird, en route from one location to another.

Pelagic bird - A bird that spends most of its time at sea, only coming to land to breed (similar to a seabird, but more ocean-going in its life history).

Raptor - A general term for a bird such as an owl, hawk, eagle, or vulture that eats live prey or carrion.

Red-necked Phalarope - A small migratory shorebird that winters at sea in ocean waters off Peru, then flies north in spring to nesting grounds on Arctic tundra.

Resident - A bird that doesn't migrate, but remains locally to breed year round.

Rufous - The color reddish-brown, often used to describe certain feathers of a bird.

http//www.Sbcobirding@groups.io - Santa Barbara County listserve used for discussion of unusual sightings and other issues to do with Santa Barbara County birds. Moderator: Jamie Chavez.

State list - All the birds a birder has seen in a state; a "state bird" is one of these.

Status and Distribution - Refers to a bird's abundance and its home range, i.e., how many of a species are seen in an area (status) and where the species is most likely to be found geographically (distribution).

Summer visitor - A bird that visits the Santa Barbara region to breed, usually from April through September, then departs.

Supercilium - A stripe or eyebrow that runs from the base of a bird's bill over its eye and toward the back of the head.

Vagrant - A bird that is out-of-range or off course, often seen during migration.

Waterbirds - An informal way of referring to species of birds that live near water, further divided into seabirds, marshbirds, waterfowl, and shorebirds. Examples of seabirds are loons, pelicans, gulls, and terns. Marshbirds are herons, egrets, and rails. Waterfowl are geese and ducks. Shorebirds are plovers, oystercatchers, avocets, and sandpipers.

Winter visitor - A bird that visits the Santa Barbara region to spend the winter, usually from September through April, then departs.

Year list - All the birds a birder has seen in a particular year, often but not always pertaining to one area.

Selected References

Books

Baldwin, Bruce G., editor, et al. *The Jepson Manual: Vascular Plants of California*. Second Edition. University of California Press, 2012.

Brittain, Vera. *Testament of Experience*. MacMillan, 1957.

Hannibal, Mary Ellen. *Citizen Scientist: Searching for Heroes and Hope in an Age of Extinction*. The Experiment LLC, 2016.

Hoffmann, Ralph. *Birds of the Pacific States*. Riverside Press, Cambridge, MA, 1927.

Howell, Steve N.G., et al. *Rare Birds of North America*. Princeton University Press, 2014.

Matthiessen, Peter. *The Wind Birds*. Viking Press, New York, 1973.

McCarthy, Michael. *The Moth Snowstorm: Nature and Joy*. New York Review of Books, 2015.

Small, Arnold. *California Birds: Their Status and Distribution*. Ibis Publishing Co., Vista, CA, 1994.

Smith, Clifton F. *A Flora of the Santa Barbara Region, California*. Santa Barbara Botanic Garden and Capra Press, 1998.

Williams, Florence. *The Nature Fix*. Norton & Co., 2017.

Wilson, Edward O. *The Future of Life*. Alfred A. Knopf, 2002.

Websites

Bratman, Gregory N., et al. *Nature and Mental Health: An Ecosystem Perspective.* Science Advances, July 24 2019, https://www.advances.sciencemag.org/content/5/7/eaax0903

Lehman, Paul. *The Birds of Santa Barbara County, California, June2020,* http://www.sbcobirding.com/lehmanbosbc.html

McCaslin, Dan. *Rewilding and Human vs. Geologic Time Scales.* Noozhawk, April 2, 2018, https://www.noozhawk.com/article/ dan_mccaslin_rewilding_and_human_vs._geologic_time_ scales_20180401

National Oceanic and Atmospheric Administration. *Tiny shells reveal waters off California acidifying twice as fast as the global ocean.* December 16, 2019, https://www.noaa.gov/stories/tiny-shells-reveal-waters-off-california-acidifying-twice-as-fast-as-global-ocean

Nature Alley. *Schedule of 2020/21 and recap of 2019/20 California Christmas Bird Counts.* January 5, 2020, http://www.natureali.org/cbcs.htm

The Cornell Lab of Ornithology. *Bird Migration Forecasts in Real-Time: When, where, and how far will birds migrate? Our migration forecasts will answer these questions for the first time.* June 2020, https://www.birdcast.info

Who Was Who in California Birding: A History and Chronology of the California Birding World, 1960-1989. http://www.crea-grus.home.montereybay.com/CAwhoswhointro.html

My Website

Joan Easton Lentz, http://www.joaneastonlentz.com/

Acknowledgments

I want to thank my editor, Kathy Jean Schultz, and book designer, Anna Lafferty, of Lafferty Design Plus, for their enormous help in moving the book forward. Their dedication to the project made the book a reality.

William B. Dewey, photographer and friend, was a significant part of the team. His talent for managing all the photos so they were easily accessible to Anna and me, deserves kudos.

Patti Jacquemain and David Gledhill at Mission Creek Studios, my distributor, were wonderful. Without their guidance, I would have been lost, and so would the book.

To all the birders who've taught me, befriended me, chased a rarity with me, and listened to me teach — you are my heroes and I wouldn't have written this book without your contributions to my life.

To Larry Ballard, who read several early drafts of the book and whose meticulous comments I heeded, thank you.

To Alex and Annabel Gerson, my beloved grandchildren, thank you for visiting me in Santa Barbara and letting me share the natural history I love so much. Your mother, my daughter Jenny, knew what pleasure those times together gave me.

To Ellen Easton, my cherished sister, who encouraged me from the start that this book should see the light of day. Without her invaluable help, I would not have persevered. Her husband, Greg Giloth, had eagle eyes for proof reading, which I appreciated.

And to Gib, my husband, who left me free to "go to the cottage and write" every afternoon; who prepared dinner if I wasn't feeling well; who took care of the laundry and the shopping, especially when the COVID-19 pandemic put us in lockdown; to Gib I say once more, I couldn't have done it without you. Thank you, thank you.

Joan Easton Lentz
July 2020

Made in the USA
Las Vegas, NV
10 November 2020